Endorsements of *Begin Again*

FR. GALLAGHER HAS WRITTEN of the Founder of his religious order with a personal sense of the particular charism of the Oblates of the Virgin Mary and with a historian's sense of the context of its birth and development.

Quite ordinary events in Lanteri's life are unified by his strong sense of spiritual purpose often obstructed by a body weakened with constant ill health; these same events are played out in the tension between Church and State in France and Piedmont in an age of revolution; they are reflected in the lives of his co-workers and companions in the various societies and communities he formed part of.

A man who sought always to remain in the background is brought forward in this book so that all can begin again to discover his virtues and appreciate his influence today.

—Francis Cardinal George, O.M.I.,
archbishop of Chicago

FR. TIMOTHY GALLAGHER HAS RESPONDED admirably to the call of the Second Vatican Council to those in religious life to return to the charism of their founder. With his impressive scholarship, pastoral prudence, theological acumen, and pellucid prose, Gallagher has made available to English-speaking readers a biography of the Venerable Bruno Lanteri (1759–1830), the founder of the Oblates of the Virgin Mary.

Tracing this remarkably holy and dedicated figure's lifelong fidelity to prayer that led to contemplative union with God, Gallagher shows how, from this center, the fruitful priestly ministry of this "man of a hundred tongues and a hundred arms" arose. When an emperor attempted to subjugate the Church to state policy, Lanteri defended the Church, to the point of willingness to lay down his life. Fr. Gallagher presents Lanteri through a careful reading of the original documents and offers readers the story of a life that will awaken in many the courage to begin again in times of struggle and draw near to the God whose love this man so effectively taught. **—Harvey D. Egan, S.J.,**
professor emeritus of theology,
Boston College

A CLEAR AND DELIGHTFUL PORTRAIT of Venerable Bruno Lanteri, rich and engaging on three counts:

As biography, Fr. Gallagher provides an exact and full life of Lanteri, replete with important passages from the letters.

As history, he investigates his subject's activities in the Napoleonic aftermath of the French Revolution as it affected the papacy and the Piedmont region.

And to the spiritual benefit of the reader, he explores Lanteri's spiritual journey into deep union with God and his rich spiritual teaching with its message of mercy and hope.

—David Beauregard, O.M.V., author and professor of church history, St. John's Archdiocesan Seminary, Brighton, Massachusetts

EVERY OBLATE OF THE VIRGIN MARY, and all who know Fr. Lanteri and seek to live according to his spirituality, will find strength, consolation, and spiritual joy in reading Fr. Gallagher's biography of our Founder. As I read, I was struck by Fr. Lanteri's unwavering efforts to follow more closely Him whom he loved above all else. These efforts, and at times these struggles, never hindered him from persevering on this path and constantly "beginning again" in what grew to be a deep love for Christ.

He personally experienced God as a Father who loves and forgives, and so, throughout a lifetime of intensely active ministry, he became an apostle of God's mercy, in particular toward those who themselves struggled spiritually. As founder of the Oblates of the Virgin Mary, he unceasingly taught his spiritual sons that there is nothing greater than God's mercy.

—Fr. Louis Normandin, O.M.V., member of the general council in the Oblates of the Virgin Mary

IT WAS TIME FOR AN ENGLISH-LANGUAGE BIOGRAPHY of Venerable Pio Bruno Lanteri, and Fr. Timothy Gallagher was the natural choice of an author. His research and acquaintance with the person and spirit of Lanteri started as early as his doctoral studies at the Gregorian University in the late 1970s. He has chosen a unique approach among existing biographies, seeking to uncover the spiritual journey of the Founder of the Oblates of the Virgin Mary. He has done a wonderful and poignant job!

At a time when the Oblates of the Virgin Mary, especially in the English-speaking world, continue to seek a deeper personal understanding of a man of the Church who has profoundly influenced their ministry to this day, Fr. Gallagher's timely work is of immense importance. His biographical approach will most certainly further reveal the mind and heart of Lanteri for a growing number of lay men and women who want to associate themselves with the spirit and ministry of the contemporary sons of Venerable Lanteri. This work will also contribute to a deeper appreciation of the life of the Church in southern Europe during the second half of the eighteenth and first half of the nineteenth century. Bravo, Fr. Gallagher!

—**Ernest Sherstone, O.M.V., vicar general of the Oblates, director of the Lanteri Center for Ignatian Spirituality**

Begin Again

The Life and
Spiritual Legacy of
Bruno Lanteri

TIMOTHY M. GALLAGHER, O.M.V.

A Crossroad Book
The Crossroad Publishing Company
New York

This printing: 2021

The Crossroad Publishing Company
www.crossroadpublishing.com

Printed in the United States of America.

ISBN 978-0-8245-2579-8 (alk. paper)

Library of Congress Cataloging-in-Publication Data is available from the Library of Congress.

Cover image: Stained-glass window portraying Bruno Lanteri, from the sacristy of Our Lady of Grace Church, Carignano

Cover design: George Foster

Photo credits: Yves Morin, O.M.V., and the Oblates of the Virgin Mary

The painting of the Marchesa Giulia di Barolo and the sketch of Constance de Maistre are reproduced with permission.

Maps: Kirsten Harper

In continuation of our 200–year tradition of independent publishing, The Crossroad Publishing Company proudly offers a variety of books with strong, original voices and diverse perspectives. The viewpoints expressed in our books are not necessarily those of The Crossroad Publishing Company, any of its imprints or of its employees. No claims are made or responsibility assumed for any health, or other benefit.

Books published by The Crossroad Publishing Company may be purchased at special quantity discount rates for classroom and institutional use. For information, please e-mail sales@crossroadpublishing.com.

Contents

List of Illustrations

Preface

FROM THE DAY I LEARNED of Bruno Lanteri, he captured my interest. When I joined his religious community, the Oblates of the Virgin Mary, he became central to my life. I wanted to know everything about him. I read every book and article I could find. I learned the necessary languages, and focused my graduate studies on him. Twelve years in Italy provided familiarity with the places, history, and culture that shaped his life. Teaching and publications in subsequent decades built on that foundation. Five further years of research and writing have led now to this book.

One evening during those years of research, I joined a group in conversation. Others asked about the biography, and I described Bruno Lanteri's life: his faith, his struggles with poor health, his persevering search for spiritual growth, his courage in dark times when Rome was occupied by foreign troops and the pope held captive, his willingness to risk his life in defense of the Church, his resolve to begin again in times of failure, his message of mercy and of hope to the discouraged, and, above all, his deep love for Christ. As we spoke, one woman said, "The story of this life needs to be told." She was right: the story of Bruno Lanteri's life does need to be told.

That story has been told in the past. The most significant biography was published in Italian nearly 150 years ago; no biography has ever been written in English.[1] This book tells the story of Bruno Lanteri's life for contemporary readers in the English-speaking world. It tells a story that speaks, as in Bruno's lifetime (1759–1830), to men and women of all vocations: priests, religious, and laity.

As the subtitle indicates, this book focuses on the person and spirituality of Bruno Lanteri. His person: Who was he? What were his interests? To what did he dedicate his life? How did he interact with others? What were his struggles? His accomplishments? His failures? How did he respond to these? What did it mean to live with shattered health? And his spirituality: What place did faith have in his life? How did he discern his vocation? How did he pray? What was his relationship with Christ? What means did he employ for spiritual growth? What ministries did he see as crucial for his times—the age in which the modern world was shaped? What message did he offer those who sought his guidance?

The primary source of this book is the Archive of the Oblates of the Virgin Mary.[2] Thousands of manuscript pages offer direct access to Bruno Lanteri's prayer, spiritual striving, works, relationships, joys, and sorrows. I have utilized them abundantly. In the past seventy years, the more significant of these have been published with critical apparatus, permitting deeper insight into Bruno Lanteri's life.[3] Additional archives and the many studies published in recent decades amplify the understanding of these documents.[4] I am deeply grateful to the authors who composed them: this biography could not have been written without their dedicated labors.[5]

All translations of primary texts—the many quotations from original documents—are the author's, and the source is noted in each case.[6] In this book I have included only evidence I have judged beyond dispute. When a document or incident is attributed to Bruno with unclear or disputed evidence, I have omitted that evidence in my text, and supplied references to the dispute in the endnotes.[7] I have likewise accepted the limitations of the documentary evidence when that evidence is incomplete.[8] My goal has been to present all that the sources contain regarding Bruno's person and spiritual legacy, and only what those sources, with their richness and limitations, authorize.[9]

This biography situates Bruno's life in the often dramatic context of his times. During his lifetime, the French Revolution spilled violently into his own nation, the small Italian kingdom of Piedmont. Nearly twenty years of military occupation ensued, a time of great struggle for the Church. The false peace of the Restoration followed, as cultural and political energies gathered for sweeping change in Europe. As we will see, the tumult of his times directly affected Bruno's life and service.

Throughout, the call to *begin again* recurs, a teaching Bruno himself lived and repeated to countless men and women. In times of darkness and failure, when discouragement burdens the heart, new effort appears useless, and unhappy surrender of hope seems the only choice, Bruno gently, firmly, almost relentlessly repeats that nothing can ever impede us from *beginning again*; that when, in such times of failure, we open our wounded hearts to him, God's love and mercy draw even closer to us. His teaching instilled hope in the many persons who approached him.

ONE SUNDAY MORNING, as I was writing this book, I sat in our community chapel. It was early, my time of quiet before Mass in the parish and immersion in the lives of the parishioners. Subdued sounds of traffic filtered through the walls of this fifth-floor chapel. Outside the window, I could see the gray, overcast sky of a cool fall day.

I was glad to be in the chapel, glad to have time for prayer. I looked forward to meeting the people in the parish whom I knew so well. As I sat, however, I sensed a heaviness in my heart, a feeling that something was wrong. Brief reflection revealed its source: the preceding day, a person had asked my help, and I had failed to respond. I knew that opportunity might not return. As I reflected, I realized I had carried a sadness since then, buried in busyness, but now felt in the silence. That sadness stood between me and full freedom to be glad in the Lord's presence.

The quiet time ended, and I was about to leave the chapel. I knew the grayness in my heart would not stop me from serving the parishioners; I knew, too, that it would quietly burden the day.

Suddenly I realized that this was exactly the spiritual situation in which Bruno spoke of *beginning again*: when persons want to be faithful, want to grow closer to God, and, in small things or great, must face their failures and their faults. *It is then*, Bruno taught, that we have more reason than ever to turn to the God who loves to forgive, loves to be merciful, and to begin again. Of himself he would write, "If I should fall a thousand times a day, a thousand times a day I will begin again."

As I remembered his teaching, my heart began to lift. I could ask God's forgiveness, I could begin again, confident that his grace would open new spiritual doors. I understood afresh the impact of Bruno's teaching on so many throughout his nearly forty-nine years of priesthood.

This book tells the story of a man who inspired human hearts with new hope and energy in God's service. His story continues to inspire that same hope today.

Acknowledgments

I am deeply grateful to the many persons who made this book possible: to Fr. William Brown, O.M.V., who, as provincial, asked that I write this book and who supplied the necessary conditions; to his successor, Fr. David Nicgorski, O.M.V., who supported this process to its conclusion; to the Oblates of the Virgin Mary who accompanied the writing as readers: Ernest Sherstone, O.M.V., Louis Normandin, O.M.V., Thomas Carzon, O.M.V., William Neubecker, O.M.V., David Beauregard, O.M.V., Gregory Staab, O.M.V., James Walther, O.M.V., and Oseni Ogunu, O.M.V.; to Daniel Barron, O.M.V., David Guza, O.M.V., Gerardo Joaquin, O.M.V., and Jeremy Paulin, O.M.V., for their assistance with technical and practical matters; to the Oblates in Pinerolo and Rome who so generously assisted me during my stay with them and throughout the years of writing: Sergio Zirattu, O.M.V., Rector Major of the Oblates, Agostino Valentini, O.M.V., Andrea Brustolon, O.M.V., and Alan Hall, O.M.V.; to the staff of the Oblate library in Pinerolo and archive in Rome: Paola Dema, who tirelessly responded to my many requests for materials in the library and elsewhere in Piedmont, and Antonietta Marongiu and Giorgina Ciocca who repeatedly supplied documents from the archive in Rome; and to Yves Morin, O.M.V., and John Wykes, O.M.V., for their expertise in taking and preparing the photographs for printing.

I acknowledge with gratitude the scholarship and archival labors of the many Oblates, living and deceased, upon whose contribution this book depends, in particular: Giuseppe Loggero, O.M.V., Luigi Dadesso, O.M.V., Tommaso Piatti, O.M.V., Giuseppe Roberto Claretta, O.M.V., Paolo Calliari, O.M.V.,[1] Vittorio Moscarelli, O.M.V., Andrea Brustolon, O.M.V., Agostino Valentini, O.M.V., and Armando Santoro, O.M.V.; and others whose works are invaluable resources for a biography of Bruno Lanteri: Msgr. Amato Frutaz, Candido Bona, I.M.C., Jean Guerber, S.J., and the many scholars cited in this book.

To those who read the manuscript and offered suggestions for its improvement, I express my sincere thanks: to Claire-Marie Hart, for her insightful comments and encouragement, to Harvey Egan, S.J., Richard McKinney, Cabrini Pak, James Gallagher, Gill Goulding, C.J., Gertrude Mahoney, S.N.D., Robert Irish, Geoff Groesbeck, Terry Wong, and Kathleen O'Brien.

I am deeply grateful, once again, to Joseph Schner, S.J., to the Jesuit community of Pedro Arrupe House, and to Regis College, Toronto, for their warm hospitality during the writing; likewise to Fr. Dan Caruso and the parish of St. Mary of the Assumption, Binghamton, New York, for their gracious welcome during the months of writing I spent with them; and to my own Oblate community of St. Clement's, Boston, who assumed the tasks that would have limited my freedom to write, and accompanied me throughout the process.

I thank Carol McGinness and Scott Gullicksen for their indispensable aid with technical matters, Bernadette Reis, F.S.P., for her expert assistance with issues regarding publication, and Edward Casey for the digitization of thousands of Bruno Lanteri's manuscripts.

Finally, I express my heartfelt thanks to John Jones, editorial director of The Crossroad Publishing Company, who encouraged this project from its beginning and supported it at every stage. His passing through illness prevented him from seeing the fruits of his editorial labors in this book; to him, and to all at Crossroad who assisted in the publication of this book, I am most grateful.

Begin Again

CHAPTER ONE

Into Exile

When it is necessary to think, speak,
and labor for God, even to give my
life, let everything be lost, let whatever
may happen, happen: this I must do.
—Bruno Lanteri

ON JANUARY 11, 1811, a certain Claude Berthaut du Coin was arrested by the French police. He was brought from Lyon to Paris, imprisoned, and, four days later, underwent the first of six interrogations.

He knew that his life was at stake. He had known and accepted this risk when he first agreed to contact Pope Pius VII, held prisoner by order of the Emperor Napoleon.[1] His first journey of clandestine communication with Pius VII two years earlier had been successful, and the police had suspected nothing. This time, disaster struck.

Tensions between pope and emperor had been rising for years as Napoleon increasingly subjugated the Papal States and attempted to dictate Church policy. Open conflict had erupted when, in May 1809, Napoleon decreed the incorporation of the Papal States into his empire. Pius VII immediately responded with a bull of excommunication. Napoleon retaliated with the arrest and abduction from Rome of the pope. Since July 1809, Pius VII had been Napoleon's prisoner, detained in Savona, along the Italian coast, fifty kilometers from Genoa.

Napoleon lodged the pope in the bishop's residence in Savona. Officially he was considered a "guest" of the emperor's local representative, and treated with deference. Yet guards watched as he celebrated Mass, as he walked in the garden, and as he received visitors. His letters were opened and read. Pius was alone only in his private room.[2]

In protest, the pope employed the one avenue remaining to him. The existing agreement between pope and emperor allowed the emperor to name new bishops as dioceses became vacant. For the exercise of their authority, however, canonical institution by the pope was required. Pius now simply refused to grant that institution. As the number of vacant dioceses increased—above all, Paris itself, without a bishop since 1808—discontent among the people and paralysis in the life of the Church grew as well.

Napoleon increased pressure on the pope to yield and grant canonical institution to the new bishops. The pope was forbidden communication with the Church, his living conditions made harsh, and envoys from Napoleon verbally battered him, pressing him to yield. Pius wavered . . . but ultimately refused to submit.

Napoleon's appointee as archbishop of Paris, Cardinal Jean-Sifrein Maury, suggested a way beyond the impasse. When a diocese had no bishop, canon law permitted the naming of a vicar capitular as temporary administrator of the diocese until a bishop could be appointed.[3] Then, Maury proposed, let each diocese appoint as temporary administrator Napoleon's nominee for bishop of that diocese. In this way, the pope's authorization would no longer be required, and administration of the vacant dioceses could resume under the leadership of whomever Napoleon desired.

Pius VII, informed secretly of Maury's ploy, wrote to Maury on November 5, 1810, accusing him of betrayal, enjoining him to renounce the archbishopric of Paris, and declaring null any administrative acts he performed.[4] Maury ignored the letter, and refused to make it public.

Others in Paris, however, troubled by the confusion regarding legitimate authority in the archdiocese, desired Pius VII's guidance. Direct communication with the imprisoned pope grew urgent. Berthaut du Coin, a member of a group in Lyon dedicated to the Holy Father, was again chosen for the task.[5] For a second time, he undertook the dangerous journey to the captive pope in Savona. Berthaut du Coin received clarifying documents from the pope, and brought them to supporters of the pope in France. These, in turn, transmitted the texts to loyal Catholics in Paris.

But this time they did not escape the police. One document was discovered, and, on December 31, Napoleon was informed. Events now moved quickly, as the police uncovered an extensive network of clandestine defenders of the pope. Twenty persons were arrested; among them, on January 11, 1811, was thirty-one-year-old Berthaut du Coin.

Interrogated repeatedly by the police, Berthaut du Coin refused to betray his companions. Yet even his silence could not protect them. A search of his papers revealed a list of six names—priests and laymen of the Piedmont region of northern Italy, formerly the kingdom of Piedmont, but now incorporated by Napoleon into France. Among these six was "Monsieur l'abbé Brunon Lanteri."[6]

PIO BRUNO LANTERI, was fifty-two years old, a priest of twenty-nine years. He was 5'8"tall, of average body size, with graying hair and brown eyebrows, oval in visage, his eyes blue-gray, his forehead wide, his nose large and somewhat flat, his mouth medium-sized, and his chin furrowed.[7]

He was every inch a Piedmontese: reserved, little inclined to speak of his accomplishments, quietly focused on his tasks, accustomed to hard work, and forthright to the point of bluntness. Speaking in self-defense, as one unlikely to plot against the emperor, he would describe himself to the police as "solitary, reserved, and a man of few words."[8] When he spoke, his voice tended to be soft.[9]

He was a man of shattered health, often utterly unable to work, exhausted by an oppression of the chest, at times scarcely able to breathe, and constantly aware that physical effort might cause a recurrence of these attacks. His eyes were ruined, and frequently he was unable to read.

The French police already knew the name Bruno Lanteri. Some time earlier, a secret agent had identified him to the police as one unfavorably disposed to the French government, in particular since the rise of tensions between the emperor and the pope.[10] Signor d'Auzers, director of police for Piedmont, had ordered that Bruno be kept under surveillance. D'Auzers informed his superior in Paris, however, that "because he [Bruno] is most careful in his speech and actions, I have obtained no proof against him."[11] But now the stakes were higher, and new efforts would be made.

On January 19, 1811, Savary, Duke of Rovigo and minister of police in Paris, wrote to d'Auzers ordering him to interrogate and search the papers of the six persons named in Berthaut du Coin's text. Ten days later, on January 29, Bruno was interrogated "with the greatest care" and his papers searched.

D'Auzers informed Savary that same day that the interrogation had revealed nothing significant.[12] Bruno—carefully choosing his words—insisted that he had only seen Berthaut du Coin once or twice when he had come seeking confession, and that he, Bruno, could not recall whether he granted the request because he was ill at that time; that he had no knowledge of the reasons for Berthaut du Coin's trip; that Berthaut du Coin had indeed told him of his forthcoming journey to Savona, but that he, Bruno, had not given Berthaut du Coin any commission for that trip or for any other.

D'Auzers, however, was not convinced, and voiced his reservations to his superior. He told Savary that Bruno "is generally regarded here as a very pious and very honest man." Yet d'Auzers had learned of the existence in Turin of what he called "a certain association of priests and clerics of the Jesuits, after their suppression," bound by secrecy, with branches in Vienna and Paris, and that Bruno was their leader.[13]

Immediately following the interrogation, the police searched Bruno's papers. They found nothing except a copy of Pius VII's bull of excommunication against those—ultimately Napoleon himself—who had stripped him of the Papal States. D'Auzers sent the document to Savary, noting key passages so that Savary might perceive "what should be thought of the political opinions of a man who would keep such a manuscript among his papers."

D'Auzers continued: "I must inform you, Monsieur, that Monsieur l'abbé Lanteri has great influence here through his hearing of confessions. He is one of the most sought after in the city. Though his health has been very poor for some months now, many, among them the most influential persons, have taken him as their spiritual director."[14]

D'Auzers then presented his recommendations to his superior: the archbishop of Turin should be ordered to revoke Bruno's permission to hear confessions. Bruno himself should be removed from Turin. Because his poor health would not endure more severe exile, he should be sent either to Cuneo, his birthplace, or to his home in the countryside outside of Turin. He should be forbidden to return to Turin "since his presence may lead to harm because of the erroneous counsel he might give to those who seek guidance for their consciences."

On February 27, 1811, Savary presented these recommendations to Napoleon, suggesting as the place of exile Bruno's home, the "Grangia," in Bardassano, twenty kilometers from Turin, advising further that Bruno be kept under surveillance.[15] Napoleon endorsed his subordinate's proposals.

On March 9, Count Bigot de Préameneu, Napoleon's minister for religion, ordered the archbishop of Turin, Giacinto della Torre, to remove Bruno's faculties for confessions, and to require him to abandon Turin for his home in Bardassano, "thus forestalling the measures that the police might take in his regard"—a lightly veiled threat of police action should the archbishop fail to comply.[16] Giacinto della Torre, not one to resist the French authorities—few dared to do so in those days of Napoleon's power—obediently executed the orders from Paris. As he did so, however, the archbishop declared to Bigot de Préameneu that "there is no malice in the priest Lanteri, nor is he one ever to take part in correspondence against the government," and expressed his wish that "all my priests would be as reserved, as wise, as docile and obedient to the laws" as Lanteri.[17] His words changed nothing.

ON MARCH 25, evading the surveillance of the police one final time, Bruno met with the group that d'Auzers had confusedly described as "a certain association of priests and clerics of the Jesuits."[18] Later that day, he left Turin for his home in Bardassano, where Don Giuseppe Loggero, his faithful assistant, would join him.[19] Bruno's exile had begun.

Almost immediately he experienced severe problems of health. In early May, he informed the archbishop that "a few days ago I was once again assailed by a strong and protracted attack of oppression of the chest, such that I feared for the outcome."[20] A further problem arose in his arm.[21] Bruno requested and, after laborious bureaucratic proceedings, was granted fifteen days in Turin to attend to urgent medical needs. Compelled to depart in haste when his exile began, such measures had been impossible earlier. D'Auzers's superior ordered him to keep Bruno under surveillance during those two weeks in Turin, and to report his return to Bardassano.[22] Archbishop della Torre assured d'Auzers that Bruno would not abuse the permission received.[23]

May passed, then June . . . and the days of exile became weeks, the weeks, months, the months, years. . . . As the tumultuous events of those decisive years unfolded, Bruno's isolation and the enforced interruption of his ministry perdured.

On December 12, 1812, a year and seven months after his exile began, Bruno wrote "from my country dwelling" to his collaborator and spiritual directee Leopoldo Ricasoli, thanking him for his recent letter, encouraging him to fidelity in prayer, and asking for word regarding his spiritual practices and their fruits. "If you share this with me," he wrote, "you will give me the consolation of contributing as much as I am able to your spiritual progress." With a certain pathos, Bruno continued: "Do me this favor, my dearly beloved Signor Priore, so that in this my cherished solitude, where I have become as though useless to my neighbor, I may be at least of some spiritual assistance to you."

My cherished solitude: in these years of compulsory inactivity, something was changing in Bruno, something that no one, neither French police nor archbishop, not even Bruno himself—this man who once had sought monastic life—could have foreseen. *Useless to my neighbor:* a burden weighed on this "man of a hundred tongues and a hundred arms,"[24] who, notwithstanding his devastated health, had for thirty years spent himself for others in the capital of his nation, ever in the thick of culture and events.

Bruno felt this burden all the more "since my days will not be long because of my illnesses which, rather than diminish, persist all the more, hastening my departure from this unhappy world, and the union for which I long with my gentle Jesus."[25] Exiled from the persons and places he loved, forbidden the priestly ministry so long the center of his life, experiencing in pain the accelerating decline of his body . . . Bruno turned his thoughts to release from "this unhappy world" and to eternal union with Christ.

But the end was not yet come.

CHAPTER TWO

Beginnings

*I understand this all the more
from the special desires He has
granted me to feel for some time, to
consecrate myself entirely to Him,
and for the salvation of souls.*
—Bruno Lanteri

IN 1743, AT THE AGE OF ELEVEN, Nikolaus Albert von Diessbach left his home in Bern, Switzerland, and began his military career. His two brothers, Rudolf Anton and Ludwig, would later follow him into the army. The young Nikolaus Albert entered a Swiss regiment in the pay of the king of Piedmont, and for the next sixteen years pursued the military life. This fledgling soldier, through unlikely paths, was destined to be the decisive influence in Bruno's life.

Raised a Calvinist, in the military Diessbach gradually lost his Christian faith. Later he would describe how "I found myself in the full vigor of youth, and the permissiveness that too often accompanies military life, the stubborn vanity of a proud spirit, the impetuous stirrings of strong passions, and an excessive thirst for every kind of reading, led me by rapid steps toward the pyrrho-nian [skeptical] system of unbelief."[1]

Reviewing those years, he would recognize that in large part his unbelief derived from his indiscriminate reading: "I read the writings of the famous atheists of our days and I was, I confess, greatly impressed by them. What men! I said. These are men of courage, men who use their minds. These will be my masters! With courage they destroy empty prejudices, and ennoble a humanity that superstition weakens and degrades. What! Does the world persecute these wise men? That very persecution renders them all the more admirable in my eyes. I unite myself with all they endure for their cause."[2] Bruno would later note that in Diessbach's youth, "he read a great deal, and abandoned his Calvinism to embrace unbelief."[3]

As books contributed to Diessbach's loss of faith, so they would be the instrument of its rebirth.

In 1754, Diessbach's regiment was stationed in Nice, then belonging to the kingdom of Piedmont. His personal goodness and refined bearing made the twenty-two-year-old Diessbach welcome in society, and gained him entrance into the home of the Spanish consul, Monsieur Saint-Pierre. There his Catholic hosts both esteemed his goodness and lamented his unbelief. The family, noting his interest in reading, placed a book about the faith in a visible spot in their home. As they hoped, the young soldier noticed the book and asked to read it. When he did, a new spiritual journey began.[4]

Diessbach now began to grapple with the religious questions that arose from his reading. Because he was, as Bruno would write, "a reflective man, who made no decision without pondering it well beforehand,"[5] Diessbach brought his questions to the Jesuits in Turin. There he found a priest who answered them all. His doubts about the faith resolved, at the age of twenty-three Diessbach entered the Catholic Church. The following year, 1755, he married Monsieur Saint-Pierre's daughter; his conversion had removed the one obstacle to a marriage desired by both Diessbach and the Saint-Pierre family.

Three years later, tragedy struck as Diessbach's wife died in childbirth, leaving him with a young daughter, who also would die at an early age.[6] Years later, Diessbach would review his life and write, "I have seen . . . my plans undone and brought to nothing. . . . With my own eyes I have seen inexorable death strike persons dear to me beyond all others with the most unexpected blows, in the springtime of their years."[7]

His family life shattered and his next step uncertain, Diessbach considered entering the Jesuits, so instrumental in his conversion to Catholicism. Bruno would relate that, "After the death of his wife he consecrated himself to God in the Company of Jesus, affirming that, because, after God himself, he owed his conversion both to the Saint-Pierre family and to the Jesuits, he thought in this way to satisfy his debt of gratitude toward all."[8] Having arranged for the education of his daughter, Diessbach requested and was granted admission among the Jesuits. On October 19, 1759, at the age of twenty-seven, he entered the Jesuit novitiate in Genoa.

ON MAY 12 OF THAT YEAR, Bruno Lanteri was born in Cuneo, north and a little east of Nice, 170 kilometers from Genoa. That same day, his parents, Pietro and Margherita, had him baptized in the local parish, Santa Maria della Pieve.

Bruno was the seventh of ten children in a family that death had already struck repeatedly. The first three children died young. Bruno's oldest sister, Maria Angelica Luisa, would live to be fifty-one; another sister, Anna Maria Teresa, would die at twenty-four. Two of his brothers, Giuseppe and Giuseppe Tommaso (both would enter and would leave the priesthood), lived longer. The exact date of death of the first is unknown; the second would live to be sixty. The two other children, Agostino Luca and Margherita, like the first three, would die at an early age.

Bruno's father was a doctor, respected both professionally and as a Christian. Of his mother, from nearby Pianfei, little is known beyond the essential dates of her life. Both were faithfully Catholic. In 1759, then, Bruno entered a profoundly Catholic family, financially stable, in a time of civic peace.

BUT IT WAS AN UNEASY PEACE, troubled by a European-wide unrest that foreshadowed and prepared the explosion to come. On May 1, 1759, eleven days before Bruno's birth, Baron di Coccei, aide to Frederick the Great of Prussia, arrived in Turin. He was instructed to invite the king of Piedmont, Carlo Emmanuele III, to join with Prussia, England, and the kingdom of Naples, and together expel

Cuneo, old part of the city.

Cuneo, a street in the old city.

Former Jesuit church in Cuneo.
Bruno's baptismal font is conserved in this church.

Cuneo, Piazza Galimberti, new part of the city.

the Austrians from Italy.[9] The nations of Europe intrigued end-lessly for their own aggrandizement, and the menace of war hung over the continent.

Also in 1759, in France, Voltaire published his best-selling *Candide*; on March 8 of that year, the French government banned the *Encyclopédie* of Diderot. The cultural battle of the Enlightenment that would so deeply affect Bruno's life already agitated the continent, and would, one day, utterly destroy the peace of his small nation, the kingdom of Piedmont.[10]

On May 28, 1759, sixteen days after Bruno's birth, William Pitt the Younger was born; on October 26 of that same year, Georges Danton. The first would be an implacable foe of the French in the wars issuing from the French Revolution; the second, both an architect of the Revolution and its victim.

Across the Atlantic Ocean, France and England were already at war. On September 13–14, 1759, when Bruno was four months old, Generals James Wolfe and Louis-Joseph de Montcalm lay dying on the Plains of Abraham, as France surrendered Quebec to the English.

On the first day of September 1759, at nightfall, Portuguese troops approached the Jesuit College in Elvas, near the Spanish border. They arrested the Jesuits and, under guard, compelled them to walk the 200-kilometer trip to Lisbon, where they were imprisoned on board a ship. Others, similarly arrested, were also confined on board, and the ship filled with 133 Jesuits. They embarked with orders to sail directly to the Papal States, where the Jesuits were to be abandoned ashore. A month later, on October 24, starved and exhausted, they were cast from the ship at Civita-vecchia. On September 29, the process was repeated with another 121 Jesuits. These reached the Papal States on January 4, 1760, "in a more wretched state of filth and emaciation than their prede-cessors."[11] The Jesuits were being expelled from Portugal—the first dramatic step in a process that would, fourteen years later, radi-cally affect the novice Diessbach, and decisively shape the life of the newly born Bruno.

ON JULY 19, 1763, death struck Bruno its cruelest blow as his mother, Margherita, died after giving birth to her tenth child, Giuseppe Tommaso. Bruno was four years old when she died. Fr. Antonio Ferrero, who would assist Bruno at his own death, testified that Bruno one day told him that "I have hardly known any other mother than the Virgin Mary, and in all my life, I have never received anything but caresses from so good a mother."[12] *I have hardly known any other mother*: a human void was created in Bruno that July 19 that would never be filled.

Throughout his life Bruno sought in the Virgin Mary the maternal presence denied him at his mother's death. Shortly before his priestly ordination he would write that he desired "to have a tender love for the Virgin Mary and the confidence in her of a son toward his Mother," and the trust "of a child toward his mother."[13] Fifty years after his mother's death, Bruno would review his life and speak of "the most Blessed Virgin Mary who has always been my tender Mother."[14] Ten years later, Bruno would again refer to "Mary Most Holy, my dear Mother."[15] Here, as so often in Bruno's life, human tragedy opened new spiritual avenues.[16]

References to Bruno's relationship with his father, Pietro, focus on their shared study. Giuseppe Loggero, Bruno's assistant for twenty years, wrote that "he himself, speaking of when he lived with his father, said that his father (who was a noted doctor) always read, even at table during lunch and supper."[17] And Antonio Ferrero quoted Bruno as saying that "my father and I studied even at table."[18]

Most probably, Bruno attended the primary and secondary schools of Cuneo, directed and largely taught by priests.[19] Later witnesses cite the young Bruno's penchant for mathematical studies, an interest he would pursue at the university.[20] The clarity, precision, detail, and organization of Bruno's later writings support such affirmations.

On November 28, 1772, the thirteen-year-old Bruno received the sacrament of confirmation in his home parish of Santa Maria della Pieve.[21] In keeping with contemporary usage, he most likely made his first Communion close to that date.[22]

In 1776, now seventeen, Bruno attempted to join the Carthusians in Chiusa Pesio, fifteen kilometers from Cuneo. His stay lasted only eight days. The superior quickly perceived that Bruno's health was unequal to the rigors of Carthusian life with its prolonged fasts, penitential diet, nighttime prayer, and almost continual solitude. At the end of those days, Bruno was obliged to return home.[23] His desire for consecration to God and for the solitude that facilitates prayer, denied him because of fragile health, remained. But his first attempt to dedicate his life to God had failed, and, for the moment, the next step was unclear.

As BRUNO GREW FROM CHILDHOOD into young adulthood, Diessbach's Jesuit training progressed. He concluded his novitiate in Genoa, and traveled to Milan for studies in philosophy and theology. On September 22, 1764, after his first year of theology, Diessbach was ordained a priest.[24]

In 1768, after completing his studies, Diessbach was sent to Germany, most probably for his final year of training after ordination.[25] A passage in his later writings suggests that during that year he conceived the project that would become his life's work.[26]

Diessbach was then assigned to Turin. There he passed five active years as confessor, preacher of parish missions, and catechist to the German-speaking people of the city.[27] Bruno would later write of these years that "at times he [Diessbach] preached in Italian, French, and German on the same day in different churches. He was a deeply learned man, and was aware of all that occurred in the culture around him, noting immediately how these events related to the glory of God. He was gifted in his speech, and his conversation was warm, well-mannered, cordial, discreet, and prudent. He knew how to win the hearts of all, whence all sought him and took pleasure in being with him."[28] Among those whose hearts he would win was the writer of these words, Bruno himself.

But now the time had come to propose a project born of years of experience and reflection. In 1771, Diessbach published his *The Christian Catholic Firmly Attached to His Religion through Consideration of Some of the Proofs that Establish Its Certitude.*[29]

Carthusian monastery in Chiusa Pesio, where Bruno sought entrance at age seventeen.

Carthusian monastery in Chiusa Pesio.

His book envisioned a bold initiative in critical times for the faith—
"An Expedient that Can Contribute to Prevent the Further Progress
of Unbelief."[30] The design was simple: let small groups of fearless,
well-prepared, and united Catholics be formed in the key points
of Europe to employ on behalf of the faith the great weapon of its
adversaries: the printed word.[31]

The second half of the eighteenth century witnessed an explosion of reading in Europe. The Industrial Revolution decreased
the cost of publication, and books, pamphlets, newspapers, and
journals multiplied. The development of commerce, rising populations, and the growth of cities further increased the demand for
the printed word. In the 1700s, literacy rates doubled in France.
Libraries, private and state-run, spread throughout Europe and
began lending books to their patrons. A contemporary observed
that "Paris reads ten times more than a century ago."[32] Coffee-
houses—by 1700 there were more than 500 in London, and, twenty
years later, 320 in Paris—offered books and journals to their cus-
tomers.[33] Reading had become the chief means of communicating
ideas, the principal instrument of shaping culture in Europe.

Diessbach, his own faith formerly destroyed through reading, viewed this phenomenon with particular sensitivity, and witnessed with pain the effective use of the printed word to undermine
Christian faith in Europe. "In our age," he wrote, "people generally
love to read. While few engage in deep and lengthy study, they
nonetheless desire to read a little and to learn. The principles they
absorb through reading are ordinarily those that shape their way
of thinking; and, after enough time, if many people are imbued
with similar principles opposed to the system received, a crisis will
result."[34]

"This is the source," he continued, "of the great harm that the
books of unbelievers have caused and continue to cause to religion and morals. Such books have already perverted many, and
daily pervert more. They are multiplied beyond numbering. Like
an overflowing torrent, they flood Protestant nations almost without hindrance, and many Catholic nations in spite of hindrances
[i.e., civil and ecclesiastical censorship]. Even those who do not

seek them find them on their path, whether they wish or not; they can hardly protect themselves from them, and indeed do not always protect themselves. Frequently we see that their thinking gradually begins to reflect this reading."[35]

Diessbach then questioned his reader: "Do we wish to oppose the progress of this contagion in an effective way?"[36] To those whose hearts answered yes, Diessbach offered a concrete proposal.

First, he noted, "Everywhere in the world, in addition to the faithful people, there are still many true Christians, well-formed and excellent Catholics, who love their holy religion with all their heart. You, O zealous Catholics who live in Italy, are not alone in your zeal for your religion! You who live in France are not alone; you who live in Spain, in Germany, in Poland, etc., are not alone. You live in different places, but you have brothers who form one body with you, motivated by the same spirit of religion and zeal."[37]

And, second, "In all cultured languages, and especially in those which people read most frequently and most willingly, there are many orthodox and well written books of various kinds. Some formally aim to establish foundations for Religion and defend it, some to conserve and reform morals, others to discuss science and literature, but with respect for and in support of Religion and morals."[38]

From these two considerations, a project was born: "With all our energy, let us unite these two realities, the friends of religion and good books, and let the first impart to the second all the activity of which it is capable. Beyond any doubt, an immense good will arise from this, the salutary and abundant fruits of which will continue to multiply and spread."[39]

Diessbach explained further: let these dedicated Catholics form libraries—large or small, according to their means—of books that defend the faith (polemical books), that explain Church teaching and move the heart (spiritual books), or that indirectly strengthen religion and morals (well-chosen books of literature, history, philosophy, and lighter reading).

Let these dedicated Catholics, Diessbach urged, then go forth with "a gentle and prudent zeal"[40] to offer these books to others:

to their own friends, to zealous priests who will share them with their people, to the young, beginning with books they enjoy and moving progressively to books of greater substance, to those who would read willingly but have no books, to military chaplains who will disseminate them among their soldiers, to those on vacation with time to read, to the unoccupied whose empty hours weigh upon them: "Give them some good books suitable to their condition, and I promise you they will read them at least in their most unoccupied hours, and this will not be without fruit."[41]

Is good will enough? What of the expense? Is this not prohibitive for most dedicated people? "In the first place," Diessbach replied, "the expense does not exceed the resources of many of those with zeal for religion, especially if they join together." Second, he continued, "The implementation of this project can be divided among various persons, each participating according to his means." Finally, he explained, "We can spend for this project the money that in other times we might have spent on good works of supererogation.[42] The money that from devotion you wish to spend in decorating the altars will be spent more usefully in defending them. If you multiply the number of true Christians, you will multiply one hundredfold the number of good works."[43]

Three years later, Diessbach would conclude a second book on this project with a heartfelt cry: "Oh! If I had the consolation of seeing some generous soul of great heart who loves God, who meditates deeply, and who would seriously ponder the . . . desires I have just expressed! Then I would hope to find a person who would take these desires to heart and I would hope to see them become reality."[44] The moment was approaching when Diessbach would find such persons and, prominent among them, Bruno Lanteri.

CHAPTER THREE

A Gathering of Friends

*Oh, what a great thing it is, and
how consoling, to serve as an
instrument to glorify God!*
—Bruno Lanteri

ON JULY 21, 1773, two years after Diessbach published his *The Christian Catholic*, his Jesuit life came to an end. On that date, Pope Clement XIV, yielding to pressure from the Catholic monarchs of Europe, declared the Society of Jesus "perpetually broken up and dissolved."[1] His decree completed the process begun in Portugal fourteen years earlier; it was an act of appeasement for which the Church would soon pay the price. In the words of historian Leopold von Ranke, "since the outworks had been taken, a more vigorous assault of the victorious opinions on the central stronghold would inevitably follow."[2]

With the dissolving of the Society, Diessbach's Jesuit ministry likewise ceased. He moved to the Cistercian Abbey in Rivalta, outside Turin, where he would remain until 1777. From this base, he continued his ministry of preaching and hearing confessions, now as a simple priest.[3]

During these years, Diessbach's project matured, and the time came for his first concrete initiative. He created a *Pia Associazione* (Pious Association) for the promotion of Catholic books that, by 1779, had spread to thirty Italian cities.[4] Subscribers annually received theological, philosophical, and spiritual books selected and printed by the *Pia Associazione,* and offered at low prices. Diessbach was exploring the terrain, preparing the more defined project soon to be inaugurated.

EVEN AS DIESSBACH SOUGHT NEW PATHS, Bruno returned home from the Carthusians. In Cuneo, he pondered his life's vocation. By 1777, the eighteen-year-old Bruno had found his answer: he would seek ordination as a diocesan priest. He asked permission to adopt clerical dress, a sign of his intention to pursue the priesthood.[5] On September 17, his bishop, Michele Casati, granted the request. Shortly after, Bruno left Cuneo to begin studies for priesthood at the University of Turin.[6]

In Turin, Bruno began the five years of studies required for a doctorate in theology.[7] Problems of health immediately surfaced once more: the weakness of the eyes and chest that would burden his entire life. Often too worn to write and at times unable to read, Bruno would later say that he learned theology more with his ears than his eyes, listening attentively to the lectures and conversing with his fellow students.[8]

His interaction with one of them, Giovanni Carlo Pellegrini—like Bruno from Cuneo and, like him, studying for priesthood—prepared the encounter that would shape Bruno's theological identity and determine his life's work.[9] Together they read the theological works then in vogue; among them were writings tinged with Jansenism.[10]

Jansenism had arisen in France one hundred and fifty years earlier as a theology marked by pessimism regarding fallen human nature. Now, in Italy, it assumed a new shape: severity in sacramental practice, and resistance to papal authority.[11] It was hostile to the Jesuits, and harshly criticized devotion to the Sacred Heart. Italian Jansenism grew increasingly resistant to the Holy See, and many of its clerical adherents embraced the political system created by the French as the Revolution overran the peninsula.[12]

Such thinking inevitably affected pastoral practice. Preaching and spiritual writing in the early 1800s in Piedmont, "with their severe and austere tone, at times fostered among the faithful a state of terror and anguish concerning the destiny of their souls."[13] Fr. Charles Plowden, a Jesuit until the suppression, noted that, before the suppression, most of the high-ranking persons in the royal court of Piedmont had Jesuits as confessors. After the suppression, when they discovered that their new confessors denied them absolution, "they ended by abandoning confession and becoming unbelievers."[14] In 1786, Bishop Scipione de Ricci held his Synod of Pistoia—later condemned by Rome—attended by 234 clergy of Jansenist sympathies. Predictably, the Synod attacked devotion to the Sacred Heart, denied the authority of the Holy Father, and adopted a rigorist approach to the sacrament of confession.[15]

On February 24, 1823, Jesuit Pierre Le Blanc wrote of the clergy of Savoy, then part of the kingdom of Piedmont, that "the priests are good and well-instructed, but long ago adopted an extraordinary rigorism in administering the sacraments."[16] Le Blanc recounted a conversation with a parish priest who "told us that for three years he had not given absolution to a parishioner because three or four times a year he attended Mass in another church in the city rather than in his own parish, and, while in the city, dealt with some small personal matters. At Easter time, he would not give Communion to anyone who, though instructed in the faith, was not instructed according to his sermons. He does not give absolution to young women who curl their hair. He does not give absolution to anyone who occasionally frequents a cabaret, even though his behavior is completely appropriate when there. For an occasional mortal sin out of human weakness, he will delay absolution for months, even for years. He gives penances for venial sins that last for days and even months."[17]

Jansenist literature was widely disseminated in Italy in the 1700s, and the University of Turin constituted the center of Jansenism in Piedmont.[18] That Bruno, therefore, should encounter Jansenist thinking at the university was no surprise. As they read, Bruno and Pellegrini began to gravitate toward Jansenist principles.[19]

Bruno was now twenty years old and in his third year at the university. From his family he had received and embraced a solid Catholic upbringing, as his desire to join the Carthusians and now his choice of diocesan priesthood witness. Yet in these university years—understandably for his age—Bruno was still searching for his theological and spiritual identity. That search, and in particular his contact with Pellegrini, set the stage for "the decisive event that shaped his entire life."[20]

In notes written four years before his death, Bruno stated concisely: "I met Diessbach in 1779."[21] A witness to Bruno's life described Bruno's and Pellegrini's reading, and wrote: "Divine Providence having disposed that the Theologian Lanteri should speak with Fr. Diessbach, with Fr. Bianchi, and with other learned religious, these showed him better books and better theological systems; convinced of their truth, Lanteri immediately abandoned the rigid system and embraced the doctrine founded on the teachings of the Catholic Church and on more benign theological opinions, that Catholic authors proposed for the good of souls and the glory of God."[22] Primary among these "Catholic" authors was Alphonsus Liguori. Diessbach affirmed that "only Liguori had the courage to oppose the theological prejudices of the day, to confront the insolent boldness of the numerous Jansenists, and uphold the cause of Gospel moral teaching."[23] After these conversations, above all those with Diessbach, Bruno completely rejected Jansenism; he would be, for the rest of his life, a resolute proponent of the mercy of God.

A deep bond of spiritual fatherhood and sonship developed between Diessbach and Bruno, ended only by Diessbach's death in 1798. In the notes cited, Bruno recounted that "I knew Diessbach for almost twenty years, always dealing with Spiritual Exercises and books."[24] Bruno would write of Diessbach that "to know good books with regard to every aspect of religion, and to use all possible means to bring every category of persons to read them, was, I could say, his passion, never forgetting the great good that he himself had received from books. His knowledge of books was remarkable, and his judgment highly refined, with a great ability to remember them."[25] In time, Bruno himself would become a master of this same knowledge. And the Servant of God Johann Roothaan, future general of the Jesuits, would write of Bruno's skill with the Spiritual Exercises that "he learned this from our Fr. Diessbach."[26] Fr. Antonio Ferrero, Bruno's confessor at the time of his death, testified that in these years, Bruno "came to know Fr. Diessbach,

Fr. Nikolaus Joseph Albert von Diessbach.

whose spirit, apostolic industry, zeal, profound theological learning, and holy occupations he inherited."[27] Diessbach "awakened
in him a love for the ministry of confessions, so that, as long as he
was able, Fr. Lanteri went with him to hear confessions in the prisons and hospitals, or heard confessions in the churches of the city
and at home, receiving any who wished to come, especially those
whose need was greatest."[28]

Ferrero continued: "He spent all the time he could with Fr.
Diessbach. He went with him for lunch in the public houses in
order to contact sinners, impede harmful conversations, and
spread good books." In the long hours that Diessbach and Bruno
shared, "they spoke together of God, and deepened their knowledge of sound doctrine." "In winter especially," Ferrero related,
"Fr. Diessbach went out to the porticos of the city and gathered
the poor who were suffering from the cold; he brought them to his
rooms, and together they [Diessbach and Bruno] warmed them,
fed them, cleansed them, instructed them in the faith, and prepared them to receive the holy sacraments."[29]

Giovanni Battista Biancotti, a witness of Bruno's last days,
affirmed in a biographical sketch of Bruno that "we cannot separate Fr. Diessbach from the Theologian Lanteri without completely
revising or at least altering to a significant degree this account, so
much did these two men live united in heart and spirit."[30] Three
years before his own death, in fact, when Bruno and his companions sought civil permission for their new religious institute, he
would explain to the king that "this project is not ours—its founder
is Fr. Diessbach."[31] Bruno would also write to his friend and associate Joseph von Penkler that this institute was formed "according
to the design inspired by and instilled in us for many years by Fr.
Diessbach."[32]

"I met Diessbach in 1779": this meeting and the lasting relationship that arose from it would mark Bruno forever. Through
Diessbach and through the institutions he directed, Bruno would
find his own identity. The time to launch the first of these institutions was now at hand.

Within months of Bruno's meeting with him, Diessbach established the new organization, the successor to the *Pia Associazione*.[33] Its name appeared in a document of July 16, 1780, in which Bruno wrote: "I, Pio Bruno Lanteri, vow before God to dedicate myself for two years to the works of the society called *l'Amitié Chrétienne* [the Christian Friendship]."[34] These two years would extend to thirty— until Bruno's exile by the French police in 1811.

The members of the *Amitié Chrétienne—Amicizia Cristiana* in Italian—were to be, Diessbach explained, educated persons able to employ the single apostolic means of the *Amicizia*: the printed word. They were to be warm in character and prudent, such that nothing would trouble the harmony of these friends in Christ: "This is the Society of Christian Friendship, and it uses no coercive means."[35]

The Christian friend "loves God ardently and so seeks the most effective means for promoting his glory. Reflecting on the Incarnation of the Son of God and on the sufferings of his death, he has learned that man's salvation is the great concern that directs the workings of Providence, and that this is, for that very reason, the great concern to which he ought to dedicate his own efforts, if he wishes to be faithful to the laws of the holy love that burns within him."[36]

When, however, the Christian friend sees so much error and vice in the world, and witnesses the lethargy of the greater part of humanity in regard to God, spiritual duties, and eternity, "he is brought up short, he is astonished, he burns with passion, and he grieves in pain, but does not yield to discouragement. To supply for his own weakness, he seeks help everywhere, and, because experience soon convinces him that there is no more effective means to respond to this situation than the cooperation of the true friends of God, and the use of good books . . . he joins himself unshakably to the first . . . in the hope that they will help him systematically distribute the second."[37]

Each local group of the *Amicizia Cristiana* was to consist of twelve members, six men (both lay and clerical) and six women, working together—an innovation for the time. A year of serious

spiritual preparation preceded admission to the *Amicizia*, including regular Communion and confession, a daily hour of meditation, and a second daily hour of spiritual reading. Once admitted,
the Christian friends dedicated a half-hour daily to meditation
and a second half-hour to spiritual reading. They made an annual
retreat of eight days if possible, and no less than three.[38]

In a conference for the *Amicizia*, Bruno elaborated: "These
are the means we habitually employ. There are many others that
we adopt only on occasion as, for example, promoting the Spiritual Exercises and parish missions, the printing or reprinting of
books, newspapers, journals, holy images, etc." "Nor," he continued, "is the *Amicizia Cristiana* satisfied with fostering these aims
in one country alone; rather, it lifts its eyes to the whole world
and desires and strives to bring Jesus Christ to be known and to
reign in all places. . . . Anywhere we can reach, we seek to further every kind of good and impede every kind of evil, since there
is no place, person, or thing related to the glory of God and the
salvation of souls, and therefore valued by the Sacred Heart of
Jesus, that is not, at the same time, also valued by the true Christian friend."[39] To this group of friends, with such spiritual long-
ings and dedicated to such works, Bruno joined himself in his
university years.

EVEN AS NEW SPIRITUAL HORIZONS opened before him, Bruno continued his progress toward priesthood. By September 1780, Bruno
had received Tonsure, the ritual cutting of hair that signified passage from the lay to the clerical state.[40] On September 28, 1780,
his father, Pietro, legally constituted his son's "ecclesiastical patrimony," that is, the requisite financial security for access to holy
orders.[41] This ecclesiastical patrimony ensured Bruno financial
freedom for his life's work, already beginning under Diessbach's
guidance and in the context of the *Amicizia*.

In the following months, between October 1780 and September 1781, Bruno received the four minor orders—porter, exorcist,
lector, and acolyte—the steps through which all candidates for
priesthood had to pass in his day.[42] And on June 27, 1781, having

completed four years of theological studies at the university, Bruno
earned his licentiate in theology, roughly the equivalent of our
master's degree today.[43]

The time for Bruno's definitive commitment to the clerical
state now had come. His ordination as subdeacon, the first of the
major orders (to be followed by diaconate and priesthood), was to
take place three months later in September 1781. Through ordination to the subdiaconate, Bruno would commit himself to perpetual celibacy in view of his future life as priest.

On August 15, five weeks before that ceremony, Bruno formally dedicated himself to the Virgin Mary through his "pact of
slavery," declaring, "Let all those into whose hands this document
may fall, know that I, the undersigned Pio Bruno Lanteri, offer
myself as perpetual slave of the Blessed Virgin Mary, our Lady,
with an unconditional, free, and perfect gift of my person and all
my possessions, that she may dispose of them according to her
good pleasure as my true and absolute Lady."[44] In the imminence
of his definitive vocational commitment, Bruno offered himself
totally to the Virgin Mary. His lifelong attachment to Mary suggests that Bruno's offering was indeed "perpetual."

The following month, on September 22, Bruno was ordained
a subdeacon. Three months later, on December 22, he was
ordained a deacon.[45] Now only the final step—ordination to the
priesthood—remained.

IN THESE SAME MONTHS, a second *Amicizia* was born of the first.[46]
Of this second *Amicizia*, too, Bruno would be a member, profoundly absorbing its spirit and works. In time, he would become
its leader.

The new group was Diessbach's *Amicizia Sacerdotale* (Priestly
Friendship), that Bruno would later describe as "a devout union of
young priests and also fervent clerics [subdeacons and deacons]
who deeply desire to live according to God's sublime plans for
their priestly vocation. Gathered together for this purpose, they
strive with all their energy to render themselves capable instruments for promoting as effectively as they can the glory of God,

that is, the salvation of souls, which is the goal of their vocation to the priestly state of life."[47] Its members, another *Amicizia* text affirmed, were to be "men totally ready for battle," "well instructed," "with deep knowledge of things and of persons, and of the spirit that reigns in that place, of its motivations, its practices, and its roots," men who were "strong, persevering, and who never yield to discouragement."[48]

The *amici sacerdotali* (priestly friends), Bruno stated, "seriously dedicate themselves to acquiring that interior spirit that unites them to God, and that must especially inspire their actions, through a persevering practice of genuine and solid virtue."[49] They seek this interior spirit through a faithful life of the sacraments, through "serious, abundant, and daily meditation on the holy truths of our religion and on the life of Jesus Christ," through spiritual reading, daily examination of conscience, and "serious study of dogmatic and moral theology."[50]

The apostolic means employed by the *amici sacerdotali* were those essential to the priesthood: the Word of God and the sacraments.[51] In their weekly meetings, the *amici sacerdotali* received a training directed toward employing both effectively. To administer the Word of God in spoken form, the *amici* prepared to preach popular missions and to give the Spiritual Exercises of St. Ignatius, or at least one of these two.[52] To spread that Word in printed form, they applied themselves to knowing books of quality and to exploring ways of distributing them, both in their priestly activity and in collaboration with the *Amicizia Cristiana*.[53]

In confessional ministry, Diessbach told them, they were "to exercise true prudence and true charity, with an implacable hatred for sin, and a fatherly and gentle compassion toward the sinner."[54] Taking Alphonsus Liguori as their guide, they would receive those who approached them in confession with the gentleness and mercy of Christ.[55]

IN THESE SAME YEARS, an association with the somewhat mysterious name "*Aa*" opened a local chapter in Turin. This organization had been founded 150 years earlier by Jesuit Jean Bagot in the

College of La Flèche, France.[56] The title "*Aa*" most probably signified "*Assemblée*" (Assembly), and derived from a doubling of the
first letter.[57] The *Aa* groups consisted of highly dedicated students
in theology, young men preparing for priesthood who quietly

dedicated themselves to growth in holiness and readiness for
priestly ministry. Its members spread widely throughout France
and beyond, and exercised fruitful ministry in positions of responsibility: pastors, preachers, seminary faculty, and bishops. Among
them was renowned spiritual author Henri Marie Boudon, whose
writings Bruno would frequently read and promote.[58]

Bruno soon entered the *Aa,* whose members, like those of the
two *Amicizie,* looked to Diessbach for guidance.[59] Not surprisingly,
in view of their common Ignatian origins and theological similari-
ties, many members belonged to both the *Amicizia Sacerdotale*
and the *Aa.*

In the *Amicizie* and the *Aa,* Bruno developed a group of friends
and co-workers who would play key roles in his life: Luigi Virginio,
whom Bruno would call "the greatest friend I ever had";[60] Carlo
Giuseppe Sappa de' Milanesi, a close friend and later a bishop; Jean
Baptiste Aubriot de La Palme, also later a bishop;[61] Pierre-Joseph
Rey, a future bishop and key figure in Bruno's last years; Louis-
Guillaume-Valentin Du Bourg, a spiritual guide of St. Elizabeth
Seton and the first bishop of Louisiana in the United States, who
would seek Bruno's aid in procuring priests for his mission territory; Servant of God Giovanni Battista Rubino, future founder of
a religious congregation, who would preach Bruno's funeral discourse; Luigi Guala, Bruno's disciple and close collaborator, and
first rector of the Priestly Residence (*Convitto Ecclesiastico*) whose
later members would include St. Joseph Cafasso and St. John
Bosco; and Luigi Craveri, Bruno's disciple and a future seminary
rector, who one day would break Bruno's heart.[62]

IN FEBRUARY 1781, Jacques Necker, finance minister to Louis XVI,
published his *Report to the King* on the state of finances in France.
His *Report* masked France's enormous debt, largely caused by
its support of the American Revolution, and earned him wide

popularity among the French. Successive ministers, however, revealed the precarious condition of France's finances. Louis XVI would later reappoint Necker as finance minister, and, on July 11, 1789, dismiss the popular minister a second time. At this, a public outcry would arise, and, three days later, the Bastille would be stormed.

As 1781 ended, Bruno was twenty-two years old and a deacon, in his final year at the university and six months from priesthood. A four-year search—from his failed attempt to enter the Carthusians to his brush with Jansenism—had led to the encounter with Diessbach and the discovery of a new path. Through Diessbach, his two *Amicizie*, and the *Aa*, the young Bruno found guidance, a spiritual program, and a set of like-minded friends.

Even as Bruno strove to assimilate this identity, a tempest was preparing in nearby France. These quiet years of spiritual and intellectual labor would ready him for the day when the storm would engulf Piedmont as well.

CHAPTER FOUR

"Nunc Coepi"

> *I felt a desire to know Him, love Him, and serve Him as perfectly as I can, and to make Him known, loved, and served by all.*
> —Bruno Lanteri

AS THE FOLLOWING YEAR began, Bruno reviewed a spiritual program he had composed, and wrote: "I propose on this day, January 6, 1782, to read this directory once a week until my ordination to the priesthood."[1] The twenty-four manuscript pages of this directory, together with other spiritual notes of this time, reveal the youthful energy with which Bruno sought spiritual growth in these years. They also evidence his Piedmontese personality with its strong-willed dedication to the task at hand, embrace of hard work, sense of duty, and acceptance of the personal cost of its fulfillment.

The young Bruno desired that God be the center of his life: "I am from God and for God alone. God alone contains all good. God alone can satisfy me and make me happy. Therefore, I will direct all my energy and actions to God alone. God alone will be the center of my desires and my affections."[2] Elsewhere he wrote more simply: "God alone. God alone."[3]

The new deacon sought his ideal in the saints: "Always strive to think, speak, and act as did the saints,"[4] and declared: "The truths I have embraced are those the saints embraced. These truths are and always will be the same. Neither time nor failure to reflect on them will cause them to lose their strength. As they have convinced me once, so with the help of God, they must convince me always."[5]

34

Bruno chose to belong totally to God: "I resolve before God and the whole heavenly Court . . . to give myself to him without half-measures and without reserve, to be of those who 'who have dedicated their lives to the name of our Lord Jesus Christ' [Acts 15:26]," biblical words he would later apply to the congregation he would found, the Oblates of the Virgin Mary.[6] Bruno accepted the cost of this decision: "Having resolved to serve God with perfection, I will not be ashamed of this choice but will live it openly before all. I will let others see clearly that I value living as a good Christian who has accepted God for his King, and not the world with its teachings. If I should be scorned and derided for this, I will know beyond all doubt that such scorn honors me and places a crown on my head."[7]

The youthful cleric opened his heart to God's mercy in his failures: "I will not allow myself to be discouraged, however I may fall. If God is for me, who can be against me [Rom. 8:31]? Though I fall a thousand times, each time, even the thousandth, I will rise again as peacefully as if it were the first, knowing my weakness and knowing, Lord, your great mercy."[8] "And so," Bruno exclaimed, "if I should fall even a thousand times a day, a thousand times, with peaceful repentance, I will say immediately, *Nunc coepi* [Now I begin], my God, my God!"[9] The young deacon proclaimed God's goodness in the words of Wisdom 1:1: "*Sentite de Deo in bonitate*" ("Think of God in a spirit of goodness").[10] As a spiritual guide, Bruno would repeat these teachings and often these very words to those who sought his aid. In these notes, we glimpse the forging of his spirituality.

Bruno desired to reflect God's goodness to others: "I will seek always to be zealous, magnanimous, open, faithful, simple, sincere, warm, peaceful, resigned to the will of God, intent on pleasing him alone and gaining souls for him, joyful, compassionate, accommodating in all that is not offensive to God, gentle, and humble of heart."[11] As we will see, this gentleness would cost Bruno much effort.

The young Bruno energetically proposed "to be completely faithful to my daily exercises of prayer,"[12] and specified these exercises: meditation, Mass, Divine Office, spiritual reading, visit to the Blessed Sacrament, examination of conscience, and weekly confession.[13] He was profoundly conscious that failure to *reflect seriously* on the truths of faith causes grave spiritual harm, and so resolved "never to omit my meditation, and to make it faithfully in accord with the method I have chosen."[14] The importance of such reflection would be a central theme of his spirituality.

The careful detail with which Bruno programmed his spiritual life appeared in his approach to receiving Holy Communion: "For Communion, I will prepare the content of my preparation and thanksgiving the evening before. I will call these sentiments to mind immediately upon awaking, and will do all this with method and fidelity. I will return to these sentiments throughout the day and in my visit to the Blessed Sacrament."[15]

Bruno desired to pray the Divine Office "with attention, devotion, and trust." "I will see myself," he continued, "as an ambassador of the Church, praying for her needs, offering supplications in words given by God himself or taught by his beloved Spouse, the Church."[16] "When I say the Office," he added, "I will note attentively those verses which particularly serve to awaken or strengthen my devotion."[17]

Bruno proposed "never to omit my spiritual reading,"[18] and to do this "as though the page I am reading is a letter from God to me. I will say, 'Speak, Lord, for your servant is listening' [1 Sam. 3:9]. I will pause from time to time to reflect on what I am reading, and will dwell on those places where my heart is stirred."[19] Sacred Scripture was central to this reading: "I will read a chapter of the Gospel of Jesus Christ daily."[20] The young deacon identified specific titles for this spiritual nourishment: "I will read the entire works of St. Teresa of Avila from the beginning until I have finished them all. I will always carry with me either *The Imitation of Christ* [Thomas à Kempis] or *The Spiritual Combat* [Lorenzo Scupoli] in order to read them in free moments, or when I feel the need."[21]

Bruno proposed to pray regularly before the Blessed Sacrament: "When possible, I will make a daily visit to the Blessed Sacrament."[22] During such visits, he wrote, "I will make an act of faith and of adoration; I will ask his help in my concerns, or meditate on a phrase of the Our Father, or will say the Our Father itself with the help of his grace; I will express my gratitude, and say the *Sub Tuum Praesidium* ['We fly to your protection, O holy Mother of God...']."[23]

An examination of conscience, both of the day in general and of particular areas of growth, also entered this program.[24] Bruno specified one such area as "the practice of union with God."[25] In free moments, Bruno continued, "I will reflect on my situation or on the duties of my state in life, or I will say the Rosary."[26] In a further proposal he stated: "I will go to confession weekly."[27] He resolved to lead others to make the Spiritual Exercises, and added, "I will make the thirty-day retreat."[28]

Bruno planned to adopt penitential practices in the struggle against temptation,[29] and to seek God's grace for the *Aa*.[30] Abbreviated words in these notes suggest that Bruno proposed a weekly use of the cilice and discipline, classic forms of penance taught— with wise moderation—by St. Ignatius of Loyola, and practiced by many figures of holiness through the centuries.[31] Antonio Ferrero, Bruno's confessor in later years, confirmed his use of such instruments of penance.[32] When the young Bruno wrote that "my life is solemnly consecrated to God and totally dedicated to his service," and that "to this alone I must devote all the energies of my body and soul,"[33] he clearly intended to live this consecration fully.

The twenty-three-year-old Bruno expressed the "tender love ... and confidence" he desired to have for Mary as his Mother and his Lady.[34] He planned to keep a picture of her at hand, to speak to her often, and to greet her frequently,[35] and added, "I will strive to promote devotion to the Virgin Mary when opportunities arise, and especially in giving talks."[36]

Bruno's notes in these years reveal a spiritual identity in its youthful beginnings. His quiet, persevering efforts to live this program in coming decades would deepen that identity and shape the spiritual heritage he would transmit to others.

EVENTS NOW MOVED SWIFTLY toward Bruno's ordination to priesthood. In 1782, at the age of twenty-three, he would complete his
final year of theology. On January 22 of that year, Rome granted
Bruno permission for ordination, dispensing him from the canonically required age of twenty-four.[37]

That final year, however, would not be completed in the calm
of university studies. For the first of many times, the service of a
beleaguered pope interrupted the peaceful flow of Bruno's life.

Emperor Joseph II of Austria, since his accession to the throne
in 1780, had radically interfered with the life of the Church. He
claimed the right to approve papal documents prior to their prom-
ulgation within his empire, demanded that priests be trained in
seminaries run by the state, suppressed religious orders, unilaterally restructured dioceses and parishes, reduced marriage to a
civil contract, and subjected the behavior of priests and Church
property to state control.[38] In hopes of resolving their differences,
Pius VI decided to travel to Vienna and meet with the emperor.

Having learned the pope's intention, Diessbach journeyed to
Vienna to defend the pontiff and prepare for him a warm welcome
among the people. He chose Bruno as his companion, and the two
departed from Turin for Vienna, arriving in mid-February.[39]

Pius VI reached Vienna on March 22. His meetings with
Joseph II, though cordial, changed nothing in the emperor's
actions. Wherever the pope traveled, however, he met enthusiastic popular acclaim. In Vienna, Diessbach and Bruno helped prepare that reception. Years later Bruno would recall the days "when
I was in Vienna with Fr. Diessbach,"[40] and Antonio Ferrero would
attest that, "Having learned that Pius VI was to travel to Vienna
and the reason for his trip, Fr. Lanteri, together with Fr. Diessbach,
resolved to precede Pius VI to Vienna, and to accompany him, in
order to reawaken the fervor of those well-disposed, and to enkin-
dle devotion for him among the people by disseminating books
that refuted the widespread errors of Febronius, Richer, Eybel,
and the Synod of Pistoia."[41] These three authors and the Synod of
Pistoia contested papal authority; characteristically, Diessbach
and Bruno countered their teaching with appropriate books.

City of Turin. Bruno lived and worked here for fifty years.

Royal Palace in Turin.

Bruno would later designate Febronianism and Richerism, together with Jansenism, as the "current errors" of his day, and would relentlessly combat all three. Through contact with Diessbach and through experiences like his trip to Vienna, the young Bruno's theological identity was taking shape.

Bruno returned to Turin, and on May 25, 1782, was ordained a priest.[42] Two months later, on July 13, he gained his doctorate in theology. From this time, Bruno would be known as "the Theologian Lanteri," a title given to those who earned their doctorate in theology.[43]

On November 23, the archbishop of Turin granted the new priest, originally from Cuneo, permission to reside in the Archdiocese of Turin.[44] The city of Turin, capital of the kingdom of Piedmont, would remain Bruno's center of activity for the next forty-five years.

Once ordained, and in keeping with Diessbach's program for members of the *Amicizia Sacerdotale*, Bruno prepared to give the Spiritual Exercises of St. Ignatius. In the spiritual notes quoted above, he wrote, "I will give all the time I can to preparing my talks for the Spiritual Exercises,"[45] and again, "I will apply myself first to completing my talks on the meditations of the Spiritual Exercises, and then to studying moral theology, so that I may begin my ministry as soon as possible."[46] A list of Bruno's expenditures for books reveals that in his first ten years of priesthood he acquired the works of thirty-six commentators on the Spiritual Exercises.[47] Clearly, his effort to learn the Spiritual Exercises was serious and prolonged. In time, it would make him a master in his own right, who would prepare many others to give the Ignatian Exercises.

During these same years, Bruno dedicated himself to the study of moral theology. In the Archdiocese of Turin, newly ordained priests were allowed to hear confessions only after three further years of studies in moral theology, and after passing the corresponding examination. Now, in his first years of priesthood, Bruno undertook these studies.[48]

In the summer of 1784, when Bruno was twenty-five, his father, Pietro, fell gravely ill. Bruno returned to Cuneo to assist him in his illness. These were difficult months, as Bruno accompanied his father and, in the measure possible, strove to fulfill his responsibilities in the *Amicizie* and *Aa*. On September 18, Bruno wrote to his friend and fellow *Amicizie* member Luigi Virginio, describing the measures counseled by the doctor and their ineffectiveness: "For the past two weeks we have applied the remedies prescribed by the doctor . . . but thus far they have brought my father no improvement. Humanly speaking, I have never had any hope nor do I now, because I visit my father several times a day, and have seen no substantial improvement during the three months that this illness has confined him to bed, though forceful medical measures have been applied."[49] In the same letter, Bruno wrote that he could not return to Turin "since if my father continues in this condition, it is impossible for me to leave," and asked that others in Turin provide for his many *Amicizie* tasks.[50] Bruno signed the letter, "In haste, Cuneo, September 18, 1784, Lanteri."[51]

Six weeks later, on October 31, Pietro Lanteri died at the age of sixty-three.[52] In a letter to a priest friend three days later, Bruno wrote simply: "Last Sunday I lost my poor father. I recommend him to your prayers when you celebrate Mass."[53] As his father's principal heir, many administrative tasks fell to Bruno. Having completed them, and having entrusted the further administration of his inheritance to relatives, Bruno returned to Turin.[54] Throughout his life, Bruno would employ these financial resources in the service of the Church; at the time of his death, nothing would remain.

Signs of Bruno's steady growth now began to appear. He requested of the Holy Father, and, on December 20, 1784, was granted permission for life to read books listed on the Index of Prohibited Books.[55] Bruno sought this permission, "desiring to deepen his understanding" of erroneous writings, in order to better uphold the truths they assailed.[56] "According to the *Amicizia* mentality," one commentator notes, such permission "made of this priest, notwithstanding his notably young age, a qualified writer."[57]

And, in fact, Bruno's ministry with books continued to expand. His close associate, Giuseppe Loggero, attested that "he had a library of several thousand volumes, of books of the best authors in every branch of knowledge, and especially of books against the errors of the day, Jansenism, Febronianism, and Richerism."[58] Some years later, Bruno himself would refer to the "more than 5000 books" of his library.[59]

Bruno's disciple Luigi Craveri affirmed that Bruno "spent large sums of money" for such books.[60] In fact, Bruno's expenses for books during the fourteen years 1781–1794, included 716 titles, with an average expenditure of $3,000 per year.[61] Of this library Craveri wrote: "I remember that he constantly encouraged us to study, to labor, and to seek holiness in order to win souls for God. To this end, he invited us to use his library which was always open to priests and seminarians."[62] Bruno, Craveri asserted, "read books with deep insight and quickly grasped not only the content of the book, but also the spirit of the writer."[63] Through extensive reading in these early years of priesthood, Bruno was developing his ability to employ the printed word on behalf of the Church.

On October 22, 1785, Bruno received permission to hear confessions. That day, a further ministry opened for the young priest, one that would absorb his energies for decades to come.[64] Giuseppe Loggero related that "although his health was very weak, he dedicated himself tirelessly to hearing confessions, especially in church and in places where many were likely to approach this sacrament."[65] Loggero continued: "He directed souls toward holiness with great wisdom, and so had many spiritual sons and daughters whom he guided to a deep life of the Sacraments. He heard confessions day and night in church and at home, so that it may be said that his life was continually dedicated to the good of souls."[66]

Luigi Craveri told of Bruno that "he not only dedicated himself personally to spiritual reading and meditation, but recommended these spiritual practices to all, both in personal conversations and in the confessional. He was tireless in hearing confessions, as I can attest as one who was present and witnessed this."[67] Bruno's confessor Antonio Ferrero affirmed that "he received grace from

God to comfort the anxious, enlighten the confused, gladden the sorrowful, and encourage the diffident . . . he consoled many religious in their sorrows, and his penitents left him filled with consolation."[68]

Bruno would later transmit his love for confessional ministry to his Oblates of the Virgin Mary, who, he wrote, "dedicate themselves tirelessly to hearing confessions, ready to welcome all at any time, especially those in greatest need, with a glad and willing spirit."[69] His further counsels to his Oblates manifested Bruno's own ideal as confessor: "In particular, they strive to imitate the Divine Master in welcoming and treating all, especially those in most need, with great gentleness and goodness, and the scrupulous with great charity and unalterable patience. They judge no heart invulnerable, but with persistent and fervent prayer and with enterprising charity, do all they can so that not one be lost."[70] That a confessor who "directed souls toward holiness with great wisdom," who sought "to imitate the . . . great gentleness and goodness" of the Divine Master, and whose penitents "left him filled with consolation," would attract many spiritual sons and daughters is readily understandable. In his first years of priesthood, Bruno laid the foundations of a lifelong ministry as confessor and spiritual director.

Bruno's growth also appeared in a letter Diessbach wrote at this time to a priest whom he named "my dearly beloved friend in Jesus Christ"—most likely, therefore, a member of the *Amicizia Cristiana* or the *Amicizia Sacerdotale*. On February 6, 1786, Diessbach replied to this priest: "I am sending your letter to Lanteri as you desired, and, if you wish, send him this one as well. I earnestly recommend that you make the Spiritual Exercises; you can discuss with Lanteri how to do this."[71] Diessbach encouraged the priest to learn to give the Spiritual Exercises, and to acquire the art of disseminating good books. He concluded: "If you undertake this with a great heart and persevere in this with constancy, you will find abundant help from God, great consolation, and great peace. Lanteri will help you in all, all that you wish from him, and trust God, whose voice you will certainly be following in this way."[72]

Diessbach's confidence in the twenty-seven-year-old Bruno, now his spiritual son for seven years, manifests Bruno's increasing ability as a spiritual guide.

The following year, Bruno traveled to Switzerland for the *Amicizia*, and stopped briefly in Chambéry along the way. While there, he visited the *Aa* confrères of that city. Bruno's arrival found them on retreat with their bishop, and time for sharing was limited. His visit, nonetheless, proved welcome.

On April 25, 1787, Chambéry *Aa* member Louis Tellier wrote to an *Aa* confrère in Turin that Bruno "rekindled our beloved *Aa* by his presence alone. His wise counsels and the words of consolation that came from his lips made a great impression on the hearts of all. We listened to him with pleasure and we proposed to imitate his zeal, if not entirely, at least in part."[73] Three weeks later, on May 14, a second Chambéry *Aa* member, Benoit Guillet, wrote that Bruno's visit, "although short, gave us much joy. Monsieur Murgeray [founder of the *Aa* in Turin] had the pleasure of seeing his old friend, and the others that of seeing a confrère they had not yet met. We decided to convene the *Aa* and gathered with much pleasure on his part and ours. We have seen for ourselves the inspiring qualities in Lanteri you described to us, and it was not hard for us to see that grace has not worked in vain in him."[74] A week later, Jean Baptiste Aubriot de La Palme, also present during Bruno's visit, described the *Aa* confrère as "a man with whom it is impossible to associate without becoming better," and concluded, "Monsieur Lanteri is most likely such a man, and such as I would wish to be myself."[75]

In the years preceding the French Revolution, now only two years away, the young Bruno labored to grow spiritually and apostolically. The fruitfulness of these efforts indicated, as Guillet affirmed, that grace was indeed working richly in him.

In retreat notes from these years, after meditating on Jesus's passion, Bruno wrote: "I adored, and I proclaim that I wish to adore, Jesus mocked in his passion. I will renounce all human respect and all desire for the esteem of men; I will be honored to be treated as was Jesus."[76] Contemplating Jesus's physical sufferings,

Bruno added: "I felt a desire to give everything for God and for my neighbor, either to become a saint, or to die."[77] The following day, Bruno pondered the love of Jesus Christ, and noted: "I felt a desire to know him, to love him, to serve him as perfectly as I can, and to make him known, loved, and served by all. I no longer want any limits in my love for Jesus and for my neighbor."[78] *I no longer want limits. . . .* The day was fast approaching when these desires would be put to the test.

CHAPTER FIVE

Spiritual Struggles

> *Let him walk at the pace God wishes in his spiritual practices, holy though they be, neither hurrying ahead nor holding back.*
> —Bruno Lanteri

ON JANUARY 24, 1789, BENOIT GUILLET, who had met Bruno in Chambéry two years earlier, wrote to an *Aa* member in Turin: "I received word regarding Monsieur Virginio [Bruno's close friend and associate] and the *Aa* members in Paris. . . . I thank God that matters are going well there. We must work as diligently as we can for the glory of God and the good of the Church, to compensate in some measure, if possible, for the growing harm caused by lax moral behavior, weakening of faith, and thirst for novelties. God certainly desires more from us than simply to lament these evils. The spirit of the world is spreading in the colleges, and the dispositions required for a member of the *Aa* are becoming harder to find. Rather than let ourselves be discouraged, we must increase our zeal all the more."[1]

That same day, Louis XVI convened the Estates General, the French legislative assembly. His act initiated a dramatic process that would shake France and the Western world. The storm in France was about to break; soon it would overwhelm Piedmont as well.

On May 5, the Estates General met in Versailles, the first gathering of this assembly in one hundred and seventy-five years. In convoking the Estates General, Louis XVI admitted to the nation his inability to resolve the financial crisis facing France. Tensions quickly arose and, on June 17, the third estate (commons) declared itself a national assembly.[2] Ten days later, Louis XVI capitulated and formally recognized the new national assembly.

Events now precipitated rapidly. On July 14, the Bastille was stormed. On August 11, the assembly abolished all class privileges and, on August 27, adopted the Declaration of the Rights of Man and of the Citizen.

Quickly, however, the Revolution revealed itself hostile to the Catholic Church. On November 2, 1789, the assembly nationalized Church property and, three months later, on February 13, 1790, suppressed religious orders in France.[3] On July 12 of that same year, the assembly enacted the Civil Constitution of the Clergy, in effect creating a national French church independent of the pope.[4] And when, on November 27, a further decree ordered all clergy to swear fidelity to the Civil Constitution, those faithful to Rome faced a crisis of conscience.[5] The lives of those who refused the oath—the "non-jurors"—would soon be in danger. The first measure would be deportation; bloodier measures would follow.[6]

ON JUNE 12, 1789, five weeks after the Estates General convened in Versailles, Bruno began an eight-day retreat.[7] He was thirty years old and intensely active in the works of the *Amicizie* and *Aa*: disseminating books, giving the Spiritual Exercises, hearing confessions, guiding lay men and women spiritually, and assisting seminarians and young priests to prepare for ministry. In these eight days of prayer, Bruno reviewed his life and prepared for the coming year. Even as the storm drew near, Bruno's effort to grow spiritually continued.

The days of retreat were full: three one-hour meditations, two one-hour instructions, Mass, Divine Office, rosary, spiritual reading, and examination of conscience, with intervals between these times of prayer and two hours for relaxation and rest after lunch.[8] Bruno planned to rise each day at 6:00 a.m. and retire at 10:00 p.m.[9] He focused his retreat on classic themes of the Ignatian Spiritual Exercises: the purpose of life, sin, the last things, mercy, the incarnation and birth of Jesus Christ, his hidden and public life, the two standards, the passion of Christ, and the love of God.[10]

Bruno's prayer led to concrete spiritual proposals: "In every action I will seek God's will. I will look to see whether he desires this action and how he desires it done."[11] And again: "I will renounce all unnecessary bodily comforts, always keeping before my eyes Jesus Christ in his humiliation, poverty, and suffering. I profess that my desire is to share these with him."[12]

Bruno examined himself unsparingly in this retreat, named his defects in detail, and chose corresponding remedies. "My defects are," he wrote, "negligence in the things of God, such that I do them lightly, without commitment; severity and roughness with my neighbor, little charity and little concern for his spiritual and bodily well-being; too much concern for temporal matters, too much attachment to things, to honors, to pleasures; fear of discomfort, of suffering in my health, little courage in arduous and difficult things. These make it harder for me to have a living faith, a great confidence in God, and the love I owe God."[13]

The remedies were, Bruno continued, "to test myself often during the day, that is, with frequent examinations, to see whether I truly love God above all things, whether I love my neighbor as myself, and whether I dedicate myself seriously to self-denial,"[14] to act "with great freedom of spirit, moved by the desire to die to myself and to please God, by knowledge of God and of the emptiness of material things, by comparison of what is temporal with what is spiritual,"[15] and to grow in "a spirit of prayer, frequently representing the Lord before me saying to me, 'Until now you have not asked anything' [John 16:24], examining myself at various points during the day as to whether I have asked anything of the Lord."[16]

Bruno's resolutions grew more specific: he would rise at 5:00 a.m. on ordinary days, and at 4:30 a.m. on feast days. His day would begin with prayer: the Divine Office, meditation, and Mass. Later in the day he would continue the Divine Office and dedicate time to spiritual reading. At 9:00 p.m., he would conclude the Divine

Office, examine his conscience, and prepare the next morning's meditation.[17]

In his relationship with God, Bruno wrote, "I desire to have great reverence and great fidelity, with a persevering effort to please him and do his holy will," and added, "I will avoid negligence in God's service and strive for purity of intention in serving him."[18] "In regard to myself," Bruno continued, "I will practice my usual mortifications and fight against seeking comforts and satisfactions of the senses."[19] "In regard to my neighbor," he concluded, "I will strive for great gentleness in my way of acting and for great love in my heart as I serve him in his material and spiritual needs."[20]

I will strive for great gentleness in my way of acting. . . . We have already seen Bruno accuse himself of "severity and roughness" toward his neighbor. The frequency with which Bruno returned to this proposal suggests that such gentleness did not come easily.

In undated spiritual notes, Bruno described himself as "rough, with little compassion . . . impatient, oversensitive in things not to my liking, and therefore sharp in replying to others."[21] In another such examination, Bruno depicted his "melancholy and impatience that lead to roughness, make it harder for people to approach me, hinder the accomplishment of so much good, and cause scandal."[22]

Bruno's effort to overcome such roughness was persevering. In other notes, he proposed "to examine myself often on charity toward my neighbor and on gentleness."[23] On November 24, 1800 he again determined "to make my particular examination on gentleness and humility of heart, and to renew this often, especially in my principal actions."[24]

In further undated spiritual proposals, Bruno returned yet again to this quest: "I will treat all with gentleness, and this will be the subject of my particular examination."[25] His program for growth in gentleness reveals Bruno's seriousness in this endeavor: "For my particular examination on gentleness, I will read in Rodriguez[26] or elsewhere about the nature, kinds, acts, degrees, aids, obstacles, means, and examples of this virtue; from time to time, I will compare my response to others with the way Jesus Christ

responds to those he meets; immediately upon arising, I will
renew my proposal to grow in this virtue and will ask God's help;
I will examine myself often on this virtue and note my failures in
writing, even when walking through the streets; before going to
bed I will make my particular examination on this and review my
progress day by day and week by week."[27]

Bruno pursued this gentleness throughout his entire life. In
1827, at the age of sixty-eight, just three years before his death,
Bruno returned once more to this quest: "I will strive to grow in the
virtues of humility, gentleness, and confidence."[28] Such lifelong
proposals suggest that for Bruno, growth in gentleness required
persistent effort. We will witness his struggle to attain this virtue at
further points in his life.

Bruno's notes provide insight into his ongoing quest for spiritual growth, and the importance of his annual retreat in that
effort.[29] In the summer of 1789, as the French Revolution began,
Bruno continued to pursue such growth.

A MANUSCRIPT WITH CHRONOLOGICAL ANNOTATIONS for the years
1787–1813 reveals Bruno's close attention to the French Revolution and its impact on the Church.[30] As the Revolution unfolded,
its persecution of the Church grew increasingly violent; and when
on April 20, 1792, the French declared war on Austria, a European
conflict began that would end only twenty-two years later, in 1814,
with the fall of Napoleon.

Reviewing the year 1792, Bruno cited Pius VI's brief of March
19 in support of those French priests and bishops who had refused
the oath of fidelity to the Civil Constitution of the Clergy and
who were undergoing severe penalties.[31] He noted the legislative
assembly's decree of April 6 (Good Friday) proscribing religious
and clerical dress, and added, "Priests deported."[32] For August 10,
he observed, "Louis XVI and his family take refuge in the Legislative Assembly,"[33] the incident that effectively ended the monarchy.
Recalling September 2–3, he commented soberly, "Massacre of
priests,"[34] a reference to the mass killings of September 1792. These
began when a mob in Paris attacked and killed twenty-four priests

on their way to prison. A total of 1,400 prisoners were slain in those two days, of whom 223 were priests.[35] For September 21, Bruno wrote, "The Royalty is abolished, and the Republic established."[36] On that day, the legislative assembly voted to dissolve the monarchy and inaugurate the First Republic.

A letter of an *Aa* member written from Vienna on November 28, 1792, reveals the growing concern within *Aa* circles as the Revolution sent armies against Europe, and word spread of persecution of the Church in France.[37] The *Aa* confrère had learned of the advances of the French armies, and wrote: "May God spare us the same calamity. It is possible, and even likely that this will happen."[38] Aware that French military success might signify persecution of the clergy beyond France, the confrère added: "I know that all of our *Aa* groups have fortified their courage and are ready to accept even martyrdom, should events go badly. May God grant us this most special grace."[39]

The confrère described the arrival in Vienna of refugees fleeing persecution in France: "The other day the Bishop of Nancy arrived here, a truly apostolic man and a worthy confessor of Christ. Many priests who have emigrated from France have come here, as they have to other countries as well."[40] Seven Sisters of the Visitation, the confrère related, also in flight from France, would arrive in a few days, homeless and in need of shelter.[41]

He shared a further concern: "We are anxiously waiting word about Virginio, as I asked of you before. His long silence awakens many fears. May God grant that they not be verified."[42] In fact, three months earlier, the members of the Seminary of St. Nicolas du Chardonnet in Paris where Luigi Virginio resided had been arrested.[43] Only later would his *Amicizie* and *Aa* friends learn that Virginio had escaped arrest and had survived the days of terror in Paris.[44] The confrère concluded his letter: "My beloved friend, I embrace you with all my heart and, with you, all the members of the *Aa*. Let us remember that they who suffer persecution are blessed [Matt. 5:10]."[45] Even as the confrère wrote these lines, French troops were invading the kingdom of Piedmont.

ON SEPTEMBER 20, 1792, the French defeated the Prussians at Valmy in northern France. That evening Goethe, who witnessed the defeat, pronounced his celebrated words: "Here and today a new epoch in the history of the world has begun."[46] The following night, French troops invaded Savoy.[47] The Revolution had now entered Piedmontese territory; a new epoch was indeed beginning for the Piedmontese people and, together with them, for Bruno.

Five days later, on September 26, the French fleet approached Nice, at that time part of the kingdom of Piedmont.[48] Hostilities quickly followed and, three days later, Nice fell to the French. Shortly after, the French army marched east toward the Alps, Piedmont's last line of defense.[49] On November 27, the French annexed the whole of Savoy.[50] The territory of Piedmont itself, with its capital city, Turin, would be their next objective.

AS TENSIONS GREW and Piedmont prepared its last defense, Bruno's quiet application to spiritual growth continued. On August 6–13 of that year 1792, Bruno again made his annual retreat.[51] He was now thirty-three years old, the man "of a hundred tongues and a hundred arms,"[52] engaged in endless apostolic activity in Turin and beyond. According to his custom, Bruno withdrew from his ministry for eight days of silence and prayer.

As in other years, Bruno meditated on the classic Ignatian themes, and again his prayer led to concrete decisions.[53] He reviewed his activities, and resolved to ensure time for daily meditation.[54] As before, he examined his defects unsparingly, and wrote: "My principal vice is sloth, from which arises my roughness of character, so that if the first is remedied, the second will be as well. In reality, all my defects with respect to God and my neighbor arise from this: that I do not have a great esteem and a great love for God and my neighbor, and I do not have this esteem and love because I do not apply myself seriously to understanding what I do, and I do not apply myself because I do not want the effort this requires, that is the serious mental application."[55]

"And so," Bruno continued, "I need a means to help me overcome this spiritual sloth. If I simply attempt to force myself to overcome it, this will create a strained effort that will not endure. It is better (as experience shows me) to approach this with freedom of spirit and generosity of heart. I find no better means to do this than to try to seek God's greater glory in all things, examining myself often as to whether what I am doing is the best that can be done to glorify God, and whether I am doing it in the best way possible, always keeping Jesus Christ as my model."[56] "In this way," Bruno wrote, "I will rise above myself, and will have a noble and effective motive for rejecting my own comfort or any other human goal in my actions, since these are the obstacles to the application I desire, and my defects have always arisen from fear of effort or of being belittled by others."[57] To ensure constancy in this application, Bruno adopted two daily practices: "an hour of meditation made well," and "the particular examination of conscience according to St. Ignatius's method, on purity of intention in the sense just described."[58]

ON JANUARY 21, 1793, Louis XVI was guillotined in Paris. Eight months later, in September, the Reign of Terror began. A year of carnage followed, in which 40,000 were slain and 300,000 imprisoned.[59] Priests were put to death, and national leadership strove to dechristianize France.[60]

Year by year, the French armies made further inroads into the kingdom of Piedmont.[61] In September 1795, as total defeat neared, Bruno wrote: "Time is pressing, life is short. Opportunities to do good to our neighbor are at hand; we find them in every time and place. Let us always be ready to do all the good we can, without setting limits to our hearts or to our charity."[62]

On March 27, 1796, a young officer of twenty-seven, Napoleon Bonaparte, arrived in Nice to command the French army of Italy.[63] Within weeks, he crushed the Piedmontese army, and, on April 28, Piedmontese King Vittorio Amadeo III signed the humiliating Armistice of Cherasco. The Treaty of Paris that followed two weeks later effectively ended Piedmontese independence for the next eighteen years. During that time, apart from 1799–1800 when Napoleon was in Egypt, Piedmont would remain under French

rule. For Piedmont—and for Bruno, ever in the thick of events—
these would be years of oppression, exploitation, fear, and social
unrest. Surveillance by the French police and danger of arrest
and exile, or worse, would be constant for nearly two decades.
Bruno would now be obliged to shroud his activity on behalf of the
Church in deep secrecy.

During these troubled years, Bruno served as spiritual guide
for the young Luigi Craveri who, in 1795, began preparation for
priesthood.[64] Craveri asked Bruno to be his confessor, initiating a
spiritual relationship that would continue during Craveri's seminary years and long into his priesthood.[65] Not surprisingly, Craveri
joined both the *Amicizia Sacerdotale* and the *Aa*.[66]

Reflecting years later on the French occupation, Craveri would
affirm of Bruno that "with regard to conserving the faith and transmitting both faith and devotion to others, it was not only my opinion but also that of many who knew him that, like a confessor of
the faith, during the difficult years from 1796 to 1814, he contributed more than any other to preserving the faith and strengthening people of good will in the practice of their Christian faith.
So true was this, that those of high rank in society who remained
faithful, and indeed the greater part of all who remained faithful
to their religion . . . were distinguished by being directed by the
Signor Theologian Lanteri, as were many other men and women
of the highest rank, more than I could name, whom he directed by
his letters."[67] As we will see, Craveri would personally witness the
wide range of Bruno's activity during the occupation—an activity
that would not escape the attention of the French police.

In that critical year 1796, Bruno's quest for spiritual progress
continued. On November 13, six months after Piedmont's defeat,
Bruno reviewed his spiritual life and planned for the coming
months.[68] On that day, he wrote: "My particular examination for
the next month will be on gentleness. I will satisfy for any failures
in this with alms or some other penance, and will strive to grow
in this gentleness through frequent reading about this virtue, frequent proposals in prayer, and by rendering an account to my confessor."[69] Bruno continued: "I will dedicate some time each day to

spiritual reading, about a half-hour, and will discuss the choice of this reading with my confessor."[70]

Bruno further resolved "to set aside one day a month as a day of retreat, to review the proposals of my Spiritual Exercises during that day, and to render an account of this."[71] "Every week," he added, "I will go to confession, and will dedicate one morning to reflecting on how to promote the cause of God, of my soul, and of my neighbor."[72] In yet another proposal, Bruno wrote: "Every month I will review the book of the Spiritual Exercises of St. Ignatius, choosing from it the material for my meditation."[73] And again: "I will try to ensure at least an hour of study daily."[74] When walking the city streets, Bruno proposed "always to have with me a small book for reading should the opportunity arise, and the rosary so as to pray at least a part of it daily."[75] He planned to live with spiritual vigilance: "I will keep watch to see how the hours of the day are passing and how I am spending them, to note whether there might be more fruitful ways of employing them."[76]

As such pages witness, throughout these chaotic years Bruno perseveringly strove for spiritual growth. Such growth would be critically important in the tasks he was about to undertake.

CHAPTER SIX

"The Calamitous Circumstances of the Times"

> *Be of good heart, because the Lord*
> *is with you, and he loves you.*
> —Bruno Lanteri

AT 2:00 A.M. ON DECEMBER 8, 1798, Carlo Emmanuele IV, under pressure from the French, abdicated as king of Piedmont.[1] At 10:00 in the evening the following day, together with Queen Maria Clotilde, the king took the road to exile.[2] The circumstances of Carlo Emmanuele's departure matched the sadness of the event: the darkness of night, the heavily falling snow, the slowly moving carriages, the torches carried by soldiers no longer his subjects, the poverty and danger of death that lay ahead on the road.[3] It appeared, as one author called it, "the funeral of the monarchy."[4] The grip of French power over Piedmont was tightening.

Two weeks later, on December 22, 1798, worn by his labors, Fr. Diessbach died in Vienna at the age of sixty-seven.[5] In the years before his death, Diessbach had dwelt in Fribourg, Switzerland, as the guest of Fr. Claude Gendre, rector of the church of Notre Dame.[6] During the eighteen months that Diessbach spent with him, Gendre conceived great esteem for him, and later wrote: "I admired and recognized in him a man completely given to God, totally dedicated to works of charity, and entirely unconcerned about himself."[7] "His charity toward others," Gendre related, "was without limit. From morning to evening, his room was crowded with persons who came to him for confession or to seek his counsel, or with those who, ashamed of their poverty, came to seek alms. He received them all with the same goodness."[8]

On one occasion, Gendre attested, Diessbach "spent two consecutive nights in the military hospital, laboring without pause to console, confess, and counsel those wounded and suffering men, packed into hospital rooms. Returning home about 9:00 in the evening on the third day, though utterly exhausted, having had no time for rest and quite possibly no food, he was troubled about not spending the third night also in the hospital, and it was only by strenuously insisting that I was able to keep him from returning. He was also concerned that he had not said the Divine Office. I reminded him that, after three days and two nights of such exhausting labor by one himself burdened with infirmities, he was certainly dispensed, and that he himself would dispense anyone else in such circumstances, and that it was time to rest. I do not believe my counsels had much effect."[9] "In a word," Gendre wrote, "his life was entirely focused on the things of God, and he truly could have said with St. Paul: *It is no longer I who live, but Christ who lives in me* [Gal. 2:20]."[10]

Bruno attested that Diessbach "was esteemed as a holy man."[11] St. Clement Hofbauer, another of Diessbach's disciples, likewise described him as "a deeply learned and holy man."[12] In a time of physical suffering, Bruno once commented to a friend that "we must console ourselves with the words of Fr. Diessbach that paradise pays for all."[13] *Paradise pays for all*: it was a fitting epitaph for a man so dedicated to God, and one whose life so profoundly blessed Bruno's own.

WAR AGAIN RAVAGED PIEDMONT in the months following Diessbach's death. In May 1799, while Napoleon was in Egypt, Austro-Russian troops defeated the French and entered Turin. The brief rule of the Austro-Russians worsened the already precarious conditions in Piedmont: hunger, brigandage, and now depredation by yet another army brought Piedmont to the breaking point.[14]

Three months later, on August 29, 1799, the eighty-two-year-old Pius VI died exhausted, a prisoner of the French in Valence, France.[15] As one historian comments, "Rarely in all her history had the Church undergone a more critical time."[16] Europe was torn by revolution and war. The cardinals were scattered, some imprisoned, others deported. Rome was occupied by the armies of the kingdom of Naples.[17] How was a new pope to be elected? How were the cardinals to be assembled? And where? Some spoke mockingly of Pius VI as "Pius the Last."[18]

On November 30, 1799, thirty-four of the forty-six cardinals gathered under Austrian auspices in Venice for the conclave that, on March 14, 1800, elected Cardinal Barnaba Chiaramonti as the new pope.[19] Chiaramonti took the name Pius VII. Exactly three months later, on June 14, Napoleon crushed the Austrians at Marengo, and French rule returned to Piedmont. In November of that year, Napoleon was named first consul of France, the initial step in an ascent that would make him emperor. Pius VII and Napoleon: the chief actors of the coming struggle were now in place.

As war consumed Piedmont and social structures collapsed into chaos, Bruno's already intense activity grew. His confessor Antonio Ferrero attested that "dangerous errors prevailed increasingly in Piedmont under French rule, and Fr. Lanteri allowed himself no rest. He organized Spiritual Exercises in every city and town he could reach, distributed books, had others suitable to the times printed, and, if these books were lacking in any way, edited them to remove their deficiencies. He gained the good will of the heads of the War Office in Turin, and induced them to give books in support of the faith as gifts to their officers, and to urge these officers to go to confession with their soldiers before leaving for the deadly battles that awaited them."[20] These were the classic *Amicizia* activities—Spiritual Exercises and books—applied to the critical circumstances of the times.

Ferrero continued: "When military hospitals were established, if he himself was unable to visit the soldiers, he found priests to assist them, both French and Austrian, in their sufferings from the cold and from their wounds; he desired that none be lost. He raised large sums of money to provide them with a little food and wine, and with other means to alleviate and ease their pain. He supplied them with books to instruct and strengthen them in their faith, so that their hearts might be won to the Lord."[21]

Bruno's close associate Giuseppe Loggero elaborated: "When his physical weakness hindered him from personally assisting the ill and imprisoned, as he so greatly desired, he sought young priests to undertake this work. He guided them spiritually and trained them to hear confessions effectively in such settings. He sent those priests whom he knew to be capable to the French military hospitals, to win these men for God and to endure (with great merit) mockery and mistreatment for the love of God."[22] Loggero noted a further aspect of Bruno's ministry: "With the help of these priests he also organized the Spiritual Exercises, especially for those detained in prison.[23] With great difficulty and notwithstanding his sufferings from the oppression in his chest, he often heard confessions on these occasions."[24]

Luigi Craveri referred to these years (1799–1800) and related: "It was about this time that he acquired or adapted the Grangia, his country home in the hills of Bardassano [outside Turin], for giving the Spiritual Exercises. In those unhappy days when nearly all retreat houses were closed, he often gave the Spiritual Exercises there to priests, and these men returned home with renewed fervor. At times lay people also went there to make the Spiritual Exercises. He would receive up to seventeen or eighteen priests in his house for this purpose, as I think I remember hearing in 1807 from the Signor [priest] Lawyer Rossi, Don Rocco, the Signor Theologian Guala, and others who took part in the retreat; I was unable to be present since I had fallen ill with a fever."[25]

Craveri described Bruno's attention to current events and his defense of the Church as these unfolded: "If I speak of his faith, I will say that he labored unceasingly to lead others to embrace the teaching of the Roman Church. To this end, he distributed as widely as he was able a volume of the most effective pastoral letters of the French bishops against the schismatic Civil Constitution of the Clergy, and those that explained the obedience of heart

Chapel of the Grangia.

owed to the teaching of the Holy See of Rome in general."[26] Bruno would write, compile, and disseminate other texts as well to guide consciences in these troubled years.[27]

In the midst of activity, Bruno's constant search for spiritual progress continued. Proposals of November 24, 1800, witness to this commitment in the forty-one-year-old Bruno.[28] He would rise at 5:00 a.m. when hearing confessions, and at 5:30 a.m. on other days. His particular examination—that is, his specific focus for spiritual growth—would be on "gentleness and lowliness of heart," and he would "renew this often, especially during the principal actions of the day."[29] In the evening, Bruno wrote, "I will set aside a half hour for a little reading; I will prepare the next day's meditation, and make my examination of conscience."[30] Bruno closed this page with the reminder to "pray always."[31]

TWO DAYS BEFORE BRUNO WROTE THESE NOTES, on November 22, 1800, the French initiated the suppression of women's religious orders in Piedmont: it was the first step in a process intended to suppress all religious communities in Piedmont.[32] On that day, the Sisters Canons Regular of the Lateran were expelled from their Monastery of the Holy Cross in Turin.[33] On March 5, 1801, the same lot fell to the forty Sisters of the Most Holy Cross.[34] The community's diary described "their grief, their tears, and their sighs as they left the holy cloister they loved, and parted from one another."[35] A new ministry now began for Bruno, as Loggero related: "Before this time, he had guided sisters spiritually in their monasteries; after their expulsion, he encouraged them, assisted them, and supported them."[36]

For the Sisters of the Holy Cross, "reduced to the ultimate desolation,"[37] Bruno requested a delay of twenty days to prepare new lodgings.[38] His letters of spiritual direction to one member of this community, Sister Crocifissa Bracchetto, witness to the spiritual and material assistance he offered these suffering religious.[39]

Seventeen months later, on August 31, 1802, the government ordered a general suppression of monastic orders and religious congregations in Piedmont.[40] Rome instructed the religious not to resist, to leave their religious houses, and to relinquish religious garb as the government commanded. They were to seek dwellings suited to religious, to observe their vows as best they were able, and to profess obedience to diocesan authorities and to their spiritual directors.[41] A number of these religious sought Bruno as their spiritual director, and, through these difficult years, he supported and guided them.[42]

The Jesuit writer Antonio Bresciani, who most likely met Bruno in later years, recounted: "This was the time when religious orders were suppressed by the French Empire and the Kingdom of Italy. In those difficult days, Fr. Diessbach formulated a rule of life for women who wished to consecrate themselves to God, and could not do so for lack of monasteries. Guided by these wise rules, they lived as spouses of Christ in their homes, as had the women of early centuries when the Church was persecuted by tyrants. Fr. Lanteri greatly assisted Diessbach in this work so dear to God. He guided many of these women who, remaining at home, served God and took vows secretly in Lanteri's presence."[43] In those tumultuous times, Bruno's already multiform activity expanded further.

TWO MANUSCRIPTS FROM THESE YEARS reveal Bruno's approach to spiritual direction. A woman whom Diessbach had entrusted to Bruno's spiritual care had written, expressing sentiments of discouragement.[44] Bruno replied: "Holiness does not consist in never failing, but in rising immediately, recognizing our weakness and asking God's forgiveness, and in doing this with peace of heart, without letting ourselves be troubled. . . . It is very important to understand deeply how good God is, and not to measure him by our own limitations or think that he tires of our wavering, weakness, and negligence; that because of our sins he withdraws his help and denies his grace. . . . Our God is not such. . . . Let us think of him as he truly is, filled with goodness, mercy, and compassion, and let us know him as the loving Father he is, who raises us when we have fallen, who never tires of forgiving us, and to whom we give great joy and honor when we seek forgiveness."[45] "And so,"

Bruno wrote, "be of good courage. Let your heart be joyful, give yourself as completely as you can to God, banish any doubts, and tell God that you never wish consciously to do anything that would displease him. For the rest, do not be troubled. God is with you and will help you, and will not let you fall."[46]

In a second manuscript, Bruno outlined a spiritual program for a married woman.[47] Following the Ignatian Spiritual Exercises, Bruno asked this woman to consider that "I am created by God, and for this purpose alone: to praise and serve him, and so enter eternal life; and not only to praise and serve him in any state of life, but in this state in which he desires me, and to which he has called me."[48]

Bruno provided her a program of prayer: "I will go to Confession and receive Communion weekly, as I have already done for years. These sacraments are the channels through which God chooses to communicate his grace and light to me. . . . Every day I will make faithfully a quarter of an hour of meditation, and another of spiritual reading. I will examine my conscience every evening, and will go to Mass if I can."[49] Bruno called her to courage in living her faith: "I will seek to live always with that profound awareness of the majesty and goodness of God that the saints have in heaven, and will glory in professing openly and without fear that I wish to live as a good Christian, and that I take God as my King, and not the world with its teachings."[50]

What then of failures as she lived her married vocation? Bruno repeated a central tenet of his spiritual direction: "When I fail, I will never be discouraged; knowing that I will fail often, I will be always ready to turn to God immediately and ask forgiveness. . . . And if I should fall a thousand times a day, a thousand times a day I will begin again, with new awareness of my weakness, promising God, with a peaceful heart, to amend my life. I will never think of God as if he were of our condition and grows weary of our wavering, weakness, and negligence. . . . Rather, I will think of what is truly characteristic of him and what he prizes most highly, that is, his goodness and mercy, knowing that he is a loving Father who understands our weakness, is patient with us, and forgives us. I will be convinced that discouragement is the greatest obstacle in the spiritual life."[51]

Bruno articulated for this woman a Christian way of relating to others: "Generosity of spirit, freedom of heart in my actions and in bearing suffering, fidelity to my spiritual resolutions, peace of heart, joy, love of my neighbor, compassion for the weakness of others, goodness, patience, forbearance, warmth, openness to others in all that is not offensive to God ... this is the character I seek and that I will continually ask of the Sacred Heart of Jesus and of Mary."[52]

Many of Bruno's key teachings emerge in these passages: adherence to God as the origin and goal of life, faithful practice of the sacraments and daily prayer as the source of spiritual strength, refusal to accept discouragement ("If I should fall a thousand times a day, a thousand times a day I will begin again"), joyful awareness of God's infinite mercy, and courageous living of one's Christian identity in the world. These themes will return in Bruno's spiritual direction.

ON SEPTEMBER 8, 1801, Napoleon, now first consul of France, signed a concordat with the Catholic Church.[53] After protracted negotiations, and with significant concessions in the temporal order, the Catholic Church regained legal status in France.[54] Although Napoleon signed the agreement for political ends and would quickly betray it, nevertheless, after years of bloody persecution, the Church in France began its life anew. In all their subsequent conflicts, Pius VII never forgot that Napoleon had restored the Church to France.

The Concordat stipulated that the first consul would name new bishops as need arose, but that these could not govern their dioceses without canonical institution by the pope.[55] Another piece of the coming struggle was in place.

On July 21 of the following year, Bruno's one surviving sister, Maria Angelica Luisa, died in Cuneo at the age of fifty-one.[56] Two months later, on September 11, 1802, a decree of the French Senate incorporated Piedmont into France.[57] As a result, Piedmont ceased to exist as an independent nation and was absorbed into France, sharing its civil and religious laws. France now began to pressure the Piedmontese clergy to accept Gallicanism, a view of church-state relations that minimized papal authority and considered a general council superior to the pope. In particular, France imposed the four gallican propositions of 1682, which expressed this understanding.[58] Not surprising, Bruno reacted vigorously to this attempt to "gallicanize" the clergy of Piedmont.

Giuseppe Loggero attested of Bruno that "when the French Government ordered that the Four Gallican Propositions of 1682 be taught in the archdiocesan seminary of Turin, he composed a kind of dissertation in which he summarized the strongest and most fundamental reasons against these Propositions, and sought with much success to introduce copies into the seminary. As a result, almost all of the seminarians were theologically equipped to resist this teaching."[59]

Luigi Craveri likewise related: "When, in those unhappy times, the four propositions found in the purported defense of the declaration of the Gallican Clergy were taught, he countered this teaching with an edition of the work by [Pietro] Ballerini entitled *On the Authority and Theological Justification of the Primacy of the Roman Pontiff,* of which he gave me a copy as a gift. He distributed copies of the *Theological Conclusions* of Honoré Tournely, who taught that union with the See of Peter, that is, with the Roman Pontiff, is necessary for salvation, and that the Pope is infallible in his doctrinal decisions."[60]

Antonio Ferrero testified more succinctly: "When the teaching of the four propositions was ordered, he composed a manuscript and had copies made and distributed in the seminaries and cities of Italy and France, to reveal the fallacies in these propositions and prevent the harm, errors, and weakening of faith that might otherwise have resulted."[61] Bruno would later say of himself, "I am only a watchdog in the flock of the Lord who cries out to his last breath."[62] Ever vigilant in all that concerned the Church, Bruno had already assumed that role. He would need that vigilance in the critical times fast approaching, and that would lead to his own arrest and exile.

ON DECEMBER 22, as 1802 drew to its close, a twenty-four-year-old man named Leopoldo Ricasoli wrote to Bruno from Florence.[63] Ricasoli loved art and the classics, was prone to discouragement, and was, above all, a man of deep faith. He and his wife, Lucrezia, would have seven children, two of whom would become Jesuits.[64] Bruno would call him "one of the two principal supporters" of the *Amicizia Cristiana* of Florence, in those months beginning its life.[65]

The letter was brief. In it, Ricasoli sought Bruno's aid with practical concerns facing the Florentine *Amicizia*. So began a relationship that would span twenty-four years, and would become one of spiritual father and son.[66]

CHAPTER SEVEN

Laborers in the Vineyard

*You have only one heart with which
to love God, and, in this way, you
will love God with all the hearts
you have gained for him. And who
can say how many other souls
those hearts you have enflamed
with love of God will save?*
—Bruno Lanteri

IN SEPTEMBER 1803, BRUNO TRAVELED to Florence on *Amicizia* business.[1] Once arrived, he discovered that many he had planned to meet were absent, and that he faced a difficult decision: to return to Turin with the *Amicizia* business in Florence unfinished, or to prolong his stay in Florence and relinquish commitments already taken in Turin.[2] On October 1, Bruno wrote to Ricasoli: "I assure you, Monsieur and honored friend in Jesus Christ, that I have spent some days in much uncertainty about God's holy will in this matter. If I stay, I will miss, among other things of great importance in Turin, a retreat for young priests that I was to give this month, and that promised great fruit. If I remain here, the retreat will not take place this year."[3] Bruno chose to extend his stay in Florence, and wrote to Ricasoli: "So I will miss the activities planned in Turin. I hope that you will help me with fervent prayer to obtain some compensation for them from the good God."[4]

Now days of waiting in Florence began. They would not be idle: "I will spend this month in copying the *Utili* [document of the *Amicizia Sacerdotale*], in making my own retreat, in studying several books, in reading, and in dedicating time to prayer. I will

67

also compose a text for the *Amicizia Sacerdotale* as I await the joy of seeing you once again, and the beginning of the retreat you so desire; certainly, there is no occupation in this world more desirable than time spent in such retreat."[5]

During those October weeks, Bruno composed his *Idea of the Pious Union of Priests Called the Amicizia Sacerdotale* for the new chapter of the *Amicizia Sacerdotale* he planned to inaugurate in Florence the following month.[6] In this document, Bruno offered these young priests assistance in preparing for the two principal ministries of the *Amicizia*: disseminating good books and giving the Spiritual Exercises.[7]

How were they to judge whether a book was truly good or not? Bruno explained: "We always reject and will never use any book by an author not obedient to the Holy See, or in any way suspect, or containing anything contrary to a decision of the Church, or even simply opposed to the spirit and practices of the Church. A single false principle heedlessly accepted or proposed to others can cause harm beyond describing in private and in public."[8] "And so," Bruno continued, "we also exclude any book that tends more *ad destructionem* [to tear down] than *ad edificationem* [to build up], that is, books that tend to discourage the reader rather than animate him in the practice of virtue. Such books are not only useless for our purpose, but even harmful. In particular, we praise and use books which encourage the reader and are written with living faith, especially if they are also written well."[9] The great harm caused by bad books demonstrates, Bruno wrote, the corresponding fruitfulness of spreading good books.[10] He concluded with a cry from the heart: "It cannot be possible that the sons of darkness be wiser than the sons of light in this work!"[11]

The *amici* were to prepare to give the Spiritual Exercises and allow nothing to distract them from this. From long experience, Bruno affirmed that "preparing to give the meditations of the Spiritual Exercises is not a light task, but a long and laborious undertaking that, if not pursued unswervingly, will not be completed."[12] In preparing these meditations, Bruno taught, "we must always keep before our eyes the words of the Holy Spirit, '*Sentite de Domino in bonitate'* [Wisdom 1:1: 'Think of the Lord in a spirit of goodness.']. We must, therefore, procure sentiments worthy of God in our own hearts so as to inspire them in others, and thus attain our goal of loving God ourselves, and leading all to love him."[13] "The minister of the Word of God," Bruno wrote, "must be able to say to his listeners with the Divine Master, 'My teaching is not my own but is from the one who sent me' [John 7:16]. He must faithfully proclaim the teaching of the Church in all that concerns the doctrine of faith and moral precepts."[14]

Such pages testify that at age forty-four and in *Amicizie* circles, Bruno had become a formator of priests. Antonio Ferrero affirmed that, "For many years and with great dedication he guided a devout gathering of young clergy . . . called the *[Amicizia] Sacerdotale* . . . that included those priests who wished to dedicate themselves to giving the Spiritual Exercises. They met weekly and read in turn before the others the meditations they had prepared following the method of St. Ignatius. They examined these texts together and offered any necessary corrections. Then they would see where the greatest need for preaching or confessions might be, and divide themselves among the prisons, hospitals, and soldiers' barracks. Many qualified priests emerged from this gathering, effective laborers for the Lord, who preached great numbers of retreats and parish missions, and whose ministry bore great fruit."[15]

Luigi Craveri related that "He gathered many seminarians and young priests, and, in his own house or in that of a member, held a weekly Academy in which the members prepared the meditations of the Spiritual Exercises according to the method of St. Ignatius. Each in turn read them before the others, who offered their observations. In every meeting a member also presented a description and judgment of a book or another literary work. If the book was found useful, it would be promoted, and, if dangerous, rejected. In this they could not have had a more able guide."[16]

Many qualified priests emerged from this gathering: Bruno's labors with seminarians and young priests would bear fruit in Piedmont for decades to come. As Antonio Bresciani would write,

"In this work of forming young priests in a spirit of religious perfection, Fr. Lanteri fulfilled Diessbach's aims in a marvelous way."[17]

DURING THAT MONTH OF WAITING, Bruno traveled to Montepulciano, 110 kilometers from Florence, where he hoped to found a further chapter of the *Amicizia Sacerdotale*.[18] His trip was unsuccessful, and he returned to Florence. Those October days left Bruno weakened. On November 1, he wrote to Ricasoli: "My health, which has suffered in no small measure these past days, causes me to think seriously of shortening my trip to avoid traveling in the cold season, which would harm me even more."[19] Bruno signed his letter "in haste," an indication of the intense activity that filled these days.[20]

In early November, Bruno guided the new *Amicizia Sacerdotale* of Florence in its first steps.[21] He attended three of its meetings, and was pleased with the quality of its eight members.[22] Before leaving the city, Bruno gave the Spiritual Exercises to three *amici* of the *Amicizia Cristiana* of Florence.[23] A year later, Bruno remembered this retreat and wrote to Ricasoli, one of the three: "At times I find myself in spirit at your villa in Fiesole [outside Florence], deeply regretting that we could not hold a retreat there again this year, since there is nothing so desirable in this world as to spend several days in peace, occupied only with the things that matter most—God, the soul, and eternity."[24]

His work in Florence complete, Bruno departed for Turin. On November 18, he reached Parma where he made a brief stop. There he met well-known writer Fr. Juan Andrés to ask his collaboration with *L'Ape* (the Bee), a periodical begun that year by the Florentine *Amicizia*.[25] A monthly publication, *L'Ape* offered a "Digest of Literary and Moral Works Drawn Primarily from French Publications," and would later be expanded to include original articles.[26] Bruno described *L'Ape* as "an excellent religious periodical" that served to "promote good principles more widely and make good books better known."[27] It was a modest independent voice raised in Napoleon's Italy, and an early expression of lay Catholic involvement in the media.[28]

The *Amicizia* member Cesare d'Azeglio, editor of *L'Ape*, wrote under the pseudonym of Ottavio Ponzoni. Bruno commented to Ricasoli: "The Abbé Andrés expressed some curiosity regarding the identity of Ottavio Ponzoni, and I replied that he was a person who did not wish to be known, but simply desired to promote good principles. I would not know how else to answer when speaking to scholars of this kind (whom I find somewhat odd in these matters) to dissuade them from further investigation, if that is even possible."[29] After some initial hesitation, Andrés agreed to collaborate with *L'Ape*.[30] Bruno concluded this letter also "in haste."[31]

As November ended, Bruno reached Milan where he spent a week and where he was "able to arrange many matters of importance for the life of the *Amicizia Cristiana*."[32] On December 28, Bruno told Ricasoli that "I left Milan very satisfied."[33]

In this letter to Ricasoli, Bruno addressed spiritual matters: "Forgive me if I have not yet sent the method for prayer I promised you, nor the list of books for your spiritual reading and that of Madame the Marquise, your worthy spouse. I have no time at present, but will send them on another occasion. Until then, I await positive news of your spiritual progress, of the fruits of your meditation, of your regular reception of Communion, of your courage in the service of God, of your firmness in adhering to the established order of your daily occupations, and of whether you have been able to free yourself suitably from some occupations and worldly concerns, so as to dedicate yourself more readily to the affairs of God. I cannot be indifferent to anything that matters to you."[34] On a different note, Bruno added: "I have written to the Marquis Cesare d'Azeglio and have sent him some chestnuts from our region, asking him to share them with you."[35]

IN 1804, A YOUNG MAN of twenty-seven named Giuseppe Loggero sought Bruno's spiritual assistance.[36] Loggero, a worker and then partner in a small clothing firm, chose Bruno as his confessor. For years to come, he would approach Bruno weekly for this sacrament, finding in Bruno the "teacher and father of his soul."[37] In 1807, Loggero entered the seminary of Turin and, in 1809, was

Fr. Giuseppe Loggero.

ordained a priest.[38] From that time, Loggero lived with Bruno as his faithful assistant and secretary, sharing his labors, struggles, and exile.[39] None would be closer to Bruno than Loggero in the twenty years that lay ahead. In 1816, when Loggero considered entering the Jesuits, Bruno wrote to the superior: "I find nothing contrary to that calling except what the loss of him means for me."[40] After Bruno's death, Loggero would describe him as the father "whom we deeply venerated and deeply loved."[41]

Living in what he termed "the calamitous circumstances of the times," Bruno remained attentive to prayer.[42] A page of spiritual notes from 1804 reveals his desire to make "every day, at least a half-hour of serious and well-prepared meditation according to the order proposed by St. Ignatius. In this meditation, I will plan the activities of my day so that I may do more surely the will of God and give him glory in all that I do: *non aliud sed aliter* [not different things, but the same things done differently], *non ex more sed ex amore* [not doing things simply out of habit, but out of love]."[43]

Bruno planned each day "to make the examination of conscience even while walking through the streets if I cannot at another time,"[44] and "to enter a church to adore the Blessed Sacrament and ask for grace of Jesus and Mary."[45] He would dedicate himself to "spiritual reading and study as much as time allows."[46]

Bruno proposed "to dedicate a morning each week to young priests, and at least a half-hour for reflection on the spiritual and material affairs of the *Amicizia Cristiana*, and my own."[47] He would practice his habitual penances and "make a day of retreat each month if possible."[48] In the events of his life, Bruno would ask, "*Quid haec ad vitam aeternam?*" (How do these things relate to eternal life?), and would follow the maxim, "*Quod vult Deus et quomodo vult*" (That which God wills and in the way he wills it).[49] Bruno desired "to assimilate the spirit of the Heart of Jesus in all things," and to attain "gentleness even in my external appearance."[50] He concluded with the classic spiritual adage "*Vince teipsum*" (Conquer thyself).[51] As the years passed, constant review and renewal of his prayer fostered in Bruno a deepening relationship with Jesus.

BRUNO WAS NOW FORTY-FIVE years old. Frequent letters to Leopoldo Ricasoli in this year, 1804, reveal both his intense *Amicizia* activity, and the essential tenets of his spiritual direction.

On February 29, 1804, Bruno told Ricasoli that "I do not want to let this mail coach depart without sending you a few lines in haste. I usually wait for the day the coach leaves to write, and usually some unforeseen occupation hinders me from writing as I planned. That is what happened last week, and that is what is happening today."[52] In a final paragraph, Bruno added, "There is no time for me to write anything more," and signed this letter too, "in haste."[53]

The letter testifies to the bond between Bruno and Ricasoli: "I will not hide from you the real and heartfelt joy I experienced when I received your valued letter, which means so much to me. I awaited it with impatience, and I hope that you will renew this joy for me every week if you can, all the more since it is not just a matter of satisfying my wish and my concern for you, which certainly is not slight since I can never forget the great goodness you showed me. But this is a question of the glory of God that can be promoted by this means, so, do not refuse me this joy."[54]

Bruno addressed Ricasoli's struggles: "In your letter I sense discouragement in God's service. I beg you to be on guard against this since there is no enemy more to be feared than this."[55] And he offered Ricasoli the remedy: "A holy tenacity in the faithful practice of your daily exercises of prayer, especially in meditation and spiritual reading, will always be a source of great blessing for you. Add weekly Confession to this, and more than weekly Holy Communion, with a firm and unshakeable resolution always to begin again, and to hope ever more firmly in God, and I guarantee you safety from major failings, at least from their unhappy consequences."[56]

A month later, on April 2, Bruno replied to a further letter from Ricasoli: "I am writing a few lines in haste so as not to miss this mail coach. Forgive me if I have not replied more quickly; for over a month, all my free time has been dedicated to my books and to having them moved to another house with as little confusion as possible, since I have had to change my residence. I have moved over 5,000 of them in these days. The greater part is now done, and I hope to resume my affairs, and, if it pleases God, our correspondence will be more regular."[57]

But on April 25, three weeks later, time was again short: "I write these few lines once more in haste, unhappy that I never have the freedom to write without such hurry."[58] Bruno described his occupations: "I will be leaving soon to give a retreat to young priests. Going from one activity to the next, I have not yet had time even for my own retreat, which I very much need. I often consider whether I might visit the *amici* of Florence as I so desire, but to my great regret, foresee that it will be impossible this year. Pray with me that I may know and do God's holy will."[59]

Regarding Ricasoli himself, Bruno added: "I have no doubt that you will continue to serve God with a great and generous heart even in the midst of daily failings—all the more since, according to St. Francis de Sales, perfection itself does not consist in never failing, but in never persevering in the will to fail. Not a day passes that I do not remember you and all the *amici* before God."[60]

A month later, on May 23, Bruno replied to Ricasoli once more: "Today I received your letter of May 7. I cannot tell you how welcome I always find your letters, and I do not want to let this mail coach leave without sending at least a few lines in reply."[61] Bruno explained his delay: "I have just arrived from giving, with great consolation, the Spiritual Exercises to a group of young priests. On my return, I found the package of books you sent me."[62]

Bruno continued to ponder travel to Florence: "I remain quite uncertain as to whether a trip this year will be possible. I will write to Virginio for greater clarity about this, so that I may understand and be able to do the holy will of God, which is all I desire. Pray therefore that the Lord be pleased to enlighten us."[63] Bruno concluded with a desire: "Until such time, I wish you every true good, and I am consoled in seeing you ever more dedicated to the glory of God, since, in this world, there is no purpose greater than this, and none more consoling."[64] Bruno signed the letter "with great esteem, affection, and gratitude," and, almost inevitably, "in haste."[65]

Six weeks passed, and Bruno received no word from Ricasoli. On June 26, he expressed his concern: "I am deeply troubled because I have not had the consolation of hearing from you since mid-May. I hope this does not mean that you are in poor health; I would be very unhappy to think that was true. Let me recommend once more, in this regard, that you take serious care of your health, especially by asking the help of others with a part of your tasks, so that you can enjoy at least some moments of peace during the week. Otherwise the bow that is always bent will finally break. Know that the *Amicizia Cristiana* has great need of you, so that the greater glory of God requires you to take such care of your health."[66] Bruno explained his own delay in writing: "I too accuse myself of having let so much time pass without writing to you, but it was truly almost impossible to write, all the more because I wanted to spend some days making my own Spiritual Exercises, which did not go very well because my health is not in the best condition."[67]

Bruno's poor health also clarified God's will regarding a return trip to Florence: "This is also the reason, with many others of importance, why I believe I should not risk a trip to Tuscany again this summer. Yet you may be sure that this decision costs me a great deal, and that renouncing the trip is a true sacrifice. But I believe I have seen God's will in this matter, since, by God's grace, I want to seek nothing else."[68] On September 4, Bruno again cited physical limitations: "I had hoped to be able, and looked forward with great joy, to giving the Exercises again last month to priests, but my health did not permit it. I must be patient: the will of God is above all else, provided that I have not hindered it through my failings."[69]

In a final letter of 1804 written on November 28, Bruno rejoiced in positive news from Ricasoli: "May the Lord be eternally blessed for the special graces he continues to pour out on you. Oh! If only we could understand clearly how precious the state of grace is, what sacrifices would we not make, and what victories over ourselves would we not be ready to win, to keep ourselves in that state.

This is why I can never recommend enough to you daily meditation on the holy truths of our religion, made with true application, with affection, and pursued with a holy tenacity, and always, as much as possible, at a fixed hour of the day."[70] Bruno called Ricasoli once more to "daily spiritual reading done without hurry," and to frequent reception of the sacraments, "which are the channels through which God especially communicates his graces to us."[71]

"Above all," Bruno insisted, "I recommend with all my strength that you guard against discouragement, disturbance, and sadness, and so constantly seek to keep your poor heart in peace, and encourage it, and always to serve God with holy joy. Always keep before you these two proposals that I urge you to renew often, and with a holy tenacity: first, never to offend God knowingly, and, second, if you should fall, never to persevere in this with your will, but, with humility and courage, to rise immediately and begin again, firmly convinced that God forgives you in the instant itself that, with humility and trust, you ask his forgiveness."[72] Through such teachings, Bruno encouraged the many who, like Ricasoli, sought his spiritual guidance.

As Bruno wrote to Ricasoli, events in Europe, now centered on Napoleon, pursued their precipitous course. In Paris, on December 2, 1804, Pius VII crowned Napoleon as emperor. Traveling to the coronation, Pius VII stopped briefly in Turin. There Bruno met him, as he told Ricasoli: "I had the consolation of kissing the feet of His Holiness, who showed himself well pleased with the piety he found in our people."[73]

On October 19, 1805, Napoleon won a great military victory at Ulm and, on December 2, his greatest victory at Austerlitz. Yet between Ulm and Austerlitz, on October 21, Nelson destroyed the French Navy at Trafalgar, a defeat from which Napoleon would never recover.

After the coronation, tensions between the pope and emperor rapidly intensified. Pius VII would later recall his time in Paris and write to Napoleon: "Ever since Our return from Paris We have experienced nothing but bitterness and disillusionment, whereas the personal knowledge that We had acquired of Your Majesty, and Our own invariable conduct, had promised, by contrast, something quite different."[74] For his part, Napoleon declared that "I expect the Pope to accommodate his conduct to my requirements. If he behaves well, I shall make no outward changes; if not, I shall reduce him to the status of the bishop of Rome."[75] He was convinced that Pius VII would comply. Events would prove otherwise.

CHAPTER EIGHT

"Our Stand Is Irrevocable"

> *I have asked the Lord to give you*
> *great courage and firm hope in God.*
> —Bruno Lanteri

ON AUGUST 9, 1806, A YOUNG MAN AND WOMAN stood before the Emperor Napoleon and Empress Josephine in the Palace of St. Cloud, as the agreement for their marriage was signed. The wedding was celebrated nine days later. The groom was twenty-four-year-old Carlo Tancredi, and his bride twenty-year-old Juliette Colbert.

Juliette, born in the Vendée, France, was three years old when the Revolution exploded. A painting of the day depicted her grandmother, a victim of the Terror, quietly praying her rosary as she and her companions awaited the guillotine.[1] Others of her family would undergo the same fate. The Colberts were stripped of their property, and only exile saved Juliette's father from death. At age four, Juliette joined her father in Germany, fleeing in disguise to avoid capture.

Proclaimed emperor in 1804, Napoleon called various members of the former aristocracy to his court. Thus, at age eighteen, Juliette joined the imperial household as a lady-in-waiting to the Empress Josephine. There she met Carlo, called from his native Piedmont, who served as a page to Napoleon.

Following their marriage in 1806, the couple spent several months each year at court and the remaining months in the family home in Turin. Here Juliette was welcomed warmly by her mother-in-law, Paolina. Here too, for the first time, she met Bruno Lanteri, whom Paolina had taken as spiritual director.[2] In those early days in Turin, Juliette could not have guessed how this meeting would affect her life and, through her, the lives of many others.

IN THESE YEARS OF SUBJECTION to France, the Church in Piedmont presented, as a contemporary document related, "a spectacle of desolation."[3] The churches of religious orders were closed. Convents and monasteries were destroyed or converted to barracks. Religious, evicted from their dwellings, struggled to survive. Preachers and confessors were lacking, and vocations declined. Seminaries were closed, and seminarians subjected to military conscription. Over all things lay Napoleon's heavy, controlling hand.[4]

Notwithstanding poor health, and in spite of political and religious oppression, Bruno spent himself apostolically with remarkable energy. A part of his ministry was public; another was carefully hidden from the French police.

The pace remained intense. On August 17, 1807, Bruno told Ricasoli: "I write this short note in great haste because I am overwhelmed with tasks. I returned just the day before yesterday from giving the Exercises, and I leave tomorrow to give them again." Once more Bruno concluded "in all haste."[5] And a month later: "I write these few lines in all haste. . . . Tomorrow I leave to give the Exercises of St. Ignatius."[6] This letter, too, was signed "in haste."[7]

Ministerial occupations pressed, as Bruno confided to his friend and *Amicizia* member, Joseph von Penkler: "In the last three months, my continual travel for retreats and assistance to the sick has left me barely time for even the shortest stays in Turin. These have not been enough to deal with even half my affairs. This is the real reason for my delay in replying to you, my dear and respected friend."[8] To another friend, Cesare d'Azeglio, Bruno specified that during these months he had stopped in Turin only two or three days of each fifteen—brief "apparitions" at home in the midst of almost constant travel.[9]

Even half my affairs. . . . Among them were initiatives Bruno would never mention in his letters. The French police monitored all correspondence, and detection would mean arrest and exile, if not death. Bruno shrouded in secrecy his meetings with the *Amicizia*, his writing and diffusion of manuscripts in defense of the Church, and his mobilization of persons and funds on her behalf. Witnesses, among them Giuseppe Loggero and Luigi Craveri, would later describe Bruno's hidden activities; at the time, little was preserved in writing.[10] The wisdom of this precaution soon would be apparent.

On February 2, 1808, Bruno's "continual occupations" again caused him to conclude a letter "in haste."[11] And likewise, on July 4, to spiritual directee Gabriella Solaro della Margarita: "I do not have time to write to you more at length, as I would wish."[12]

But these were not days of uninhibited activity. Physical problems, at times severe, emerged repeatedly. In 1806, Bruno explained to Ricasoli that he had not written or visited earlier "because in that time I was ill, and my illness required a long convalescence during which I was unable to do anything at all: in fact, the doctor expressly forbade it."[13] On July 4, 1808, Bruno wrote to Gabriella Solaro della Margarita: "I may be able to visit and so learn how things are with you. It would be a great consolation for me and I am hoping it will be possible, all the more because my eyes grow constantly weaker, and this hinders me from dedicating myself to other activities that might make a visit impossible, as happened last year."[14]

By May 1809, Bruno's eyes had worsened, as he told Ricasoli: "I have not written before because of problems with my eyes. They are now in very bad condition, and continually grow worse. I am in danger of losing my sight entirely."[15] Lest Ricasoli fear to write, Bruno added: "Please do not let this cause you to deprive me of the consolation of hearing from you. As long as I have even a little use of my eyes, I will not fail to serve you with them."[16] Bruno explained why his letter was brief: "Forgive me if my eyes compel me to end this letter. I know you will understand the other things I would have wished to write."[17]

A month later, on June 12, Bruno answered a letter from Ricasoli: "How happy I am whenever you send me news of yourself! I thank you from my heart for sharing this with me, and beg you to do this often. I am sorry that I cannot always reply as quickly as I would wish, and write all that I would wish, because my eyes have continued to worsen since I last saw you [nine months earlier]. At times, even the slightest use of my eyes becomes painful and remains so for many days."[18] Bruno concluded, "My eyes tell me it is time to finish."[19]

Weakness of the eyes made recitation of the Divine Office difficult, and Bruno turned to Rome for help. His request read: "The priest Pio Bruno Lanteri of Piedmont, suffering from great weakness of the eyes, asks His Holiness to be allowed to recite other prayers in place of the Divine Office."[20] Rome responded affirmatively on April 26, 1808.[21]

IN JUNE 1805, Napoleon had bequeathed a precious tiara to Pius VII. It was his last gesture of homage in a relationship that grew increasingly difficult.[22] That same June, Napoleon, now crowned king of Italy, promulgated for Italy the French civil code. The code included provisions contrary to Catholic principles, primarily with regard to divorce.[23] When Pius VII protested, Napoleon wrote bluntly: "I will not change the measures I have taken."[24]

That summer, too, Napoleon, furious at the marriage of his brother Jerome with the American Elizabeth Patterson, demanded that Pius VII declare the marriage null. The pope, judging the union valid according to canon law, refused. Ill accustomed to denial of his wishes, Napoleon's anger grew.[25]

On October 18, 1805, following Napoleon's orders, French troops occupied the port of Ancona in papal territory.[26] When Pius VII wrote to Napoleon regarding this "cruel affront," and described it as irreconcilable with continued relations between Rome and the French empire, the existing tension mounted.[27] The pope's letter was, Napoleon declared, "ridiculous" and "lunatic."[28] He pressured Pius VII to comply with imperial policy: "Your Holiness is the sovereign of Rome, but I am its Emperor. All my enemies must be yours as well."[29] To this, Pius VII replied with firmness: "We are the Vicar of a God of peace, which means peace toward all, without distinction."[30]

Affront followed affront as Napoleon ordered his army to march across papal territory and occupy the port of Civitavecchia. The emperor placed his brother Joseph on the throne of Naples, thus threatening the pope from both north and south. He broke off correspondence with the pope, provoked the resignation of Pius VII's secretary of state, Cardinal Consalvi, and confiscated revenues belonging to the Holy See. French forces occupied the papal provinces of Urbino, Ancona, and Macerata.[31] The threat to Rome itself and to the personal safety of Pius VII grew daily.

The pope's response to Napoleon was resolute: "Our stand is irrevocable, and nothing will change it—neither threats nor the execution of those threats.... These are our sentiments, which you may regard as our testament, and we are ready, if necessary, to sign it with our blood, strengthened should we undergo persecution, by these words of our Divine Master, 'Blessed are those who suffer persecution for justice's sake.'"[32] The pope now employed a spiritual means of resistance: he refused canonical institution to French nominees for bishops in Italy, a refusal he would later extend to France with grave consequences for Napoleon.[33]

On February 2, 1808, French troops marched into Rome and occupied the fortress of Castel Sant'Angelo. They overran the city, despoiled churches, and seized precious objects. They dispersed the cardinals, and trained cannons on the apartments of the pope. Pius VII was now a prisoner in his own palace.[34] The breaking point between emperor and pope had come; soon Bruno Lanteri would enter that struggle.

ON DECEMBER 31, 1805, death stripped Bruno of his closest friend, Fr. Luigi Virginio. Three years older than Bruno, Virginio was, like him, a native of Cuneo and a disciple of Diessbach. Giovanni Battista Biancotti, who knew Bruno in the last days of Bruno's life, attested: "Fr. Diessbach, Fr. Virginio, and the Theologian Lanteri were bound by constant friendship. All three held similar views and shared a common goal: to serve God and help their neighbor in every way they could. Consequently, they worked together and helped each other. Whatever each did was as if done in the name of all. Because of this, it is impossible to separate Lanteri's labors from those of his friends."[35]

Bruno shared his sorrow with Ricasoli: "The news of the loss of the greatest friend I ever had was completely unexpected and deeply painful. Oh, how I marvel and thank Divine Providence that I was able to rejoice and profit from seeing him last fall, though it was the last time. He urged me to visit him there [Vienna] in many of his letters, saying that this visit might be the last. Only one thought consoles me, that like a person who lives far from the capital finds it very helpful to have a trusted person there who sees to his personal and public affairs, in the same way we will receive great help from heaven (where I am sure he already enjoys the fruit of his untiring and unlimited zeal for souls), and he will not fail to promote our interests effectively. Nonetheless, his loss now leaves a great void in the vineyard of the Lord, and especially in a time when we need such laborers more than ever."[36]

Four months before Virginio's death, Bruno had written to Ricasoli, explaining that difficulties in obtaining a passport and complications from the wars had rendered the proposed trip to Vienna impossible. He added: "With deep regret I have had to renounce the great consolation of seeing the Friends [*Amicizia Cristiana*] there again, and of embracing Virginio, whom I may never see again."[37] After December 1805, Bruno would indeed never see him again. A chapter in his life had closed, and, of the three, Diessbach, Virginio, and Lanteri, only he now remained.

His spiritual writings of these years reveal that, notwithstanding endless activity, struggles with health, and critical times, Bruno quietly pursued spiritual growth. On June 10, 1806, he began his annual Ignatian retreat. He resolved once more "to make my meditation daily according to the Exercises of St. Ignatius," and "to examine whether my actions adhere to those of Christ, my model and exemplar."[38] Bruno's struggle for gentleness continued: "I will examine whether I have treated my neighbor with Christ's gentleness, whether I have helped him spiritually and materially, and whether I have acted with proper moderation."[39]

The following year, 1807, Bruno determined to make "at least a half-hour of meditation, as often as possible before lunch," and noted, "An hour for prayer can be found just as the lunch hour is found."[40] He planned "to make my particular examination on imitating Jesus Christ," and sought "greater application in celebrating Mass and during the thanksgiving afterward."[41] In February 1808, Bruno renewed his focus on Christ: "I have chosen to live like Jesus, with Jesus, and for Jesus."[42]

On September 14, 1807, Bruno notified Ricasoli that "Tomorrow I am leaving to give the Exercises of St. Ignatius in a shrine dedicated to St. Ignatius himself, located in the mountains near us. The theologian Guala will come with me, and we will give the retreat together. What a wonderful thing it would be if we already had the direction of this shrine, but we will be returning at the end of the month."[43] With this retreat, Bruno and his disciple Guala launched a process that led to reopening this shrine as a retreat house in 1808, a significant step in a time when the French had closed retreat houses in Piedmont.[44] That September retreat also inaugurated a new chapter in Bruno's own retreat work, as he would note years later: "I gave the Exercises . . . for seventeen years in [the Shrine of] St. Ignatius."[45]

The retreats that began that September 1807 would play a lasting role in Piedmont. One scholar affirms: "In the quiet of the shrine, sanctified by the voice of men like Lanteri, Compaire, and, above all, by the memorable St. Joseph Cafasso, whole generations of priests and laity came to be renewed."[46] Among them were St. John Bosco, St. Leonardo Murialdo, Blessed Federico Albert, Blessed Clemente Marchisio, Blessed Giuseppe Allamano, Blessed Giacomo Alberione, and many others.[47]

Bruno's apostolate with books continued in these years, as Luigi Craveri noted: "I cannot sufficiently express how watchful and vigilant he was in examining new books for anything contrary to the sound and one true teaching of the Church. I remember that in 1807, he helped a priest, a professor of philosophy, to see such pitfalls by guiding him to read the works of the Venerable Cardinal Bellarmine regarding the authority of the Pope."[48] Bruno's

Shrine and Retreat House of St. Ignatius in the Valley of Lanzo, north of Turin.

Main entrance to the Shrine and Retreat House of St. Ignatius.

correspondence at this time records his ongoing effort to provide books to those in spiritual need.[49]

ON MAY 22, 1807, Bruno answered a letter from a laywoman, Gabriella Solaro della Margarita. She was married and the mother of six children, one of whom, Clemente, would become minister of foreign affairs under King Carlo Alberto.[50] Gabriella was talented, energetic, and resolute, with a good heart and a love for the good; she was also susceptible to impatience and sharpness.[51] She was a woman of sincere faith and desirous of spiritual growth.

In his reply, Bruno wrote: "Your letter just arrived; I was glad to receive it, and it gave me real joy. I am happy to hear that your trip went well, and that your whole family is in good health."[52] Bruno gave counsel on a family matter, and then addressed spiritual concerns. He urged Gabriella to receive Communion "as often as you can," and encouraged her "to be persevering in your meditation and spiritual reading, and also in your examination of conscience which you can do even while you work."[53] He asked Gabriella "to remember to lift up your heart often to God, but gently and with peace," and to make "acts of mortification, above all interior acts, which for you consist in a constant practice of gentleness and devotion."[54] Bruno continued: "I beg of you to wage continual warfare against negative moods, and never fail to begin again."[55] *Never fail to begin again. . . .*

Gabriella could undertake this without delay: "Do not wait until you have devotion to begin these things. Begin even without devotion since that will come with time, and this is precisely the means to attain it. Devotion must be the fruit and not the cause of the practices I have recommended. For the rest, you know that true devotion consists in readiness to be faithful to the Lord, and not in sentiment. I hope that soon you will send me consoling news in this regard."[56]

On July 4, 1808, Gabriella's son Clemente returned home from Turin, and Bruno sent with him a note for his mother.[57] Since, Bruno told Gabriella, he did not know her present spiritual condition, "I will take a sure part, and that is to urge you to begin each day, leaving the past to the mercy of the Lord, and the future to his Divine Providence."[58] In her various tasks, Bruno advised, "Do not let yourself be troubled by anything, not even by your own failings, taking care to overcome them immediately by an act of love of God." Bruno addressed Gabriella's personal struggle: "Be attentive to practice the virtue of patience and gentleness. You can make a special examination on this in the evening and at midday."[59]

Bruno offered Gabriella counsel for daily prayer: "Make at least fifteen minutes of meditation if you can, and lift up your heart frequently to God throughout the day. Do not omit spiritual reading, if only one page. Finally, try to receive Communion at least two or three times a week."[60] It was an apt program for a wife and mother of six.

Tragedy struck Gabriella's family when, in 1818, her young son, Enrico, died. Bruno wrote: "When I learned from your mother-in-law that you had lost your little Enrico, I felt great sorrow for what you must be undergoing, since no sacrifice could be more painful for you. He had such wonderful qualities that he won the love of all, and how much more the love of his mother. And so, because of this, you have every reason to feel his loss and to weep for him."[61]

Bruno then turned to the level of faith: "Yet, in another way, I share with you a joy that you have surely gained a protector in heaven who cannot fail to care for you, because he is your son. And because you love him so deeply, turn your thoughts to his eternal happiness, share in his glory, and do not imagine that you have lost him. It would be wrong to think so, because you have lost him only from sight, and not in reality."[62] Bruno continued: "Consider that he is at your side like another angel, that he encourages you to dedicate yourself to the things of heaven, and to share in his joy; that he assures you of his efforts before the throne of the Most Holy Trinity for you, for his father, his brother, and his dear sisters, to obtain for all of you great and abundant graces for your eternal salvation."[63]

Bruno invited Gabriella to lift her heart to Enrico in the communion of saints: "Remain in continual and loving conversation with him. Speak to him about all that you experience in your own heart, all that happens in your family, and anything of importance for you. Be on guard against thinking that he does not care about you, or that he is powerless to help you. That would be a misunderstanding of the immense love and almost infinite power that each of the Blessed enjoys, with all the other divine perfections that God shares with them in the greatest possible abundance."[64]

Bruno offered this grieving mother a final word of encouragement: "And so, if before you had no reason to be discouraged in the service of God, you have much less reason now. I would add that if it were possible for your little Enrico to feel any sorrow even now in heaven, it would be to see you discouraged and saddened because of him, because of your own failings, or because of the difficulties you encounter in the service of God."[65] "This," he wrote, "will be the remedy for any sadness or lack of courage you may feel: the thought that, with the grace of God and the protection of your little Enrico, you can do all things."[66]

IN 1808, BRUNO WAS FORTY-NINE years old. He had lived in Turin for thirty-one years, twenty-six of them as a priest. Year after year, in times of fragile peace and now of defeat and foreign occupation, from Turin he had exercised a multiform apostolic activity. The coming year would see the crisis between pope and emperor explode—an explosion that, in its aftermath, would demand of Bruno the sacrifice of both the city and his life's work.

CHAPTER NINE

The Pope in Captivity

*This concerns the Pope, and so the
unity, the center, and the foundation of our faith. We cannot, and
we may not remain silent.*
—Bruno Lanteri

ON THE MORNING OF JUNE 10, 1809, a herald on horseback proclaimed from the Capitol in Rome the end of papal sovereignty
and the annexation of the Papal States to the French empire. At
10:00 that morning, to the discharge of artillery, the papal flag was
lowered at Castel Sant'Angelo and the French flag raised. Cannons
boomed incessantly and, to the accompaniment of trumpets, her-
alds declared in the streets the end of the papal dynasty. It was
the execution of Napoleon's decree, issued on May 17, that Rome
was to become an imperial city. The pope would remain bishop of
Rome, retaining his palace and an appropriate revenue, but without temporal power.[1]

Cardinal Bartolomeo Pacca, then serving as secretary of state
for Pius VII, heard the tumult in the streets and grasped its significance. He related what followed: "Immediately I hastened to
the chamber of the Holy Father, and entered with a palpitating
heart, as may well be imagined. There, if my memory serves me
right, the first words that both of us uttered simultaneously were
the words of the Redeemer—'It is finished' [John 19:30]."[2] That
day, Pius VII signed the bull of excommunication against the per-
petrator of "this violent sacrilege" and all who collaborated with
it.[3] Ten days later, having learned of the excommunication, a furious Napoleon wrote: "I have just received word that the Pope has

excommunicated us. It is an excommunication that he has brought upon himself. The time for half-measures is past. He is a raving lunatic who must be confined."[4]

Three weeks later, the French acted. In the early hours of July 6, three parties of French soldiers assaulted the papal palace. They climbed the walls, shattered windows, and demolished the doors of the pope's apartments with axes.[5] Pius VII was arrested together with Cardinal Pacca, placed in a carriage, and hurried out of Rome. After forty-two days of chaotic and often painful travel, the pope was brought to Savona on the Italian coast near Genoa, and held under close surveillance in the bishop's palace.[6]

In a statement signed that same July 6, Pius VII quoted Jesus's words to Peter, "Truly, truly, I say to you, when you were young, you girded yourself and walked where you would; but when you are old, you will stretch out your hands, and another will gird you and carry you where you do not wish to go" (John 21:18).[7] He told the Church that he was indeed compelled to stretch forth his hands "to the force that binds us and carries us where we would not," asking all "to follow the example of the faithful of the first century, by whom, while Peter was kept in prison, 'Earnest prayer for him was made to God' [Acts 12:5]."[8] "We feel confident," he wrote, "that all our loving children will perform this pious and perhaps last act of duty to their affectionate and common father."[9] One who would actively answer that call, regardless of cost to himself, was Bruno.

ABDUCTED FROM ROME, held prisoner, stripped of his advisors, denied access to Church documents, and forbidden communication with the Church, Pius VII had recourse to the one arm that remained: he refused canonical institution to Napoleon's nominees as bishop. The Concordat of 1801 between Rome and France empowered Napoleon to nominate new bishops as dioceses became vacant. These, however, could not administrate legitimately their dioceses without canonical authorization (institution) from the pope. This institution Pius VII now refused to give.[10]

In 1806, the pope had already adopted this measure for Italy. In 1808, he had extended it to France and its annexed territories—much of Western Europe.[11] As years passed and diocese after diocese lost its bishop, ordinary administration in the Church was increasingly disrupted. In June 1808, the archbishop of Paris, the capital of Napoleon's empire, died, and no successor could be appointed. A crisis developed in Napoleon's empire; lacking bishops, dioceses fell into disorder, their members troubled and divided.[12]

In 1808–1810, an angry Napoleon devised measure after measure to break the resistance of "that old imbecile."[13] The pope was isolated, incessantly pressured to surrender, and his living conditions made harsher. Napoleon created commissions of bishops and theologians in Paris, and ordered them to find a favorable solution. He sent envoys to Savona to harass and intimidate the pope. Under the assault, Pius VII grew physically and emotionally weaker, nearly capitulated . . . and held firm.[14]

But he was not alone. A network of Catholics in France and Italy, fully aware of the risks, assisted the pope in his critical hour. Turin, south from Paris and Lyon, and on the road to Savona, played a key role in this effort.[15] From Turin, dedicated Catholics supplied the pope crucial canonical and financial resources. One historian writes: "In Turin as well, a group was formed to meet the need; its heart was Fr. Bruno Lanteri."[16]

In Paris, Cardinal Maury now suggested his new tactic: in the absence of a bishop, canon law permitted the priests of a cathedral to elect a vicar capitular with authority to administrate temporarily the diocese.[17] Let these priests appoint Napoleon's nominee for bishop as vicar capitular. In this way, the emperor's nominee could administrate the diocese without institution from Pius VII. Independently of Pius VII, the implementation of this tactic in Paris (with Maury himself as Napoleon's nominee) and Florence soon followed. Napoleon had found his answer.

Dedicated Catholics recognized the urgency of the moment: Pius VII had to be informed of Maury's ploy. And the pope, denied access to advisors and documents, would need the necessary canonical texts to demonstrate its nullity. Bruno, profoundly competent in such matters, identified these texts in the decrees of Pope Boniface VIII and the acts of the Second Council of Lyons. These forbade, under pain of losing their nomination, those proposed as bishops to administrate their dioceses prior to papal confirmation.[18] The texts had been found. Now police surveillance must be eluded, and the texts brought to the captive pope.

Bruno entrusted this dangerous task to his spiritual son Renato d'Agliano, a member of the *Amicizia* and the brother of the Gabriella mentioned in the preceding chapter.[19] Giuseppe Loggero attested that this mission entailed "the greatest difficulties, and, for both, the risk of death or at least imprisonment."[20]

D'Agliano brought the documents safely to Savona. Pietro Gastaldi, Bruno's first biographer, described D'Agliano's encounter with Pius VII: "He carried the texts concealed on his person and, when he approached the pope and bent down to kiss his foot, adroitly slipped them into the folds of the Holy Father's garments."[21]

On November 5, 1810, Pius VII wrote to Maury in Paris ordering him to renounce the administration of the archdiocese, and declaring null his previous administrative acts. On December 2, the pope sent similar instructions to Florence.[22]

Pius VII had acted, but word of his decision had yet to reach the wider Church. New dangers arose in this task, as firsthand witness Luigi Craveri related: "Once the decree of Pius VII to the archbishop of Florence concerning this matter, and his letter to Cardinal Maury were written, he [Bruno] labored to make them known. Though he took every precaution to avoid detection, he faced the danger of death in this task."[23] The pope's letters effectively negated Maury's tactic.

When he learned of the pope's action and of the assistance that had made it possible, Napoleon grew furious. He mobilized the police to find the persons responsible, and many arrests followed. As we have seen, the French police already knew the name "Monsieur l'abbé Brunon Lanteri." They had characterized Bruno as "one not having a very favorable opinion of the [French]

Government, especially since the difficulties with the Pope."[24] And for some time, the police had kept him under watch.

Their suspicion was not without basis. Prior even to Pius VII's captivity, Bruno had defended the Holy Father. Loggero attested that "during the time of the French Government in Piedmont and in Italy, and especially when the Holy Father, Pius VII, was captive, he [Bruno] labored ceaselessly to supply priests with writings that clearly revealed the artifices and deceptions of the persecutors of the Church."[25] Ferrero likewise affirmed that, "When Pius VII was imprisoned, Fr. Lanteri disseminated great numbers of books in defense of his pontificate."[26]

Bruno assisted the Holy Father in other ways as well. Stripped of his own revenues, Pius VII steadfastly refused financial assistance from his captors. Knowing the pope's need, the faithful in Turin came to his aid. Ferrero recounted that Bruno "organized that association that brought such honor to the Catholic Church and to the Pope, and that, through the voluntary contributions of dedicated Christians, supplied the Pope with the abundant means that freed him from dependence on the Emperor Napoleon."[27] In later years, Pius VII would recall with gratitude the generosity of the Turinese during his captivity.[28]

In past efforts, Bruno had successfully evaded the police. This time he did not. On January 11, 1811, Claude Berthaut du Coin was arrested, and from his papers emerged the name of Bruno Lanteri. On January 29, Bruno was arrested, interrogated, and his apartments searched. Loggero recalled that day: "The search of his house was sudden and rigorous. He had composed a lengthy, forceful, and persuasive text to alert the bishops of that time to the tactics of the government in their regard. The text was not found because one of his spiritual sons [Loggero himself], who had made the copy, had removed it, and packaged and sealed it for mailing to the prepared address."[29]

Bruno was permitted no trial, no defense, no recourse, and no limit was set to his sentence. No proof was necessary; suspicion was enough. On February 27, Napoleon endorsed the director of police's recommendations. The archbishop was ordered to remove

Bruno's permission to hear confessions. Bruno was to depart from Turin and reside in his rural dwelling, the Grangia, in the hills twenty kilometers outside the city. The exile would endure as long as Napoleon—or political events beyond his power—should decide.

On March 25, Bruno set out for "my isolated country dwelling," as he called it.[30] With his departure, the *Amicizie* scattered, and the activity of the preceding decades collapsed.[31] At age fifty-two, deprived of ministry, distanced from friends and collaborators, and burdened with poor health, Bruno faced an unknown future. In demanding circumstances, beyond his power to change, he would need to find a new way.

IN HIS HELPLESSNESS, Bruno turned to prayer. Prayer had always accompanied his priestly life; now it would come to the fore. From the beginnings of his priesthood, Bruno had resolved to "enter the way of prayer" and to "grow in the habit" of prayer.[32] He had sought "the faithful practice of my daily spiritual exercises, which are meditation, Mass, the Office, spiritual reading, the visit to the Blessed Sacrament when possible, and the examination of conscience."[33] Antonio Ferrero described Bruno's practice of prayer: "Every day he spent an hour or more in meditation, and made two examinations of conscience. . . . Every month he made a day of retreat, and every day he dedicated time to abundant spiritual reading, which he chose with care."[34] The retreat notes we have seen testify to Bruno's faithfulness to prayer through the years.

Now a spiritual deepening occurred. Luigi Craveri recounted his experience of Bruno during his exile: "In the years he spent withdrawn there [the Grangia], I visited him more often than before, and always returned from our conversations warmed by the encouragement he gave, and with greater desire for the good. It was then that I came to admire more deeply, and with many confirmations, the great degree to which the theological and moral virtues were at work in that soul."[35]

Craveri continued: "He nurtured his love for God in the time he spent before the Blessed Sacrament, and, during the years

View of the Grangia from the adjoining fields.

A part of the Grangia buildings dedicated to farming the surrounding fields.

he spent at the Grangia, meditated deeply on the things of God through the writings of St. Bonaventure, with such savor and penetration that he said he had never known so much of God as after reading those sublime writings; consequently, I do not doubt that his soul reached the highest levels of contemplation, and I have seen that he could discern the degrees and nature of such prayer with great ease."[36]

In the years he spent withdrawn there.... This was no longer a monthly day of retreat or annual spiritual exercises of eight days. Month after month, year after year, Bruno's enforced exile offered him time to "savor and penetrate" the things of God, leading him deeper into contemplative prayer. St. Bonaventure's writings emerged in this deepening, and, in fact, among Bruno's manuscripts extensive notes on this saint's writings remain.[37] In his third year of exile, Bruno described to the local priest what he called "the system of quiet life I have set for myself," and Antonio Ferrero summarized these years as a time of prayer and study.[38] A day would come when Bruno would speak of his exile as "my cherished solitude."[39]

Confined to the Grangia, Bruno sought and was granted permission to keep the Blessed Sacrament in his chapel.[40] He explained that his "habitual problems of health, the distance from the parish, and the muddied condition of the roads made it impossible for him to frequent the parish church."[41] As throughout his life, the Eucharist would be central to Bruno's prayer in these years. Craveri testified: "The liveliness of his faith shone in his face during the long hours he spent in adoration before the Blessed Sacrament. There he often recited the Divine Office and meditated at length. At times it seemed to me that by leaving open the door of his room, which was only a few steps from the chapel, he remained constantly in the presence of the Divine Master."[42]

OTHERS TOO BORE THE BURDEN of French oppression, and, in his isolation, Bruno did not forget them. For years he had assisted religious women expelled from their convents and constrained to subsist as best they could, among them Sisters Radegonda, Prudence,

Crocifissa Bracchetto, and Leopolda di Mortigliengo.[43] Now, in his own exile, Bruno continued to aid them. He offered them retreats at the Grangia, at times difficult to arrange on account of poor roads, cold weather, and Bruno's fluctuating health. He met with them at the Grangia, wrote them letters of spiritual direction, and assisted them financially.[44]

On September 29, 1811, Bruno encouraged one of them, Sr. Crocifissa Bracchetto, to renew her retreat proposals regardless of failures, and added: "This readiness always to begin again has something heroic about it. You may be sure that you will fail often during the day, but be constant in rising again immediately each time. In doing this, you will exercise humility and confidence in God, virtues that you need to make great progress in the service of God."[45] And on February 21, 1813, again to Sr. Crocifissa: "Oh, if only you knew how much God loves these two virtues of humility and Christian hope!"[46] The heroism of beginning again, regardless of repeated failure, with humble confidence in God: Bruno would tirelessly proclaim this message in these years of suffering for the Church and nation.

On January 10, 1813, Bruno wrote to Sr. Leopolda di Mortigliengo, a faithful religious yet prone to discouragement, now troubled regarding both her spiritual past and future. Bruno assured her that her fear for the past "is without basis," and encouraged her "rather than to yield to this fear, to give glory to God and thank him from your heart for his infinite goodness in having forgiven you everything."[47] Bruno affirmed that the year just beginning would be a time of growth "if you approach it with humility and renewed hope in God, asking him constantly to grant you these two graces, that we so much need, and that already he desires deeply to give you, having promised and merited this grace for you."[48]

Bruno drew the conclusion: "Say then with boldness, *nunc coepi* [Now I begin], and go forward constantly in God's service. Do not look back so often, because one who looks back cannot run. And do not be content to begin only for this year. Begin every day, because it is for every day, even for every hour of the day, that the Lord taught us to say in the Our Father, 'Forgive us our trespasses,' and 'Give us this day our daily bread.'"[49]

CHANNELS OF SERVICE opened in other ways as well. Bruno's spiritual son Giuseppe Loggero joined him in his exile, a choice for which Bruno was deeply grateful. Bruno later would write: "He [Loggero] freely offered to come with me to my country dwelling, to stay with me and assist me, and did so for the three years of my exile. I was profoundly grateful for this, especially because my health was very poor at that time."[50]

Loggero had been ordained after one year of theological studies because, Bruno explained, "the critical circumstances of the times did not permit more."[51] At the Grangia, Bruno continued, "he resumed his studies . . . on the classical and Jesuit authors that I supplied him," with special emphasis on the errors of the day: Jansenism, Richerism, and Febronianism.[52]

On January 22, 1813, Loggero began a sixteen-day retreat under Bruno's guidance. For each of these days, Bruno chose readings for Loggero's meditation and reflection. In his retreat notes, Loggero chronicled the struggles and fruit of his retreat. On the first evening of the retreat, he prayed "without stirrings of the heart and with little desire."[53] The following morning, Loggero prayed again and commented: "Meditation moderately well made, with few and involuntary distractions."[54] A time of reflection later that day brought "spiritual savoring and a sense of the greatness of God."[55]

Later in the retreat, Loggero reflected on paradise "with affection, savoring, and attention."[56] Of a like consideration the following day, he wrote: "This truly touched my heart."[57] On the fifteenth day, Loggero meditated on the love of God and noted that "I felt stirrings of the heart and the resolution to live no longer for anything but to love God, imitating how Jesus lived. *Fiat. Fiat.* [May this be so.]"[58]

On the morning of the sixteenth day, Loggero ended his retreat: "I renewed, without affective stirrings but from my heart and firmly, the proposals I made earlier in the retreat, especially regarding diligence in a faithful practice of daily meditation, of preparation and thanksgiving for Mass, and diligence in using well the time available to me, dedicating myself to study, and in moderating my desire to go to Turin. I asked the special help of God and of the Virgin Mary and of my patron saints."[59] Loggero concluded: "How blest I will be if I am faithful to this."[60] The effort to curb his desire for Turin suggests that, despite his free choice to accompany Bruno, exile was no easier for Loggero than for Bruno.

Forbidden active ministry, Bruno wrote ceaselessly in defense of the Church. During these years, one scholar notes, "his activity as an essayist grew particularly intense."[61] Bruno strove through writing to inform public opinion, and to defend university students and seminarians from error regarding Church teaching and practice.[62] Craveri testified that when Napoleon, in a further attempt to subjugate Pius VII, convoked a "National Council" in 1811, Bruno composed his *Dissertation on the Right of the Primacy of the Sovereign Pontiff for the Confirmation of All Bishops*, printed secretly in France.[63] Some years later, a French journal published this *Dissertation* under a different author's name. Bruno, Craveri recounted, "learned of this and remained silent."[64] Craveri added: "But I can attest that this was his work because I made a compendium of it from his original manuscript before it was published."[65]

ON JUNE 4, 1812, at the height of his power, Napoleon led the 614,000 men of his Grande Armée into Russia. The withdrawal of the Russian army, Napoleon's increasingly stretched lines, the inconclusive and bloody battles, and the onset of the terrible Russian winter, led to a ruinous retreat from Moscow on October 19. On December 5, Napoleon abandoned his shattered army and fled to Paris. Of the 614,000 soldiers, only 35,000 survived the Russian trap at the Beresina River, and many of these would die in the following days.[66] In the aftermath of unprecedented disaster, Napoleon's Grande Armée ceased to exist.

A weary Europe learned of the catastrophe, and hope awakened that the Napoleonic yoke at last might be broken. The reversal of political fortunes now approaching would open a new chapter in Bruno's life.

CHAPTER TEN

Restoration

I live only for the glory of God.
—Bruno Lanteri

FOR BRUNO, HOWEVER, THE SLOW MONTHS OF EXILE persisted. Fluctuations of health marked them, as improvement alternated with more frequent lapses. On July 5, 1811, Bruno told Sr. Leopolda di Mortigliengo that "today the oppression [struggle to breathe] that I have not experienced for many days returned again. . . . At the moment it has largely subsided, and I think it is not likely to return. However this may be, we shall always say *fiat* [God's will be done]."[1]

Four months later, on October 29, Bruno planned to guide Sisters Leopolda and Crocifissa on retreat at the Grangia, but commented: "My only fear is that bad weather or my health or the cold will interfere. Whatever happens, may God's holy will be done."[2] In February of the following year, 1812, Bruno observed to Sr. Leopolda that "regarding my own retreat, as you see, everything is much delayed because of my illness, and I will barely finish it during Lent."[3]

In his second year of exile, Bruno's health worsened and, on December 10, 1812, he asserted that "my days will not be long because of my illnesses which, rather than diminish, persist all the more."[4] Again, on August 5, 1813, Bruno wrote to the local priest of "one who is close to eternity," adding, "as I am because of the illnesses to which I am subject."[5]

An unexpected improvement then occurred. On November 17, Bruno's friend and *Amicizia* companion Francesco Pertusati rejoiced: "May God be praised for the news you sent of your improved health, which we value so highly. I hope now that, by God's goodness, you will recover entirely."[6] But problems reappeared, and on February 23, 1814, in his third winter of exile, Bruno told Sr. Leopolda that "my health suffers from the cold."[7]

EVEN AS BRUNO WROTE THESE WORDS, his exile was about to end. With astonishing energy Napoleon strove to recover from the Russian disaster, raising armies, waging war . . . but France was exhausted and the power of the Allies too great. On March 4, 1813, the Russians drove the French from Berlin. Only weeks later, the English under Wellington entered Madrid. In August, Austria joined England, Russia, and Prussia in the war against Napoleon. Irreparable disaster struck at Leipzig in October, when 335,000 Allied troops defeated Napoleon's 190,000. The Allies invaded France and, on March 31, 1814, Paris fell. Six days later, Napoleon abdicated and his empire came to an end.

In Piedmont, almost beyond hope, freedom returned after twenty years of oppression. Italian statesman Massimo d'Azeglio, the son of Bruno's associate and friend Cesare d'Azeglio, described the jubilation of the people: "At last, one blessed day, came the glad tidings that Napoleon was no longer our master, and that we were, or were about to become, free and independent once more. He who was not at Turin on that day can form no idea of the delirious joy of a whole population at its utmost height."[8] For Bruno, as for so many, an enormous weight lifted that April 1814.

On April 20, Napoleon departed under guard for exile on the island of Elba. That same day, Bruno and Loggero left the Grangia and returned to Turin.[9] Five weeks later, on May 24, Pius VII reentered Rome to the acclaim of the city and Europe.

An account of Loggero's last days in 1847 relates that seminarians accompanied him, praying with him and reading to him. And "when readings from Church history recounted the sufferings of those two great Popes, Pius VI and Pius VII, they often saw him moved to tears of tenderness."[10] Loggero and Bruno had shared the pope's sufferings; now they shared his freedom.

RETURNING TO TURIN, Bruno found a ruined city and nation. Decades of revolution, war, and foreign occupation had exhausted Piedmont's resources. Financial distress gripped Turin itself.[11] Famine would ravage Piedmont in 1816-1817, with illness and death in its wake.[12]

The Church, too, lay in disarray. Seminaries and novitiates had been closed, religious expelled, parishes crippled, and the people abandoned.[13] It was necessary, one historian writes, "to provide them religious instruction . . . to teach them the Creed, the basic prayers, the fundamental truths of the faith, the Ten Commandments . . . to regularize marriages, and to prepare the young for First Communion."[14] In this work of restoration, the same author notes, "the Church had to begin again from nothing."[15] These years of new beginnings would be the most creative of Bruno's life, and the time of his most enduring works.

The *Amicizia Cristiana* resumed activity only in 1817, and under the new title—proposed by member Joseph de Maistre—of *Amicizia Cattolica* (Catholic Friendship).[16] The new group discontinued secrecy, was entirely lay in membership, and focused solely on the apostolate of the printed word. Bruno assisted the new *Amicizia* as theologian and advisor.[17] By 1825, the *Amicizia* had published and distributed without charge more than 140,000 volumes.[18] In 1821 alone, the Church in America received 6,500 volumes.[19] Five years later, the *Amicizia* would inform the king that "over 10,000 volumes have been sent to America."[20]

New forms replaced the *Amicizia Sacerdotale* as well. On February 22, 1815, Bruno instituted in Turin the Pious Union of St. Paul, a group of young priests modeled on the initiative by this name of former Jesuit Luigi Felici in Rome.[21] Its goal, Bruno wrote, "was to provide confessors, instructors, and consolers for the ill in hospitals, for the neglected poor of the city, and for those detained in prison."[22] During the two years of its existence, Bruno gathered some twenty members for the Pious Union. Among them was Don Giovanni Battista Reynaudi, whose life would affect Bruno's own in decisive ways neither could foresee.[23]

Predictably, Loggero joined Bruno's Pious Union.[24] In a letter of July 12, 1816, Bruno described the formation he offered Loggero and these young priests. Bruno wrote that "when I resumed residence in Turin after our liberation from Bonaparte, he [Loggero] continued to live with me."[25] There, Bruno added, "under my guidance and with the help of many books that I supplied him, he dedicated himself to preparing an entire series of meditations [preached conferences intended to move the heart] for the Spiritual Exercises, faithfully following the method of St. Ignatius. He is working at present to complete his series of instructions [preached conferences intended to explain the faith] for the same purpose."[26] Loggero would give the Spiritual Exercises often in coming years—150 times in 1815-1827—and repeatedly again until 1841.[27]

Bruno prepared Loggero for further priestly work: "At the same time, he heard confessions in the church of San Francesco in Turin. With diligence and much zeal, he visited, heard confessions, preached, and taught catechism in the prisons and hospitals. He has preached the meditations of the Exercises of St. Ignatius in public on various occasions with abundant fruit."[28] One who knew Loggero in later years would relate of him that "I never saw a confessor so constantly sought by so many. He was austere by nature, though with a discreet sense of humor. Yet I firmly believe that he had no equal in encouraging the disheartened, healing the scrupulous, and guiding those disposed to solid virtue and holiness. In my own struggle with scruples, I might have been in great trouble had I fallen into other hands than his."[29] The hallmarks of Bruno's priestly formation—Spiritual Exercises, confessions, visits to the poor and ill, encouragement of the discouraged, guidance of those receptive toward holiness—and its efficacy, appear in Loggero's fruitful ministry.

Loggero was one of many whom, as Ferrero related, Bruno guided to become "well prepared men" and "effective workers" in the Lord's vineyard.[30] Servant of God and future general of the Jesuits, Johann Roothaan, in 1824 would affirm that, "He [Bruno] has trained many priests; [they are] excellent men, and unshakeable in their calling."[31]

On August 7, 1814, Pius VII reestablished the Jesuits after forty-one years of suppression. Bruno exulted, and wrote to Ricasoli: "I thank God that the Jesuits are restored . . . now we must do all we can to see that they establish houses in our country [Piedmont]."[32] And Ferrero testified: "He employed every means in his power to defend the Jesuits and to send them vocations."[33] Bruno desired to support religious orders in general, as he further declared to Ricasoli: "We must also assist the reestablishment of the other religious orders, of both men and women, because this is a powerful means for promoting God's glory and the salvation of souls."[34]

During these years of restoration, Bruno initiated "a campaign of popular missions [preached Ignatian retreats]" to renew the faith of a spiritually neglected people.[35] Craveri attested that "beginning in 1814–1815, he organized the Spiritual Exercises in many places, wherever his encouragement could reach . . . and especially in the Province of Casale Monferrato, whose devout Governor, the Marchese Taparelli d'Azeglio, had agreed to cover the expenses, which he did."[36] Ferrero recounted that "after the Holy Father returned to Rome . . . he used every possible means to multiply retreat houses for the Spiritual Exercises, and to provide retreats according to the method of St. Ignatius."[37] For this purpose, Bruno gathered a group of priests in Turin, among them Loggero, Craveri, Antonio Lanteri,[38] and Giovanni Battista Genovesio—men who would share in the unexpected turn this work soon would take.[39]

Bruno relentlessly urged these men to give the Spiritual Exercises: whole populations needed to hear God's word and return to the sacraments. On April 10, 1815, he wrote to Craveri: "The Spiritual Exercises for the church of San Francesco [in Turin] are set to begin the evening of the 22nd of this month. The Theologian Guala, however, has no one to preach the meditations. We had planned on Don [Antonio] Lanteri for this, but he excused himself saying that you had denied Guala's request.[40] The only possibilities, consequently, are that you withdraw your opposition and encourage Lanteri to preach the meditations, or that you come to give them in his place, or that we renounce these Exercises."[41]

The spiritual cost of such renouncement would be great: "We are doing all we can to avoid this last, desperate choice since the harm to souls would be great, all the more because this year, as far as I know . . . no Spiritual Exercises are being given in any other church [in Turin]."[42] Bruno, convinced that Antonio Lanteri's resistance was without basis, charged Craveri to "persuade, exhort, compel Lanteri to come."[43]

The need was equally pressing eight months later when, on December 8, 1815, Bruno wrote to Craveri: "We have received here a formal request for priests to give a number of parish missions in the Diocese of Casale from now until Easter. These missions are for towns of four or five thousand people. If Signor Cocchis [a doctor] can assure Don Lanteri that this will not slow his full recovery, he could give one mission before Christmas (and you could give one after Christmas). In that case, ask him to give me a clear answer, yes or no, and when he would plan on beginning if the answer is yes."[44] Bruno then solicited Craveri's participation: "Regardless of whether Don Lanteri's answer is affirmative or negative, please let me know at what time between Christmas and Easter you would be able to begin the mission you will give. You can preach the meditations, and everything necessary will be provided."[45]

These parish missions, Bruno told Craveri, were critically important for the times: "I know that I do not need to give you reasons for making this commitment, since you know well the value of souls and the importance of their salvation. I will say only that the mission will be in a town where the poor people generally live without the aid of the Sacraments, and cannot receive them even if they wish, because, unhappily, most of the priests follow the contrary system [rigorist moral theology]. Believe me, were the need not extreme, I would never have even considered asking this of you, and I confess the truth, that I envy the lot of those who can do this work; but I am not worthy of it."[46] Bruno's health forbade the hours of preaching in packed churches and the endless confessions these eight- to ten-day missions entailed. *I envy the lot.* . . . Here, as so often in his life, Bruno was compelled to accept his physical limitations.

TWENTY KILOMETERS AWAY, a thirty-two-year-old priest pondered how best to restore the Church in his native Carignano. Don Giovanni Battista Reynaudi saw and lamented the religious decline in his town of 7,000. Under French occupation, the practice of the faith had diminished, and religious orders had been expelled. The monastery of the Poor Clare sisters was now a public school, and that of the Capuchin fathers had been destroyed. The Augustinian fathers also had been evicted and their monastery rented to private individuals.[47] The church attached to the Augustinian monastery, Nostra Signora delle Grazie (Our Lady of Grace), remained open. During the French occupation, in 1807, the archbishop had appointed a young priest, Don Agostino Golzio, as rector of this church.[48]

In the summer of 1814, Don Reynaudi gathered with Don Golzio and another priest of Carignano, Don Antonio Biancotti.[49] All were in their early thirties, all were concerned for Carignano, and all desired its spiritual renewal. In conversation, together they explored the means.

The Poor Clares wished to return but could not because the school occupied their monastery. What if the city transferred the school to the former Augustinian monastery? The school would function as before, and the sisters could then return to their monastery. Reynaudi and Biancotti would join Golzio at Nostra Signora delle Grazie. Living in common, they would strengthen each other's priesthood. Serving this church as preachers, catechists, and confessors, they would offer Carignano a new center of spiritual energy. As circumstances might suggest, they could assist in the school now adjacent to the church.[50]

By early November 1814, the three presented to the local administration their proposal of "a religious institution totally dedicated to confessions, catechism, and popular instruction."[51] Years later, Biancotti would write that "our initial project was somewhat vague: to work for the good of souls and especially to provide Carignano with priests dedicated to ministry,"[52] and Golzio would affirm that "our goal was to live together in brotherly union and work for the greater spiritual good of the people."[53] Reynaudi would add that "in the beginning, Fr. Reynaudi and Fr. Biancotti chose as the single basis of the institute the ministry of receiving sinners with charity and preaching devotion to Our Lady."[54]

The civic and ecclesiastical authorities responded favorably, and the project advanced.[55] Opposition arose, however, from the school's director, who considered the plan prejudicial to his role.[56] Others supported the director, and the conflict intensified.[57] Progress halted, months passed . . . and the three grew discouraged. By October 1815, Biancotti related, "the three priests decided to renounce their plan. It seemed that this was not God's will for them, and that they were to take a different way."[58] That October, Reynaudi left for Rome to join the Jesuits. Biancotti, too, prepared to follow.[59] The brief dream had ended.

CARLO TANCREDI AND JULIETTE COLBERT had married in 1806, and, from that time, had lived between Paris and Turin. With Napoleon's fall in 1814, their duties at court ceased and they established themselves definitively in Turin.[60] Here Juliette was known by her Italian name, Giulia.

She was young, wealthy, charming, and capable, a woman of faith, with a lively desire for goodness.[61] As Giulia would later recount, Bruno now became an inescapable presence in her life.[62] His name arose often in conversation, and she saw him in his visits to her mother-in-law, Paolina.[63] Giulia began to esteem Bruno . . . and to avoid him. She admired the devout life her mother-in-law led under Bruno's guidance. She sensed—rightly— that Bruno wished to draw her to a similar life of dedication. And Giulia was not ready to make that choice.[64]

Bruno, for whom gentleness required lifelong effort, overcame Giulia's resistance through patient goodness. She sought his spiritual guidance, and a new life began for her and for the Church of Turin.[65]

On April 17, 1814, Giulia was walking through the streets of Turin. She saw a priest bringing Communion to the sick, and knelt as he passed. In that moment, she was startled by a cry from a nearby window: "I don't want Holy Communion! I want soup to

The Servant of God Marchesa Giulia di Barolo.

eat!"[66] Giulia related: "The tone of that voice pierced me. I looked around to see from where it had come, and saw the blackened bars of the Senatorial Prison."[67] She asked to enter the prison and was horrified by "the darkness, the stench, and the sound of chains" that met her.[68]

Giulia then visited the upper floor reserved for women prisoners. The sight of women dressed in rags and packed into overcrowded cells with limited light and air, and only a corridor for exercise, forever changed her life. She wrote: "They almost threw themselves on me, crying out all at once. Their state of degradation caused me an affliction and a shame that I cannot remember without deep emotion. . . . I returned home, my heart wracked with pain, not knowing how to remedy the physical and moral conditions of these prisoners."[69]

Giulia, never hesitant and never intimidated by obstacles, began visiting the women prisoners, whose good will she gradually won.[70] She gained the government's permission to transfer the women to a more adequate building, and, in 1821, was named superintendent of the prison.[71] Under her supervision, Turin's female prison became a model for Europe.[72]

Initiative now followed upon initiative. She assisted abandoned children, orphans, young women in danger, the poor, and the ill.[73] Giulia—a married woman—founded communities of sisters to assist these persons in need: the Penitential Sisters of St. Mary Magdalene and the Sisters of St. Ann.[74] She established a refuge for women, the Hospital of St. Philomena, and the Workshop of St. Joseph to provide employment for young women without financial support. She built a church . . . the list of her undertakings grew long with the years.[75] At her death in 1864, it was said that "wherever she went, the poor and the suffering learned of her presence."[76] Giulia's cause of canonization was introduced in 1991, and, four years later, her husband Carlo's as well.[77]

Through Bruno's guidance, Giulia had opened herself to God's grace with new energy. Long after his death, the fruits of that openness would endure.

IN 1815, NAPOLEON CAST HIS SHADOW over Europe a final time. On February 26, he escaped from the Island of Elba and landed in France. The nation, humiliated in the aftermath of defeat, rallied to its former emperor, and his Hundred Days' rule began. On June 18, Wellington defeated Napoleon at Waterloo: it was his "exit from the world stage."[78] That same June, the Congress of Vienna completed its labors and Europe was "restored" after revolution and empire.

Piedmont, too, was reestablished as a nation, and a time of peace began. But seeds of unrest had been sown in the years of occupation and soon would come to fruition. Statesman Massimo d'Azeglio described the return of King Vittorio Emmanuele I to Turin in 1814: "At last, on the twentieth of May, the beloved and long-expected King arrived. The usual repeated cries of acclaim greeted the good prince, with such enthusiasm as to remove all doubt of the affection and sympathy of his faithful Turinese."[79] Only seven years later, however, a revolution in Piedmont would compel this same king to abdicate and flee.

In the uneasy calm of 1815, Bruno labored assiduously for the restoration of the Church. He was fifty-six years old. An encounter now only months away would shape definitively his remaining years.

CHAPTER ELEVEN

Carignano

God has given you to us as a father.
—Reynaudi and Biancotti to Bruno Lanteri

IN OCTOBER 1815, A DISCOURAGED REYNAUDI had abandoned Carignano and sought entrance among the Jesuits in Rome. Difficulties arose, however, attributed by one early account to physical issues: "The climate there was so harmful to Don Reynaudi's health that in the six months he spent in that city, he was never strong enough to begin the novitiate."[1] His Jesuit confessor advised Reynaudi to return home and pursue the former project in Carignano.[2] A renewed effort to join the Jesuits also ended in failure when the superior "with tears in his eyes told him that this was not God's will, and that he should return to his own city."[3] On April 17, 1816, Reynaudi reentered Carignano.[4]

There he found that two months earlier, on February 22, the king had granted the former Augustinian monastery to him and his companions, Biancotti and Golzio.[5] The others were willing to resume the project. Reynaudi, "unsure of whether he should face once again the opposition already encountered," made the spiritual exercises in the Shrine of St. Ignatius in Lanzo.[6] During those days of retreat, Reynaudi accepted the undertaking as God's will and embraced it anew.[7]

Yet questions persisted. Their community that "as yet had no name," remained also without a rule of life.[8] And, as the project revived, opposition did likewise.[9] Seeking counsel, Reynaudi approached Bruno's disciple Luigi Guala, who advised Reynaudi to speak with Bruno.[10] In the summer of 1816, Reynaudi asked to meet with Bruno; the stage was now set for the conversation that would shape the rest of both their lives.[11] Bruno was then fifty-seven years old, and Reynaudi thirty-four.

Reynaudi's request found Bruno at the Grangia. Giovanni Battista Isnardi, who shared Bruno's final years, recounted that "when Fr. Lanteri learned of the worthy initiative about which Fr. Reynaudi wished to consult him, he invited him to spend some days with him so that, in holy solitude and extended prayer, together they might examine better before God a matter of such importance, and more clearly know the divine will."[12]

Reynaudi himself, writing in the third person, related what followed. Bruno not only confirmed the initiative as of God—he proposed something new. Reynaudi remembered that day: "Turning to the Theologian Lanteri for help, Don Reynaudi was encouraged by him to this enterprise as to a work clearly of God."[13] Reynaudi continued: "Indeed, enlightening him [Reynaudi] concerning a more important aim that could be given to the Institute, he [Bruno] spoke to him convincingly of the good that could be accomplished through the Spiritual Exercises of St. Ignatius, through studying current errors in depth, and through an opportune distribution of well-chosen books, suited to the times."[14]

Isnardi described this key moment in similar terms: "Lanteri, however, who had labored tirelessly in the vineyard of the Lord for many years, and knew better the urgent needs of those troubled times, as well as the most effective means to remedy them, proposed to Reynaudi the sublime plans upon which he had long meditated, and among other things, showed him with the most moving clarity the almost irresistible power of the Spiritual Exercises of St. Ignatius."[15] Should Reynaudi's group accept this plan, Bruno added, many others he had already trained would join them or help as they were able.[16] In effect, Bruno was inviting Reynaudi and his companions to accept "the design inspired and inculcated in us for many years by Fr. Diessbach,"[17] the apostolic program Bruno had long promoted: the Spiritual Exercises, the apostolate of the printed word, and the defense of faith through combatting errors in the culture of the day.

Reynaudi not only accepted Bruno's proposal: he asked the older priest to join and lead the community. He recounted: "Don Reynaudi was persuaded by the considerations he [Bruno] raised, and proposed to the Theologian Lanteri that he take the leadership of this new congregation. He [Bruno] left him with some hope that if his companions were willing to accept the plan he proposed, he might with time resolve to join them."[18] From the wisdom of the one and the openness of the other, a new institute was born in the Church that day.

The response in Carignano was similar, as Reynaudi further related: "Upon his return to Carignano, he [Reynaudi] immediately spoke of this with his companions, and since they desired only the glory of God and his will, they readily accepted this counsel."[19] From that day, the group in Carignano considered Bruno its leader. Biancotti attested that "they sought Fr. Bruno Lanteri's advice in every doubt," and from his residence in Turin, he guided them.[20]

On September 22, 1816, Reynaudi and Biancotti wrote to Bruno, asking him to choose which of them should be superior (both had refused). They requested his counsel "because God has given you to us as a father and you have accepted us as sons to direct."[21] In his reply, Bruno named Reynaudi superior, and referred to "your beloved Congregation in honor of Mary Most Holy," telling them that he was willing "for this time" to choose the superior.[22] Bruno's language revealed his understanding of his relationship with the congregation at this time: he was one who guided, without himself belonging to the group.

Two weeks later, on November 8, Reynaudi informed Bruno of the community's affairs, and added: "We consider it a religious duty to share with you this good news so that you be informed precisely of all that is happening to us, and because we have special need of your prayers, your counsel, and your help. Have compassion on our inexperience; guide us in our youth. . . . If only we had you here among us and could depend in everything on your guidance, and constantly read from your lips the holy will of God. . . . We will pray intensely to our good Mother that, moved with pity for the great weakness of her sons, she obtain for us one day, and soon, the strength we so need from our beloved and deeply desired father!!"[23]

With Bruno's assistance, the community elaborated its first provisional rule, canonically approved for the Archdiocese of Turin on November 13, 1816.[24] The rule stated that the "Oblates of Mary, established in Carignano," would dedicate themselves to "administering the sacrament of Penance, together with conferences on moral theology; to preaching the Word of God, especially in the Spiritual Exercises; and to public instruction with catechesis for the poor."[25] The text concluded: "The principal spirit of the Congregation is to visit the sick, assist the dying, visit hospitals and prisons, receive the poor with goodness in confession, teach catechism to the uninstructed, win the conversion of sinners, and labor strenuously for the truth against the errors of the times."[26]

On that same November 13, 1816, the vicar capitular, Emmanuele Gonetti, granted formal canonical status to the "Oblates of the Most Holy Virgin Mary."[27] The new congregation now existed officially in the Church.

IN MARCH 1816, a bishop from the United States traveled to Turin.[28] Louis-Guillaume-Valentin Du Bourg was born on the island of Santo Domingo in 1766, studied in France, and was ordained in Paris in 1788, one year before the French Revolution. With the outbreak of revolution, Du Bourg fled to Spain and from there to Baltimore where he joined the Sulpicians.[29] He was named president of Georgetown College, founded by Archbishop John Carroll, and later established the college that would become St. Mary's Seminary in Baltimore.[30] Du Bourg spiritually directed Elizabeth Ann Seton on her journey toward religious life in Emmitsburg, Maryland.[31]

In 1812, Archbishop Carroll named Du Bourg apostolic administrator of the Diocese of Louisiana—then a territory comprising eleven present-day states, reaching to the Rocky Mountains and Canada—and of Florida.[32] The new administrator was given twelve elderly priests to serve his vast diocese; no others were available. After three years of struggles, Du Bourg traveled to Rome in May 1815, to seek more adequate resources, intending to resign

Our Lady of Grace, Carignano, first church of the Oblates.

Interior of Our Lady of Grace, Carignano.

Former Augustinian monastery, first residence of the Oblates in Carignano.

if these should not be available.[33] Pius VII encouraged Du Bourg in his task, and ordained him bishop. Du Bourg remained two years in Europe seeking priests, women religious, and financial aid for his diocese. In March 1816, he traveled to Turin for this purpose. Among those who strove to assist him was Bruno.

On September 17, 1816, Bruno informed Du Bourg of four Piedmontese priests willing to serve the diocese of Louisiana.[34] Though every effort had been made to free them, he told Du Bourg, difficulties remained.[35] Of these four, one would eventually reach Louisiana.[36] Other Piedmontese priests would serve in Du Bourg's diocese, and, one historian comments, "it is not improbable that they too were recruited by Lanteri."[37] In his letter to Du Bourg, Bruno inquired about the date of departure for America, discussed the need for passports, and added: "It would also be helpful if you could let me know for my guidance the approximate cost of the trip for each, so that I can procure a promissory note for them as you suggested. I hope to obtain a loan for this as a supplement to the limited funds remaining with the Signor Marchese d'Azeglio."[38]

Loggero, too, stirred by Du Bourg's visit, sought to serve in America. One year earlier, in 1815, he had requested and had been granted admission to the Jesuits, waiting only for the opening of a novitiate in Piedmont.[39] Now, fired with missionary zeal, he sought permission to enter the Jesuits in America.[40] On April 29, 1816, he wrote to the Jesuit superior: "The Most Reverend Du Bourg, Bishop of New Orleans in Louisiana, has visited us here. When he explained to us the extreme need of the Church in those places, and his desire for a foundation of Jesuits in his vast diocese, I felt renewed in that ardent longing I had experienced even before I entered the seminary, as something inborn in me, to consecrate myself totally one day to spreading the faith among the nations that are still barbarian, and especially the nation of America."[41]

The superior did not approve of such initiative in a novice-to-be, and denied the request.[42] Bruno wrote to Du Bourg: "Don Loggero, remembering you and the goodness Your Reverence showed us, asked me to present his humble respects, and to express to you his lively sentiments of gratitude, and his continuing sorrow that he cannot follow you. He has been accepted for the novitiate in Genoa which will open soon."[43] Loggero, however, would become neither a Jesuit nor a missionary in America.

Bruno expressed his own desire to assist Du Bourg: "If my age and my illnesses were not an obstacle, I would offer myself willingly, and would count myself happy to be able to take the place of those missing for this trip. But since I cannot do this, I will be satisfied with readiness to help whenever you honor me with your valued requests."[44] The pattern repeated itself: because of physical limitations—and now because of age as well—Bruno would provide resources for a work he loved but could not himself accomplish.

ON OCTOBER 4, 1815, Bruno wrote to Ricasoli that "there was never greater need than now to promote solid principles everywhere through books."[45] *Never greater need than now*: a striking statement from one who had long considered this work critically important. Bruno's letters in these years reveal his dedication to this ministry: as error increasingly threatened Christian culture, the apostolate of the printed word grew correspondingly urgent.

His friend and *Amicizia* companion Francesco Pertusati wrote to Bruno on June 17, 1814, with a request: "Yesterday I saw Don Carlo Rivapalazzi. . . . Some months ago, he was named confessor of our Salesian Sisters [in Milan] and of the many young women they teach. He asks for a list of good and useful books suited for the instruction and education of young women. You will render a great service to him and to the sisters who teach if you note on a sheet of paper the titles of at least those books you consider most helpful for the training of young women, both in piety and in forming the mind."[46] A manuscript among Bruno's writings lists 480 books under the title "Catalogue of books useful for the education and spiritual direction of young women, which may also serve them as a guide in forming a small and select library for their families."[47]

Some months later, Don Rivapalazzi thanked Bruno for the list received and requested another. On April 12, 1815, Pertusati wrote: "He [Rivapalazzi] expressed his gratitude for the list of books you sent him. He asked me to ask you if you would be willing to provide him another list of books helpful for young men studying to prepare for priestly ministry, for the care of souls, for preaching, etc."[48]

Two weeks later, Bruno's friend and future bishop Carlo Sappa de' Milanesi, asked his advice about François-René de Chateaubriand's classic *Génie du Christianisme* (The Genius of Christianity), published thirteen years earlier in 1802. Sappa de' Milanesi specified his question: "Since I have not yet read Chateaubriand's book, *Génie du Christianisme*, and since I am sure that you are informed about it, could you tell me if it is suitable reading for a young woman, especially in regard to the chapter in the third volume entitled *Atala* [a romantic novel]. Please let me know as soon as you can because I need an answer quickly."[49] All in his circle recognized Bruno's knowledge and wisdom in discerning the value of books.

Bruno never missed an opportunity to obtain new books or additional copies of those he wished to spread. On October 14, 1814, Claude Berthaut du Coin—whose arrest had caused Bruno's own arrest and exile—wrote from Lyon: "I received your letter . . . and the note of the other books you desire. I am sending a part of them since I have not yet been able to acquire the others."[50] Of his own initiative, Berthaut du Coin added recent works by the young Félicité de Lamennais, soon to gain European-wide fame, and explained: "I have not had time to read this last one, but I know that you want to see any new book that deals with such issues [church-state relations]."[51]

In September 1815, Pertusati sent Bruno a package of fifty books, asking him "to offer them as a simple gift to our common friends there [in Turin]."[52] From Rome the following April, the Jesuit novice Luigi Gianolio, a former member of the Pious Union of St. Paul, posted thirty-four books to Bruno, and in August, another forty-six, commenting, "I am sending you a further shipment of the books I have been able to find, in accord with the list you gave me before I left."[53]

Succinct notes of 1816 indicate multiple recipients of these books.[54] Bruno proposed to supply "300 bound copies and 1000 unbound to soldiers," and planned to provide "books for the prisons" as well. Bruno also reminded himself of "books to be obtained from booksellers."[55] In a text composed in these years, Bruno described the book as a "highly effective and readily available means for overcoming ignorance and error, for conversion of hearts, for strengthening good proposals, and for spiritual growth."[56] Thousands of salutary books reached such waiting hearts through Bruno's efforts.

THE OFTEN REPEATED "in haste" of earlier correspondence appeared less frequently in these years. On April 22, 1817, Bruno concluded a letter to Craveri noting, "I have no more time to write," but such references are occasional rather than recurring.[57] Later that year, a new theme surfaced in the letters: Bruno's desire for the visit of friends. On October 5, 1817, Bruno wrote to Craveri: "In these days I am at Bardassano [the Grangia] for the grape harvest. I hope that you will come to visit me soon, especially since I am still alone here."[58] The need for such visits would appear especially in Bruno's final years.

In December 1817, Bruno's cousin Agostino Eula wrote from their native Cuneo. Eula, formerly an Augustinian and now a diocesan priest, had been invited to return to the Augustinians. Unsure of what to decide, he wrote to his "dearest cousin" for assistance, concluding, "I embrace you, anxious to hear your wise advice."[59] Eula declined the invitation and remained a diocesan priest. The following year, his bishop offered him a prestigious position at the cathedral, and again he sought Bruno's aid: "Some tell me to accept, some tell me no. I would like to know what you think, and I ask you to have someone do the writing for you. That will save your eyes from strain and also allow you to express your thoughts more at length, and sooner."[60] Eula signed this letter as the preceding, "Your most affectionate and most indebted cousin, Agostino Eula."[61]

Bruno's quiet work of spiritual direction continued in these years. A letter of November 17, 1817, to Clementina Celebrini, a wife and mother, manifested that blend of directness—at times almost bluntness—and encouragement that characterized his guidance. Bruno wrote: "Forgive me if I have not replied earlier to your letter, since I could not. I have done what you asked, and you need not be anxious. You would like to live already in heaven where happy events are not followed by trials, but you must be patient since you must still remain here on earth, and suffer with patience the trials necessary to enter heaven."[62]

Bruno offered two counsels: "If you want peace in this life, you must, first of all, decide to accommodate yourself to circumstances and not demand that circumstances accommodate themselves to you. You must, secondly, strive to practice uniformity of your will with God's. It is he who disposes everything, arranges everything, and permits all that takes place. We need only seek and follow his fatherly design, which is always to provide us opportunities for practicing different virtues, at times one, at times another, so that he will have something for which to reward us."[63]

Then a word of caution and an encouragement: "I have noticed in your letters that you often turn in on yourself. Try to watch for this, and to focus less often on yourself, but to serve God with great simplicity. Instead of turning in on yourself, lift your gaze often with peace and love to God, to his lovable will, to his adorable Providence. Tell him that regardless of whether you are good or bad, you want to be totally his, and that it is his to make you become better. Cast also upon him all your concerns about your children and your husband. The more you trust in him, the greater will be his care for you."[64] Here, as always, for Bruno confidence in God was the answer to concern about self.

IMMEDIATELY AFTER THE APPROVAL of their provisional rule, the Oblates asked Bruno to prepare a definitive text. On November 15, 1816, Reynaudi wrote to Bruno, asking of him "the charity to reflect on our rule and adapt it as you judge best and more pleasing to God," declaring that "I defer to your wisdom and your charity for the decisions to be taken."[65] Reynaudi continued: "I hope to be in Turin on Monday and to bring you personally our own poor reflections. Our greatest need is that you pray for us and help us with your wisdom."[66] Bruno accepted the request, approached it with great care, and by August of the following year, completed the new rule.[67]

On December 7, 1816, the Oblate community, now grown to five members, began life in the former Augustinian monastery.[68] The next years would bring expansion; they would also lead to tragedy.

CHAPTER TWELVE

The Oblates of Mary

*They will be as apostles who desire
to be numbered among those who
"have dedicated their lives to the
name of Our Lord Jesus Christ."*[1]
—Bruno Lanteri, of the Oblates

BRUNO SENT THE NEW RULE to Carignano on August 6, 1817. The Oblates accepted it without change and, six days later, Vicar Capitular Emmanuele Gonetti approved it as the definitive rule of the Oblates of Mary.[2]

In the text, Bruno further specified the congregation's mission with respect to the earlier provisional rule. He wrote that "their principal goal is to give the Spiritual Exercises and they dedicate themselves to this form of preaching alone, except in their own churches."[3] The Oblates "attend tirelessly to hearing confessions" and "promote the practice of the Sacraments, and the reading of good books."[4]

In his directory on the rule, Bruno added: "They frequently and willingly visit the poor and ill of the city, especially the most abandoned, the infirm in hospitals, and those detained in prisons, bringing consolation and instruction to all, hearing their confessions with all goodness and patience."[5] The Oblates combat current errors, striving "through opportune and cordial conversation to enlighten those led astray and to forearm others, always exercising zeal in a spirit of charity, 'doing the truth in love,' as St. Paul says."[6]

Should he fail, the Oblate is a man who *begins again*: "Let each know that he need fear nothing except discouragement and lack of confidence in God. Let him distrust, even despair of himself, and unshakably hope for all things in God, destroying every failure immediately in the fire of charity, and let him repeat resolutely, always and in every moment, *Then I said: Now I begin* (Ps 76:11)."[7] In time of faults, "let him immediately prostrate himself before God and say, 'Lord, have mercy on me. I have acted according to who I am; now act in me according to who you are. Forgive me, help me. *Then I said: Now I begin.*' "[8]

Three days after Gonetti approved the rule, Loggero joined the Oblates.[9] A few weeks later, Antonio Lanteri did so as well.[10] The preceding April, these two had preached the Spiritual Exercises in the Oblate church of Carignano with results that Bruno described as "exceedingly abundant," and Reynaudi as "extraordinary."[11] Among the fruits of these Exercises were a gathering of young men for prayer and instruction held three times weekly, and the conversion of a former soldier in Napoleon's wars, Michele Valmino, who would later join the Oblates.[12] Now both Loggero and Antonio Lanteri entered the Oblates in Carignano.

A few days later, Bruno traveled to Carignano and, on the evening of September 9, began the Spiritual Exercises for the community.[13] Reynaudi commented: "He himself wished to give the first Exercises for the family, and spoke with so elevated a spirit, and in words so warmed by his own zeal and filled with such remarkable learning, that not only the members of the Congregation felt their effect, but also other priests who took part out of devotion."[14]

The following September, in 1818, Bruno again gave the Exercises to the community. Loggero noted Bruno's words: "The day is composed of twenty-four hours. If we give twelve to the body: seven for sleep, two for meals, two for recreation [time together when silence was lifted], one for walking; if we give four to the soul: one for prayer [meditation], one for Mass, one for the Divine Office, one for spiritual reading; and if we give eight to our tasks, how much less time we will lose, how many more merits we will gain, how many more souls will be saved, how much greater the profit."[15] The extenuating days of preaching and confessing in parish missions and retreats would, obviously, be less ordered.

A year later, again in September, Bruno offered a third eight-day retreat for the Oblates. The first evening he spoke of the purpose of life, and returned to this theme the following day. Loggero observed: "Most sublime sentiments regarding the essence and greatness of God. Sublimity of the supernatural state to which he has elevated us."[16]

A text of June 1, 1817, names the "Theologian Lanteri, Pio Bruno" among those yet to join the congregation.[17] Fifteen months later, on September 1, 1818, another includes the "Signor Theologian Lanteri, Rector Major" among the members of the community.[18] Reynaudi wrote: "Together with the priests Loggero and [Antonio] Lanteri, the Theologian Pio Bruno Lanteri, a person of much learning, great faith, and in high reputation among the good, also wished to take part, though he did not come to live in community. The acquisition of a man of such stature and such holiness gladdened the entire fledgling Congregation, adorned it, rendered it more venerable to the city, and attracted excellent vocations."[19]

Reynaudi continued: "As soon as the Theologian Lanteri secretly accepted the role of first superior of the house, everything began to be better ordered and more stable. . . . If before it could be said that the members were good men, after the entrance of the Theologian Lanteri and the first retreat he gave the community, one could see the Spirit of God at work in the Congregation and in its undertakings."[20]

Reynaudi's words illustrated the delicate balance of Bruno's relationship with the community. Bruno "did not come to live in community," and only "secretly" accepted the office of superior. Yet his role was decisive: he gave the Oblates their apostolic works and rule, directed their every decision, and strengthened them through retreats, visits, and letters. As one scholar comments, Bruno joined the Oblates "morally, but not juridically."[21]

In October 1819, Reynaudi's three-year term as superior concluded, and elections for a new superior were necessary. One contemporary document listed the "Theologian Lanteri, Bruno" among the Oblate priests with an active vote.[22] Another, in Loggero's handwriting, included him among those "aggregated" to

Attesto io infrascritto, che il Sacerd.° Giuseppe Loggero da più di dodici anni in qua si è sempre settimanalmente confessato da me.

Che essendo io stato esigliato da Bonaparte in una più deserta campagna, come soggetto di segreta comunicazione con il S. P. in Savona, e di cattivi principj contro il governo d'allora, il sud.° Sacerdote superando ogni dicería, e difficoltà spontaneam.te si esibì, e volle venir meco in detta solitudine, per tenermi compagnia ed assistermi, siccome fece pel corso de' tre anni che durò il mio esiglio; ciò che mi fu sommam.te grato, massime essendo io molto cagionevole di salute.

Che non avendo ancora fatto allora che un'anno di studj Teologici (ordinato però già Sacerdote con la debita dispensa stanti le critiche circostanze di tempi) riprese in detta solitudine i suoi studj su Autori Classici, e Gesuitici, che io gli somministrava, massime contro le eresie, e gli errori correnti de' Giansenisti, Richeristi, Febroniaristi, tanto più che non vi era mezzo altrimenti di studiare la Teologia senza pericolo di cattivi principj.

Che in seguito dopo la liberazione da Bonaparte, essendomi io ristabilito in Torino, continuò il mio ad abitar meco, ed attese a comporsi un corso abbondante di meditazioni per gli Esercizj spirituali, esattamente secondo il metodo di S. Ignazio, a tenor di quanto io gli andava suggerendo con somministrargli abbondantemente libri opportuni, e continua di presente a lavorare per compirsi il suo corso d'istruzioni per tal effetto.

Che frattanto non lascio d'attendere al Confessionale nella Chiesa di S. Francesco di Torino, e di visitare, confessare, predicare, e catechizzare assiduamente con molto zelo nelle prigioni, e negli Ospedali; e detto più volte in publico le meditaz.; dando gli Esercizj di S. Ignazio con grandissimo frutto, godendo sempre un'ottima salute —

Che finalmente, riguardo alla sua vocazione, io l'ho sempre conosciuto amantissimo della Compagnia di Gesù, ed anziosissimo d'entrarvi, nè io saprei trovarvi alcuna cosa in contrario à tale vocazione, fuorchè la perdita che io ne faccio.

Questo è quanto posso io attestare per amore della verità.

— Torino li 11 Luglio 1816

Teol.° Pio Brunone Lanteri
affezionatissimo alla Comp.° di Gesù.

Handwriting of Bruno Lanteri, 1816.

the congregation—a status that applied to external members who assisted as their own priestly occupations permitted.[23]

Consternation arose among the Oblates when they saw Bruno named an external member only. On November 20, 1819, Reynaudi wrote to Bruno on behalf of the community: "Oh, what a profound and painful surprise it was for us to read that Your Reverence, whom all of us have always considered as the father, the center, and the Rector Major of this Congregation, had quietly withdrawn and included yourself among the external members. For myself, bringing this immediately before God, I saw clearly that, without other enemies, this alone would suffice to destroy our fragile Congregation which, without your direct involvement, would quickly lose its spirit, its order, its base, its teacher, and its unifying center amid so many ways of thinking and the many situations that may arise."[24]

Reynaudi and the others begged of Bruno "that you be willing to consider seriously in these days before the election whether you judge in the Lord that the establishment of this Congregation be truly a work for the greater glory of God."[25] Reynaudi elaborated: "If you should not consider it of such importance before God, and do not see it clearly enough as God's will to be resolved to join it, and even be our superior should you be elected formally, then none of us, as you will see from our unanimous signatures at the end of this letter, has the courage to continue."[26] Should Bruno choose to stay with them, the Oblates told him, even six months each year in community would suffice; if chosen superior, Bruno could direct them in the remaining months through a vicar.[27]

Bruno was not indifferent to their appeal and, in his reply, reiterated his commitment to the community: "Your esteemed letter touched me profoundly. I do not believe that I ever gave you occasion even to suspect that I might wish to withdraw from you. I have always taken the affairs of the Congregation deeply to heart, and will continue to do so, and will always dedicate myself to its well-being with all my energy, nor will I ever spare myself on its behalf."[28]

Bruno then addressed the issue of his residence: "With respect, however, to the new system you suggest regarding my living there in a stable way, you can be sure that had I been able to do so before now, I myself willingly would have taken the initiative even before your gracious request. When we meet in person, we will be able to discuss better how to see each other more often, or at greater length."[29] Bruno then explained why the list placed him among the external members: "Having said this, you can see that from every point of view it would not be suitable that the canonical nomination as superior should fall upon me. And this is the reason why the list was made as it was."[30] In fact, all would continue as before: Reynaudi would figure publicly as superior, while Bruno would "secretly" continue to direct the congregation.[31]

SOME YEARS EARLIER, the archbishop had named a young priest, Luigi Guala, as rector of the church of San Francesco d'Assisi, in Turin.[32] Future saint Eugène de Mazenod would describe Bruno as Guala's "teacher, friend, and superior."[33] In 1806, Bruno himself characterized Guala as "a young man of thirty-one . . . with zeal beyond the ordinary, highly active and prudent, well endowed with the doctrine, prudence, and experience necessary for the direction of souls."[34] Guala was "Lanteri's spiritual son,"[35] "an illustrious disciple who in turn became a master."[36]

Already in 1808, Guala had gathered priests at San Francesco d'Assisi and taught them moral theology. In his instruction, as might be expected of Bruno's disciple, harsher Jansenist-tinged principles of confessional ministry were tempered by the gentler doctrine of Alphonsus Liguori.[37] In 1814, Guala's conferences were officially approved for priests preparing to hear confessions.[38] Yet no residence was provided for these young priests during the three years of this preparation.[39] They were, consequently, compelled to find lodgings as best they could, often in settings little supportive of priestly life. The archbishops of Turin had long recognized the need for a suitable residence.[40] In 1816, Bruno, ever concerned for the formation of young priests, believed the necessary means were now available: the church of San Francesco d'Assisi with Guala as rector, its adjacent residence, and the new Congregation of the Oblates of Mary.

With Guala's collaboration, Bruno proposed "to extend to Turin the Congregation of the Oblates of Mary established in Carignano."[41] To the Oblates' existing goals—Spiritual Exercises, confessions, visits to the ill and imprisoned—Bruno added another: "a residence for recently ordained priests."[42] He explained: "The establishment of this Congregation would offer newly ordained priests who are required to study practical moral theology, and are obliged during that time to reside in secular houses with harm to their priestly spirit . . . the advantage of an adequate room and board, equivalent to that of the seminary, which the Congregation would provide for them. Each would be free to attend the Conference of moral theology he chooses,[43] and those who desire could also gain experience in preaching, hearing confessions, and works of charity; in addition, they could receive spiritual formation according to a program to be approved by the ecclesiastical superior."[44] Bruno named a location for the project: "As regards the place for this residence, the unsold part of the convent and house of San Francesco d'Assisi would be well suited."[45] At this same time or shortly after, Bruno proposed a variation of this project for "a group of priests . . . who desire to live in community under the title of Oblates of Our Lady of Sorrows."[46]

The Piedmontese government, however, hostile to religious communities, denied permission.[47] Guala, "evidently working together with Lanteri,"[48] then requested the residence in his own name as a diocesan priest. On August 8, 1817, the same day it was presented, his petition was granted.[49] Three months later, in November, the "convitto ecclesiastico" (Priestly Residence) of Turin began its distinguished career.

In 1821, the archbishop of Turin formally approved the rule for the Priestly Residence.[50] The following year, it welcomed priests from eight dioceses and, shortly after, was enlarged to house nearly one hundred priests.[51] Others beyond those who dwelt in the residence—young priests living elsewhere and older priests desirous of learning Alphonsian pastoral practice—also attended the conferences.[52] Guala would serve as rector of the residence for forty years until his death in 1848, when St. Joseph Cafasso succeeded him. The twenty-four years of St. Joseph Cafasso's teaching and rectorate drew priests from throughout Piedmont, and the residence grew in reputation. The young St. John Bosco would study there under St. Joseph Cafasso, and Blessed Joseph Allamano would be among future rectors.

Of his three years (1841–1844) in the residence, St. John Bosco would write: "The Priestly Residence may be called a completion of our theological studies, since in our seminaries we study only dogmatic and speculative theology. In our classes on moral theology we study only disputed questions. Here we learn to be priests."[53] Giacomo Colombero, biographer of St. Joseph Cafasso and graduate of the residence, would affirm in 1875: "A little more than half a century has passed since the founding of the Residence, and already it may be said that in great part it has achieved its principal mission.... The Residence ended the spread of Jansenism and Gallicanism, and caused the clergy to abandon rigorist theology and embrace the more moderate principles of the teaching of St. Alphonsus."[54]

The residence prepared generations of young priests for ministry well into the twentieth century. A historian comments: "The Priestly Residence became a true center for the formation of young Piedmontese priests . . . contributing to disperse the last residues of Jansenism."[55] The residence was "a school of both pastoral practice and formation for the spiritual life,"[56] and with it, "a new 'spiritual school' of priests was born in Turin."[57] For decades to come, the Priestly Residence would supply Piedmont with dedicated parish priests, effective preachers, and wise confessors. Here, as so often, Bruno quietly promoted a work that would bless the Church long after his death.

IN THIS SAME PERIOD, Bruno prepared the Oblates in Carignano for their mission. Reynaudi, a talented preacher but untrained in the Spiritual Exercises, under Bruno's guidance now learned to give them.[58] He would become a skilled preacher of the Exercises, widely sought and appreciated. Michele di Cavour, father of famed Italian statesman Camillo di Cavour, would later describe Reynaudi as "one of the most distinguished orators I have ever heard."[59]

Bruno likewise guided Reynaudi as confessor: "Under Bruno's direction, he laid aside the principles learned in earlier years through study of an author of theology whose work was placed on the Index [forbidden by Rome], and, dedicating himself entirely to the theology of St. Alphonsus Liguori, accomplished great good for souls."[60] In May 1817, together with Loggero, Reynaudi preached the Spiritual Exercises to the Poor Clare Sisters.[61] It was the first of many fruitful retreats he would give.

In the latter months of 1817, twenty-four-year-old Filippo Simonino joined the Oblates. His brother Enrico would later relate that "through his relationship with the Theologian Guala . . . he encountered the Theologian Pio Bruno Lanteri as well. . . . Once he had come to know him, he entrusted himself entirely to his [Bruno's] guidance. Through that guidance, his fervor in the service of God grew until finally he resolved to dedicate himself solely to gaining souls for God."[62]

When Filippo reached Carignano, Enrico continued, "his first thought was to apply himself with all possible energy to preparing to preach the Spiritual Exercises, beginning with the meditations, and in a short time he accomplished this task."[63] Enrico elaborated: "I should add, however, that he had begun to prepare himself for this work earlier, that is, when he was living in Superga [near Turin]—as soon, in fact, as he was ordained a priest and met the Theologian Lanteri who inspired in him a love for this ministry."[64]

On April 1, 1818, Antonio Biancotti also wrote to Bruno: "I hope to be prepared to give the meditations a month from now, if such will be God's will."[65] Biancotti would give his first retreat in late 1818—for him, as well, the first of many.[66]

In the first seven months of 1817, Loggero and Antonio Lanteri, with help from Reynaudi, Craveri, and another priest, Don Genovesio, had given nine retreats.[67] Now, in November, the Oblates of Carignano were ready to begin this ministry formally.[68]

Some years later, Bruno would recall that November 1817, and note: "The retreats and parish missions begin."[69]

SUPPRESSED UNDER FRENCH RULE, religious women now struggled to resume community life. Among them was forty-eight-year-old Sister Crocifissa Bracchetto, whose community was forbidden access to its former monastery in Turin. On October 29, 1818, Sr. Crocifissa entered a monastery in Genoa, then under Piedmontese rule.[70] Bruno, who assisted her throughout these years, approved and supported her entrance into the new community. Sr. Crocifissa found the transition emotionally, physically, and spiritually difficult.[71] Bruno's counsels during her first months in Genoa reflected those struggles.

On January 15, 1819, eleven weeks after her arrival, Bruno wrote: "Do not be surprised if you find yourself dry in prayer. This is a human condition to which we are subject. You will overcome this through patience and perseverance, seeking to avoid *voluntary* negligence."[72] On the following March 7: "Your call is to become holy, but this is not possible without overcoming great difficulties. You are not alone in surmounting them, but Jesus will be with you."[73] And one month later, on April 10, with characteristic directness and encouragement, he observed: "I find you always the same, that is, prone to discouragement, and this is your principal defect. If you give in to this, it will cause you many others. It is especially in this, therefore, that you must grow in strength, by *resolving to try always to have an unshakeable hope*, whatever may happen and however weak you may seem to yourself; because on our part, the basis of hope is precisely *our misery*, and on God's part, *his mercy*, which is simply his *heartfelt compassion for our misery*."[74]

On June 27, 1819, eight months after Sr. Crocifissa's beginnings in Genoa, Bruno insisted once more: "I recommend that you renew *more than ever and very often* that holy presumption that seeks grace from the Lord to attain the holiness you would have attained had you always been faithful to his grace. At the same time, be on guard against discouragement and lack of trust. Strive to do well all that you do, but do so with respect for your humanity . . . without striving for an impossible perfection, focusing simply on the day at hand. . . . Remember that 'The just man falls seven times a day' [Prov 24:16], and so you will find it helpful to begin not only every day, but *every hour*."[75]

On that same June 27, Bruno referred to Sr. Crocifissa's physical burdens: "Keep far from you the spirit of sadness and melancholy. Show yourself joyful even when you do not feel so because of physical problems. At such times more than ever, guard against closing in on yourself, and turn your thoughts to Paradise, because it is yours."[76]

On March 26, 1820, Bruno wrote to a woman religious identified simply as "My dearest daughter in Jesus Christ."[77] The recipient may have been Sr. Crocifissa; certainly the letter is addressed to a religious with similar spiritual needs.[78] Bruno observed: "I have always thought that those shops are best in which a great volume of business is enacted. And so I must say that this monastery, which offers you so many opportunities to grow rich spiritually, is the best you could possibly choose."[79]

Bruno anticipated and answered an objection: "You, however, would wish to tell me that rather than growing rich in merit, you only acquire further demerit. To this I reply that on these occasions either you practice virtue and so grow in merit, or you commit some fault, and then you have an opportunity to gain double merit: first, in humility, through deeper practical knowledge of yourself; second, in hope, through turning with trust to your heavenly Father, saying to him, *Dimitte nobis* ["Forgive us"];[80] third, in love of God, to repair the coldness shown him in his divine service. And gaining such merit by these acts will be easier if you take care never to grow angry with yourself, nor to be upset at your continual defects, but rather to say always, with peace, at every moment, 'It is good for me that you humbled me' [Ps 119:71], and, 'Now I begin.'"[81]

Directness even to bluntness, unfailing encouragement, clear thinking, theological depth, emphasis on prayer, belief in our capacity for spiritual progress, fostering of God's glory in the world, vigilance against discouragement, trust in God, hope in his mercy, and readiness to begin again: the hallmarks of Bruno's spiritual guidance appear in these letters.

Sr. Crocifissa remained in the monastery thirty-two years until her death at eighty-one.[82] Her obituary portrayed both her struggles and her efforts to overcome them, and presented her as a faithful religious.[83] Sr. Crocifissa sought Bruno's guidance by letter throughout his remaining years. Her words in one such letter expressed her awareness of the gift received: "I thank you from my heart for the care you have for me, and I will not fail to show my gratitude in prayer before Jesus and Mary."[84] *The care you have for me:* already the years of that caring were slipping away. They would bring both life and death to the works now beginning.

CHAPTER THIRTEEN

Growth and Crisis

Nor have they any doubt that
their vocation comes from God.
—Bruno Lanteri, of the Oblates

IN EARLY NOVEMBER 1817, Antonio Lanteri crossed the streets
of Carignano to the Poor Clares' Monastery. There he preached
the Spiritual Exercises to the sisters: it was the formal launch of
the congregation's retreat ministry.[1] The Oblates gave five parish
missions and retreats in the remaining months of 1817, twenty
in 1818, and twenty-four in 1819.[2] Reynaudi, remembering those
days, related that "each parish mission . . . cost unbelievable labor
to those who gave it because, in the early days of the Congregation,
we always heard confessions with no pause, except when we were
preaching, from four in the morning until noon, and from two in
the afternoon until ten or eleven in the evening."[3] The Oblates welcomed a people abandoned during the occupation, and, too often,
discouraged by rigorist pastoral practice. Now they flocked to hear
these priests, and, sure of their reception, returned in great numbers to confession and the practice of their faith.

On February 8, 1818, Bruno asked Craveri to accompany Log-
gero to Fossano where the Oblates were to offer a Lenten mission.[4]
Suppressed fourteen years earlier under Napoleon, the diocese
of Fossano had been reestablished in 1817.[5] The mission was to
be held in the newly reconstituted cathedral of this city of 20,000.
Craveri and Loggero arrived on February 21, and remained until
March 3, a stay of eleven days.[6] Two other Oblates, Biancotti and
Simonino, accompanied them to hear confessions.

For eight days, Craveri and Loggero held five functions in the cathedral: at 6:00 a.m., the preaching of a first meditation, and, at 10:00 a.m., an instruction followed by a meditation. The schedule of the afternoon paralleled that of the morning.[7] Loggero preached the meditations, Craveri the instructions. Each typically lasted an hour, delivered (without amplification) before a packed church.[8] In this case, the church was large, accommodating one thousand people.[9]

A document commemorating the mission related that "the number of those seeking confession was so great that halfway through the Exercises, it was necessary to ask the help of three additional confessors. Don Golzio and Don Moretta were sent from Carignano, and, from Turin, Fr. Lanza."[10] The account specified: "During the Exercises, the church was opened at four in the morning, when the priests began hearing confessions. They continued until midnight, and during the night hours, the church was lit. . . . From the start of the Exercises an extraordinary number of people came to confession, and great numbers attended all the functions."[11] The pastor of the cathedral, Giuseppe Caramelli di Clavesana, wrote that "in the thirty-five years that I have been pastor here in the cathedral, years in which the holy Exercises have been given many times, I never saw so many people so eager to profit from the grace of confession as on this occasion."[12]

A link between two Oblate ministries—the Spiritual Exercises and books—was also manifest in this mission: "Those holy, exemplary, and tireless priests not only labored without seeking any recompense or gifts, but also distributed two cases of spiritual books of various kinds, all of them excellent, to conserve the fruit of the Exercises."[13] After the departure of the preachers, the written word would remain to reinforce the spoken word.

The mission closed on March 2. People continued to request confession, and the Oblates remained the following day, hearing confessions until 9:00 p.m.[14] The record concluded: "The departure of these holy priests from this city was deeply moving because many in the city gathered around their carriages and wept to see those good priests, by whom they had been welcomed with such charity and from whom they had received consolation in the sacred tribunals of Penance, depart from them."[15]

One priest of Fossano, Don Giovenale Canaveri, having witnessed those days of grace, was moved to prepare for this ministry himself. On March 31, four weeks after the mission, he wrote to Bruno: "This week, as I have some free hours, I hope to make further progress in writing my talks for the meditations. Though I am not yet able to assist the Oblates of Mary by preaching, if on any occasion you think I could help with confessions, you have only to let me know and you will always find me immediately ready to obey."[16]

Filippo Simonino's brother, Enrico, himself later an Oblate, recounted that during this mission Filippo "spent twenty-four continuous hours in the confessional with no refreshment other than a little coffee, which he took primarily to keep himself from falling asleep."[17] Filippo would soon pay the price for such physical exertions.

That same February 21, as Craveri and Loggero opened the mission in Fossano, Reynaudi and Antonio Lanteri began a retreat for seminarians in Turin.[18] Four days after leaving Fossano, Loggero had already reached the smaller town of Santo Stefano Roero, some thirty-five kilometers away, to start the next mission. Antonio Lanteri, the retreat in Turin completed, joined him; together they preached the mission, with Filippo Simonino and Don Moretta assisting as confessors.[19] The mission opened on March 7 and concluded eleven days later on March 17.

On March 19, Loggero wrote to Bruno "from my peaceful cell," describing the experience: "You will have heard already from the Signor Theologian Simonino of the marvels worked by divine grace in Santo Stefano Roero, and for the souls of fourteen or fifteen surrounding towns whose people came like the crowds of earlier days [in the Gospel] to hear the word of God, heedless of business, food, sleep, and all else. They spent the days and nights continually in church (which was never closed in the last four or five days)."[20]

The response overwhelmed the Oblates: "There were people from outside the town who spent three days and three nights continually in church without being able to approach a confessor. In short, if Fossano exceeded all the preceding missions I have preached, Santo Stefano surpassed Fossano beyond expressing, and we had to hear confessions in the streets, in public places, coming and going from the church to the house, etc. After the first Monday [third day of the mission] at midnight, we could no longer hear all the confessions, nor were we ever able to finish, though we heard confessions from four in the morning until half past midnight, without a moment of rest except from twelve-thirty to two in the afternoon when, with great difficulty and a kind of violence, we seized time for lunch and a little rest, without ever having more than fifteen minutes from the confessional to the pulpit, and five minutes from the pulpit to the confessional."[21]

At the pastor's request, the Oblates remained in Santo Stefano two days after the mission for additional confessions.[22] Loggero would later recount that "they continued to hear confessions until the moment of their departure after lunch on March 18, Wednesday of Holy Week. The pastor himself, in fact, also asked them to hear the confession of a poor elderly man who was ill, and who planned to have himself brought to a chapel along our way on the outskirts of Santo Stefano. Don Loggero heard his confession."[23]

Loggero concluded his letter to Bruno: "The bell is calling me to breakfast. I will end by saying that already I have slept at length and well for two nights, but it is still not enough."[24] Nine days later, he and Antonio Lanteri began their next parish mission in Lanzo, at the base of the Alps.[25]

Recalling these years, Reynaudi wrote: "Through these missions, word began to spread and the Congregation's members gained the reputation of being hardworking and zealous priests. . . . Requests for the Exercises were continual and increasing, and not only were they invited to small villages and cities, but bishops sought them for their cathedrals, for their priests, for seminarians preparing for ordination, for women religious, for students in the university, and for many retreat houses."[26] Reynaudi commented: "The patronage of Mary Most Holy was evident in the abundant fruit of conversions and fervor their labors bore everywhere."[27]

The letter of one pastor may stand for many. On January 3, 1818, Loggero and Antonio Lanteri began a mission in the parish of Dogliani, twenty kilometers from Fossano.[28] Nine days later, the pastor, Giovanni Battista Cauda, thanked Bruno: "I am deeply grateful to Your Reverence for having chosen such able men to give the Spiritual Exercises to my people. In these Exercises we witnessed prodigious conversions not seen in Exercises and missions given by others, and I think this was because they preached the true loving word and doctrine of Christ."[29] In Dogliani as elsewhere, the warm Alphonsian approach conquered hearts.

Some months later, Bruno expressed his joy to his friend Cesare d'Azeglio: "In these days I have the consolation of seeing the members of the Congregation committed to sacrificing themselves without rest for the Spiritual Exercises, notwithstanding these difficulties. They have given the Exercises twenty-four times in eight months, with extraordinary fruit for souls, a blessing that attests the special protection of the Virgin Mary to whom they are dedicated."[30]

Notwithstanding these difficulties . . . Even as the Oblates' ministry prospered and spread, clouds were gathering.

ON APRIL 26, 1774, a young man named Colombano Chiaveroti gained his doctorate in civil and canon law at the University of Turin.[31] He served as lawyer for the royal senate of Piedmont until, abandoning law, he entered the Camaldolese monks in Lanzo. In 1781, at twenty-seven, Chiaveroti was ordained a priest; four years later, he was named novice master.[32] Increasing responsibilities followed until 1802, when the French suppressed the monastery. The community dispersed, but Chiaveroti remained: "He did not wish to abandon the monastery he loved, but, changing his monastic garb for a short while, he continued to officiate in the monastery's church and assisted the people of those valleys in their spiritual and temporal interests, especially through his legal knowledge."[33]

In 1817, Vittorio Emmanuele I named Chiaveroti bishop for the diocese of Ivrea in northern Piedmont. Pius VII approved the nomination and, on November 23, Chiaveroti was ordained as bishop. Nine days later, the Holy See's representative in Piedmont wrote to Rome: "I am confident that Bishop Chiaveroti will be an excellent bishop. He truly has every qualification for this."[34] But Chiaveroti's life would soon alter dramatically, and that change would determine the Oblates' future.

In February 1816, the government had granted the first companions permission to occupy the former Augustinian monastery in Carignano. They had then sought Rome's confirmation of this permission, hoping also for papal approval of their new institute.[35]

On March 14, 1817, Rome confirmed the Oblates' possession of the monastery.[36] Regarding papal approval of the institute, however, the answer, though encouraging, was less definitive: "The Holy Father was most pleased with this new society of zealous priests united as a Congregation under the admirable title of the Oblates of Mary, and has sent it his pontifical blessing. . . . But his expressions of support were verbal only, and it was not possible to obtain written confirmation of his approval."[37] The Oblates' correspondent explained that "it is not the customary practice of the Church to grant canonical approval immediately to new institutes, but only after enough time has passed to show whether they are truly a work of God and not only of human initiative."[38]

As the congregation expanded, it again sought papal approval. On December 28, 1818, a new request was presented to the Holy Father. The petition was entrusted to the Sacred Congregation for Bishops and Regulars, which decreed that "the matter should be deferred, and the Archbishop of Turin contacted for more detailed information, and for his opinion on the question."[39]

The archbishop of Turin... The former archbishop, Giacinto della Torre, had died four years earlier in 1814. No successor had been named, and Vicar Capitular Emmanuele Gonetti had administered the archdiocese since then. Now, on December 21, 1818—one week before the Oblates' petition was presented to the pope—Pius VII named Colombano Chiaveroti archbishop of Turin.[40] Gonetti had already expressed support for the Oblates; as a courtesy to the new archbishop, Rome wished to hear Chiaveroti's view as well.[41]

In early January 1819, Reynaudi and Don Mana (an aggregated member of the Oblates) traveled to the diocese of Ivrea for a parish mission.[42] Chiaveroti, who would enter Turin formally in April, as yet remained in Ivrea, and the Oblates sought to meet him. It would be their first contact with their new ecclesiastical superior. Bruno later described that encounter: "Because they were to give the Exercises in Azeglio [in the diocese of Ivrea], the Oblates of Mary went to Ivrea on January 3, 1819, where the Archbishop was still present, as he had not yet taken possession of the Diocese of Turin. They desired to present the good wishes of the Congregation on his nomination as archbishop, and to ask his support for the Congregation. But the archbishop wanted time to reflect on this, giving some indication, however, that he was not overly favorable to the Congregation, for when in the archbishop's presence a priest said that upon reaching Turin he [the archbishop] would protect them, he replied, 'Let us speak of other matters.' "[43] The first contact was not reassuring.

Time passed, and Rome waited for Chiaveroti's word regarding the Oblates . . . but no word came. As public superior, Reynaudi wrote to the archbishop soliciting his assistance.[44] On April 6, Chiaveroti replied: "It is true that the Sacred Congregation of Bishops and Regulars has asked me to obtain further information about this new Institute of Oblates recently begun in Carignano. But as this is not a matter to be resolved quickly, and much less by letter, and because, in addition, I will soon be leaving for Turin, I have decided to postpone it until after my arrival in the capital, and after I will have had a brief time of rest."[45]

Chiaveroti then raised two considerations: "If the Oblates of Carignano were to become like the Oblates founded by St. Charles [Borromeo], I think there would not be much difficulty in obtaining the Holy See's approval for the Institute."[46] He added: "In fact, I hear the members of this new Congregation spoken of with much

The archbishop of Turin, Colombano Chiaveroti.

Interior of the church of St. Francis of Assisi, church of the Priestly Residence in Turin.

praise, although those who accuse them of excessively benign moral theology are not lacking. But I will not give credence to anything that has not been proven true."[47]

The first observation touched the identity itself of the congregation. The Oblates of St. Charles, founded by St. Charles Borromeo in 1578, were priests available to the bishop for any needs of the diocese: parishes, schools, seminaries, and especially preaching. They were "a body of competent and able volunteers in the diocese who responded readily to the bishop's requests, and were prepared to assume even difficult tasks in time of emergency."[48] Clearly, such priests would be valuable to a bishop, and Chiaveroti, about to assume direction of the archdiocese, saw in the Oblates of Carignano potential Oblates of St. Charles. From a congregation whose "principal goal is to give the Spiritual Exercises," whose members "attend tirelessly to hearing confessions," who "promote the practice of the sacraments, and the reading of good books," who "visit frequently . . . the poor and ill of the city," and who strive "to enlighten those led astray" by error,[49] they would become men available to the archbishop at any time for any need in the archdiocese.

Chiaveroti's second observation concerned the controversy between Jansenist-inspired rigorism in sacramental practice and the more welcoming Alphonsian approach. The latter, to which Bruno firmly adhered and which he had taught the Oblates, characterized their confessional ministry and drew an enthusiastic response from the crowds. Chiaveroti's comments questioned an essential component of the Oblates' pastoral practice.

The archbishop's first request, if accepted, would completely change the nature of the congregation. The Oblates of Mary could not recognize in the Oblates of St. Charles the institute to which they felt God had called them. Regarding the second observation, Bruno wrote and Reynaudi presented to the archbishop a letter that shared with him the Oblates' "profound affliction upon learning that Your Reverence held us suspect of unsound doctrine."[50]

Even as relations with the archbishop grew troubling, a tension in Carignano reached the critical point. Bruno referred discreetly to "a certain priest who had persecuted the Congregation earlier, and subsequently persecuted it all the more."[51] Reynaudi, writing years later, identified him as Francesco Abbate, pastor of the parish in Carignano.[52] As the Oblates' ministry expanded, the pastor's resistance increased. Bruno related that "in the pulpit he openly criticized their teaching and showed clear disapproval of their ministry, disquieting the consciences of those who had recourse to them by rendering suspect the confessions they heard."[53] In the small city of Carignano, the conflict between the parish and the Oblates intensified. For the fledgling congregation, unsure of its archbishop's support and immersed in local strife, the future grew uncertain.

Reynaudi affirmed that the Oblates strove to maintain peace and "interpreted the . . . pastor's words and actions in a positive light."[54] Bruno likewise attested that "these words and scandalous actions, known throughout the city, were constantly suffered in peace without complaint to anyone, seeking rather to calm the hearts of the people."[55]

On July 10, 1819, twenty-six-year-old Filippo Simonino fell ill with typhus.[56] Three weeks later, on July 31, he died a deeply spiritual death.[57] That same day, Biancotti wrote to Bruno: "If anyone other than God and our Mother [Mary] had done this to us, it would be unforgivable. But in all this we must humbly bow our heads and adore his unfathomable decrees."[58] Biancotti commented tersely, "God loves us very much because he afflicts us very much."[59]

In late August, Reynaudi met with the archbishop in Turin to discuss the Oblates' situation.[60] He recorded the conversation in detail, both his questions and the archbishop's answers.[61] When Reynaudi asked the archbishop "what decision he had taken regarding the Oblates of Mary Most Holy," the archbishop replied that "his desire was that we accept the rules of the Oblates of St. Charles because their work is more centered on the Diocese, [and] they serve in a greater variety of ministries."[62] Reynaudi answered that "the members were all resolved to enter a religious community," to which the archbishop rejoined that "he sees the good the institute can accomplish, but the diocese needs the Oblates of St. Charles."[63]

Reynaudi recounted the Oblates' labors in retreats and parish missions. In reply, the archbishop declared that "while they may work hard, they do not work only for the diocese."[64] When Reynaudi explained that "they always put the diocese [of Turin] first, and never preached outside it without informing him," the archbishop insisted that "the diocese continues to need priests available to help pastors in parishes, to be administrators, etc., so that the Oblates of St. Charles always would be of greater assistance."[65]

Reynaudi specified that "the Rule of St. Charles cannot satisfy us because we desire that our institute be formed of religious priests who also have vows, and all of us desire to die [remain for our entire lives] in the Congregation."[66] The archbishop replied that "for a new institute, it would be necessary to write to Rome, whereas for the Oblates of St. Charles this would not be necessary, and that Rome would not easily approve a new institute."[67] Reynaudi asked, "Would you permit us to write and seek approval from Rome?" The archbishop answered, "You will not obtain anything. Rome will always write to me." Reynaudi persevered, "And would you not write favorably on our behalf?" In reply, the archbishop stated, "No (although I will not oppose you) because I do not believe it more useful for the Diocese."[68]

The Oblates had reached an impasse. Rome would not grant approval without the archbishop's support of their request. This he firmly refused unless they were willing to become Oblates of St. Charles, a change the Oblates felt they could not accept without betraying their God-given vocation. The archbishop's reserve toward the congregation discouraged new candidates and disheartened existing members.[69] Tensions with the parish in Carignano were rising. In late 1819, the Oblates' future looked dark.

CHAPTER FOURTEEN

Dispersal

All that will happen to me,
whether favorable or unfavorable,
is prepared for me by God as an
occasion of gain, may he ever be
praised; I desire to profit from it.
—Bruno Lanteri

AS THE NEW YEAR OPENED, Reynaudi wavered. On January 8, 1820, Loggero wrote to Bruno: "With great consolation, I can now tell you that though Don Reynaudi was firm in his intention to dissolve the Congregation, or to withdraw from it himself, I found Don Biancotti and [Antonio] Lanteri equally firm in their resolve to remain."[1] For the moment, Loggero told Bruno, the crisis was averted: "With great difficulty I persuaded Don Reynaudi to continue at least until Easter, living our life as if he were to remain forever in the Congregation. Then I was easily able to persuade Don Lanteri, whom I found perfectly in agreement, and Don Biancotti also immediately concurred, that is, to make every effort to continue."[2]

In the first months of 1820, the Oblates continued to give parish missions and retreats: one in January, two in February, three in March, four in April . . . but gradually they succumbed to the mounting pressure.[3] In May, members began quietly to withdraw, and, Biancotti informed Bruno, "word has already spread in Carignano" of the dispersal of the congregation.[4]

On May 29, the city council of Carignano wrote to the archbishop "imploring his efficacious assistance to conserve for the city this devout and beneficial institute."[5] The council affirmed that the Oblates' ministry brought "countless benefits to the city, not only in spiritual matters...but also in temporal affairs,"[6] and explained: "With wisdom in their teaching and approach to moral issues, and with exemplary conduct, they have dedicated themselves without ceasing to our people through confessions, frequent preaching, tireless assistance to the sick, and all other priestly ministries. All can see that from their beginning among us, their labors have fostered not only a notable improvement in moral conduct among the people, but also in temporal affairs since, as true agents of peace, they never lose an opportunity to heal divisions among families and lead them to harmony in their concerns; and to many others they have rendered every charitable assistance in their power, even at the cost of hardship to themselves."[7] The mayor and two councilors personally presented this petition to Archbishop Chiaveroti. Their appeal changed nothing.[8]

In Turin, Bruno examined the Oblates' plight together with his associate and friend Fr. Carlo Daverio.[9] On May 29, he wrote to Biancotti: "I have related the whole matter to the Theologian Daverio. I can assure you that we share deeply in the affliction felt by all."[10] Bruno outlined their conclusion: "Having examined the matter attentively and at length . . . we have agreed on the following points as a way of proceeding with order, and of avoiding greater problems and complications."[11] Three points led to a single conclusion. First, since the archbishop had not recognized the congregation officially, "it appears that the members may consider themselves completely free to make their own decisions." Second, as "word has already been spread and very likely has reached the archbishop, he is probably waiting for the Congregation to dissolve itself." Finally, as procurator of the congregation, Biancotti would be the appropriate person to return the church and former monastery to the archdiocese.[12] A voluntary decision to disperse, Bruno wrote, "would also have the advantage of avoiding any semblance of canonical dissolution, and this could be important with time."[13]

Later that same year, Bruno explained this decision more fully: "They [the Oblates] suffered these conditions for over a year in peace and in silence, with no recourse other than that made directly to the archbishop himself through a first letter presented in April and a second in May of 1819. But these had no effect, and the Oblates of Mary could no longer endure such opposition and persecution, nor could they work in peace. As it was no longer helpful but even harmful to persevere in common life without the favor and approval of the Archbishop, for which they could no longer hope, they decided to separate with respect to their dwelling only, and to conserve the spirit of their vocation by living their Rule in the measure possible, and continuing, as they have done tirelessly until the present, to labor together in giving the Spiritual Exercises."[14] Elsewhere Bruno succinctly stated the core issue: "Vocations are to be examined by superiors, not given by them."[15] In this case, Chiaveroti was attempting to *give* a vocation rather than examine whether the Oblates' vocation, as they understood it, was truly of God.

On June 3, 1820, Reynaudi officially notified the archbishop that the Oblates, "finding in themselves neither the strength nor the vocation to change their spirit and rule, have exercised the full freedom that the nature of our Institute provides us, to take their leave and withdraw from the Congregation."[16] As the members did not feel called to be Oblates of St. Charles, Reynaudi concluded, "I have no other recourse than to inform Your Reverence of the complete dissolution of this new Congregation."[17] By June 5, two days later, Reynaudi had already left Carignano.[18] After three and a half years of life, the Oblates of Mary ceased to exist.

THE QUESTION OF THE FUTURE now faced the former Oblates. They would answer that question variously, and their answers would occasion both joy and sorrow. In coming days, this issue would be central for Bruno as well.

In the short term, from their scattered residences the Oblates pursued the ministry of retreats and parish missions. Loggero recorded these retreats in "A list of the Exercises given after they retired to their houses, constantly conserving the spirit of the Congregation and their reciprocal union, under the direction of the Theologian Pio Bruno Lanteri whom they regarded as their father."[19] The companions gave nine retreats and missions in the remaining months of 1820, and twenty-three in 1821.[20] During those months, however, four former Oblates reached the same decision: Reynaudi, Loggero, Biancotti, and Antonio Lanteri requested entrance into the Society of Jesus.[21] All traveled to Rome for that purpose.

After a brief stay with the Jesuits, Reynaudi and Loggero returned to Turin.[22] On November 22, 1821, Loggero informed Bruno of their imminent departure from Rome and added, "The consolation of seeing you soon makes these days seem very long for me."[23] Loggero would resume residence with Bruno as his secretary.[24]

Reynaudi remained uncertain of his future, as Loggero recounted: "I have not been able to induce Don Reynaudi to write to Turin. At first he was thinking of writing to the theologian Guala to reserve a room for him in San Francesco [the Priestly Residence]. Then he hesitated, and is still undecided about where he will live, whether in Turin or in Carignano. He does not know what he will do. His health is good, however, and I hope he will help me accomplish much for souls."[25] Most probably, Reynaudi chose to live in Turin, either in the Priestly Residence or in the Hospital of St. John.[26] There he resumed the ministry of retreats and parish missions, frequently preaching together with Loggero.[27]

Biancotti and Antonio Lanteri, however, persevered with the Jesuits. Bruno related that "two priests of the Oblates of Mary Most Holy, once they saw that the Congregation was dissolved, entered the Company of Jesus where, upon completing their novitiate, they were immediately made rectors of two colleges."[28] On November 26, 1821, Biancotti expressed his gratitude to Bruno: "It is time now to thank Your Reverence for the many benefits received from you, above all for having procured my entrance into the Company of Jesus. After our blessed God himself and Mary Most Holy, I owe this to you, and I cannot thank you enough. You often told me that I needed a novitiate [spiritual training for religious life], and in a vague way I knew this was true. Now I begin to see this more clearly, and my gratitude that you procured for me this means of dedicating myself to spiritual perfection continues to grow."[29] One sorrow, nonetheless, weighed on Biancotti's heart: "Amid these consolations, I have only one sadness and that is the departure of Don Loggero and Reynaudi. But I sacrifice my desire to the will of God; may it be done in all things."[30]

The rector, Biancotti told Bruno, "hardly tells me anything except to be joyful, though I am not melancholic, to conserve my strength to labor for souls, and not to expect to reach perfection so quickly, and other similar things that Your Reverence used to tell me."[31] Biancotti expressed his hope of persevering in the Jesuits and concluded, "I will always be grateful, however, to Your Reverence should you have any light or counsel for my guidance in this regard."[32] Biancotti would remain a Jesuit and hold positions of responsibility until his death in 1837.[33] A time would come when Biancotti's Jesuit vocation would cause Bruno sorrow.

On January 23, 1823, during his second year as a Jesuit, Antonio Lanteri wrote to Bruno from Tivoli (near Rome): "Although I have not written to Your Reverence since residing in these Papal States, I have not forgotten you.[34] On the contrary, every day, and often many times a day, I remember you. As the days and months have passed, in my heart, and in the presence of the Lord, a deep and never satisfied longing has grown, if not to see you, which is impossible, at least to receive sure news about you. . . . I send this letter to you with great longing that it reach you quickly, so that soon I may receive a consoling reply."[35]

Antonio opened his heart to Bruno: "My countless debts toward Your Reverence oblige me to remember you always, and to pray, and offer Masses for you, as I have several at my disposition. Forgive me, as you have forgiven so many temerities in the past, if I speak too boldly, because I have no other means of repaying in some measure these many debts, and otherwise I should remain ungrateful for so many benefits received from you. As I think of this, tears come to my eyes, and I am compelled to stop writing. I feel this all the more when I reflect that I may never see you again, to kiss not only your hands but also your feet, and to ask, on my knees, your forgiveness and pardon for all things. Until Paradise, then. . . . "[36] Antonio Lanteri would serve as rector of Jesuit colleges in Nice and Sassari (Sardinia) until his death in 1836.[37]

IN 1820, THE FRAGILE PEACE restored after Napoleon's fall unraveled as revolutions erupted in Portugal and Spain. In July, the uprising spread to the kingdom of Naples in southern Italy, and unrest in Piedmont followed.[38] Agitation among university students in Turin on January 11–12, 1821, was harshly suppressed, and tensions mounted. On March 10, soldiers in nearby Alessandria proclaimed a new constitutional government; two days later, soldiers in Turin did likewise.

As the crisis escalated, King Vittorio Emmanuele I grew hesitant and afraid. On the night of March 13, he abdicated in favor of his brother Carlo Felice and fled Turin for Nice. In the absence of Carlo Felice, then dwelling in Modena, Vittorio Emmanuele appointed twenty-two-year-old Prince Carlo Alberto as regent. The king's capitulation intensified revolutionary ferment in Turin, and agitators threatened bombardment of the city unless the regent immediately granted a constitutional government. That evening, from the balcony of the palace, Carlo Alberto promised a constitution. Enthusiasm exploded among the revolutionaries, and, on March 14, a provisional government was established. The following day, Carlo Alberto swore fidelity to the constitution.

On March 16, a new revolutionary journal, *La Sentinella subalpina* (the Subalpine Sentinel), appeared. Its purpose was "to spread the new ideas, to teach the rights of citizens, to foster love for our common fatherland, Italy, and to proclaim war against Austria."[39] That same day, however, marked the beginning of the end for the revolutionary government. On that day, from Modena, Carlo Felice made known his decisions: he himself would assume government of the nation. He rejected the political innovations, urged his subjects to resist them firmly, and ordered Carlo Alberto to withdraw from Turin and await his orders.[40]

In the absence of both king and regent, the city fell to the revolutionaries. Carlo Felice appointed General Vittorio Amadeo de la Tour as new regent with orders to suppress the rebellion. Aided by Piedmontese and Austrian troops, de la Tour accomplished his task. On April 9, 1821, he and his soldiers entered Turin and quelled the "revolution of thirty days."[41]

In October, Carlo Felice solemnly entered Turin as king of Piedmont. Four days earlier he had written to the nation: "Following the example of our predecessors, we invoke the aid of divine Providence, which has entrusted us with the government of our people in difficult times. Holy religion will be the sure guide and efficacious support of all our undertakings, of all our thoughts."[42] One historian comments that, as they read these words, "the clergy especially felt new hope that the era of revolutions was over."[43] Coming years would demonstrate the contrary.

Bruno, from his home in the heart of Turin, witnessed these troubling events. One decision of the king in the aftermath of revolution awakened a particular foreboding in his heart. In early 1822, the king ordered the leading members of the nation to swear an oath of fidelity to royal authority. Shortly after, he extended the obligation to the clergy.[44] Bruno resisted this demand with all his energy, perceiving in it—rightly, as events would prove—a new subjection of the Church to the state, and a harbinger of graver measures to come.[45]

THROUGHOUT 1821, BRUNO CONTINUED to struggle physically. On May 29, his friend Francesco Pertusati expressed his concern: "I am also afflicted by the unhappy news you give me in your letter regarding your health, which matters so much to me and to so many others."[46] Later that year, Bruno wrote to the bishop of Pinerolo, Francesco Bigex, recalling their conversation in which Bruno had promised the bishop his observations regarding "the doctrines taught in the recently instituted chair [at the University of Turin] of natural and public law, and political economy."[47] Now Bruno explained that "the circumstances of the times [the political upheaval], together with my consistently fragile health, have led me to regard that labor as pointless, and have caused me to suspend it."[48]

On May 8, 1822, Bruno again wrote to Bishop Bigex: "Forgive me if I have not replied earlier to your esteemed letter. The worsening of my habitual infirmities burdened me so much that I had to remain in bed and adopt medical remedies."[49] Bruno discussed Bigex's recent pastoral letter, commented on issues of the day, and added: "As long as the Church and the government fear each other . . . the state cannot prosper, nor can the Church flourish other than by the exercise of the virtues proper to the martyrs; nor will it be possible to change the teaching in public institutions, or to impede the continuing flow of harmful books—which is the only remedy that can heal, if this is possible, spirits that have absorbed such poison for so long—or at least to impede the spreading of this poison in the future, and disseminate in its place the balm of truth and of religion."[50]

Bruno ended on a personal note: "Forgive me if I speak with such liberty; the reason I do is the goodness that Your Reverence has so often shown me. I am only a watchdog in the flock of the Lord who cries out to his last breath, and who soon will have lost his voice completely, and will end this unhappy life in the firm hope of a better."[51]

Writing to Bigex one month later, Bruno discussed the government's assaults on "the freedom of the Church, which must be professed and defended more than ever in these times because it is so attacked."[52] History would prove that Bruno had accurately interpreted the policies of a government determined to subjugate the Church. Coming decades would witness the violent suppression of religious communities in Piedmont, confiscation of Church property, the abrogation of age-old Church prerogatives, open hostility to the Holy Father, and imprisonment of bishops and priests.[53] In his letter, Bruno shared his concern with Bigex: "Forgive the length of this letter and the liberty with which I speak. I did not intend to write this way, but this has come from a heart deeply afflicted by so many errors and by the present struggles, all the more because I see no hope of a remedy. If Your Reverence should find that I am in error on any point, I hope you will be good enough to direct me back to the way of truth because, by God's grace, I want only this as my guide, and never simply my own opinion."[54] Physical infirmity compelled Bruno to seek his secretary's aid: "Forgive me also if I have asked another [Loggero] to write for me; it was because of my weakness of the chest."[55]

The expressions in these letters—labor regarded as pointless, a burdened spirit, an unhappy life, an afflicted heart, and, strikingly, from one who instilled hope in so many others, "I see no hope of a remedy"—witness to the affliction Bruno felt in the aftermath of revolution as, from this perspective, he contemplated the future. The "watchdog in the flock of the Lord" would not fail, however, to "cry out to his last breath" in service of the Church.

On December 15, 1821, French Jesuit Didier Richardot wrote to Bruno, expressing gratitude for his assistance during an earlier stay in Turin: "You would have received this letter more than a year ago if I had known how to reach you. I was too eager to show you my gratitude not to write immediately upon my return [from Russia] to France, but I have only now been able to obtain your address from our priests. I am delighted to learn from a letter of [Jesuit] Father Grassi that you still live in Turin."[56]

Richardot longed to see Bruno again: "When I left Russia, I was first assigned to Italy. You can be sure that had that not changed, I would have traveled the additional eighty kilometers to satisfy my ardent desire to see you and express in person all the tender and respectful affection I feel toward one who, for over a year, showed such deeply touching and generous hospitality toward me. After God, it is to you that I owe my belonging to the Society [Jesuits] for which you have such affection and esteem. It was through your example, through my conversations with you, and in your library that I found the seed of my vocation."[57] And Richardot declared: "If I ever cross the mountains [the Alps], you can be sure that I will come to cast myself on your neck and at your feet to ask your blessing. I pray from my heart that God conserve your strength and the health that you employ so well for his glory and the salvation of your neighbor."[58]

ON MAY 5, 1821, NAPOLEON DIED in exile on the island of St. Helena. He was fifty-two, and had passed his final six years under British guard on the island. Early in Napoleon's exile, Pius VII had pleaded for benign treatment of the ex-emperor. In October 1817, the pope wrote to his secretary of state, Cardinal Consalvi: "We ought both to remember that, after God, it is to him chiefly that is due the re-establishment of religion in the great kingdom of France. The pious and courageous initiative of 1801 [the concordat with the Holy See] has made us long forget and pardon the wrongs that followed. Savona and Fontainebleau [the places of Pius VII's captivity] were only mistakes due to temper, or the frenzies of human ambition."[59]

On the evening of July 6, 1823, the eighty-one-year-old Pius VII rose from his chair and fell.[60] His condition worsened, and forty-five days later, on August 20, he died.[61] The death of these two men ended an era in Church history; their passing also closed a chapter in Bruno's life.

That same summer, Bruno's youngest brother, Giuseppe Tommaso, died in Savigliano, Piedmont.[62] Giuseppe Tommaso had entered the Barnabite order and had been ordained a priest. He later obtained papal dispensation from the priesthood, and died with the Church's sacraments on July 31, 1823, at the age of sixty.[63]

Bruno informed his cousin Agostino Eula of Giuseppe Tommaso's death, and on August 21, Eula replied: "I received . . . your appreciated letter of the 18th with the sad news of the death of your brother Tommaso, our dearly beloved cousin. I shared this news immediately with my brother who, like me, had not yet heard of it. Our sorrow was tempered greatly when we learned that he had died the death of the just."[64] In all likelihood, Giuseppe Tommaso was Bruno's last living brother; from that day, he alone of the family survived.[65] Another chapter in Bruno's life had also closed.

CHAPTER FIFTEEN

"His Ardent Desires"

In all things, seek the will of God.
—Bruno Lanteri

ON MAY 28, 1823, BRUNO'S FRIEND Bishop Sappa de' Milanesi replied to a letter from Bruno. Bruno had composed a manuscript on the teaching of then Blessed Alphonsus Liguori. He had asked Sappa to review it, and "to form a judgment of it and communicate that judgment to him."[1] Now the bishop answered: "I have read with the greatest interest your manuscript on the teaching and holiness of Blessed Alphonsus Liguori. . . . The information you have gathered . . . increases the esteem I have always had, and will always conserve for the teaching of Blessed Liguori."[2] The bishop then offered his recommendation: "Finally, I want only to express my hope that you will decide to publish this work. It is of such nature that it can render vitally important services to our religion."[3] Future years would confirm the accuracy of the bishop's judgment.

Later in 1823, Bruno published his text under the title *Réflexions sur la sainteté et la doctrine du Bienheureux Liguori* (Reflections on the Holiness and Teaching of Blessed Liguori).[4] The work appeared in French, both in Lyons and Paris.[5] A second edition was issued that same year, and, seven years later, a third.[6] In 1825, Bruno's volume of reflections was published in Italian translation as well. Three further Italian printings followed in the next fourteen years, and, in 1833, a Spanish translation was published in Madrid.[7]

Bruno's views regarding Alphonsian teaching later circulated through "Some Observations on Moral Theology," an article printed in 1828 and reprinted four times in subsequent years.[8] The *Observations* summarized the *Reflections* in easily readable form, and this digest was widely cited in theological discussion.[9] Through the *Observations,* Bruno gained a broad and influential audience.

Characteristically, Bruno published the *Reflections* anonymously.[10] He later explained why he issued this volume in France rather than his own Piedmont: "This book of *Reflections* was published in a foreign country for fear of encountering difficulties in publishing the work in our own country, where many strongly oppose the principles of the moral teaching of Blessed Liguori."[11]

The theological stakes were high. In these publications Bruno addressed bitterly contested questions of sacramental practice: Was God a severe God, slow to forgive human weakness and repeated failure? Was it true, as a text followed by most confessors asserted, that "experience teaches us that delay of absolution is an efficacious remedy to help men overcome their sins"—that is, that a confessor's refusal to give absolution to those who struggle is an effective means to help them conquer sin?[12] Was an Italian bishop right in declaring that "the best remedy for reducing the number of sins is to be very severe in hearing confessions, and not to give absolution until one is sure of the penitent's conversion"?[13] Was there a more effective pastoral approach? One truer to the God revealed by Jesus Christ?

Bruno proposed the gentler moral theology of Alphonsus Liguori as the answer. He cited many reasons for this choice: Alphonsus was a modern author who incorporated the teachings of his predecessors; he wrote from decades of pastoral experience, "something rare among other authors"; great numbers returned to Christ through his pastoral practice; Alphonsus espoused no particular theological faction, but "simply followed the teaching of Rome"; his moral theology "is esteemed and followed by many zealous priests who, having studied his teaching well, exercise their sacred ministry with great fruit"; Alphonsus himself "became a saint by practicing and teaching his moral theology." If so, "What more can one wish? And how can one who imitates him be lost?"[14]

But Bruno emphasized another reason above all these. The process of canonization includes a thorough examination of the prospective saint's writings. The Sacred Congregation of Rites in Rome had reviewed Alphonsus's writings, and on May 14, 1803, had decreed that "nothing worthy of censure was found in them." Four days later, Pius VII had approved that decree.[15]

Nothing worthy of censure: this decree, Bruno explained, certainly did not require that all adopt Alphonsus's theology; it did signify, however, that those who followed this theology stood on sure theological ground. Bruno wrote: "We cannot criticize a priest who follows an opinion in moral theology on a matter not yet decided by the Church, if that opinion, whoever its author may be, is founded on solid reasons. All the more, then, must we not criticize those who follow the opinions of an author venerated on the altars [beatified or canonized], opinions in which the pope has declared *there is nothing worthy of censure*."[16]

Bruno reasoned, one scholar comments, "with so dispassionate and serene a tone that he calmed the hearts of the disputants, and dissuaded them from polemics in matters not defined by the Holy See, and which therefore were to remain open for free discussion."[17] As another historian notes, there was "something prophetic" in Bruno's views on Alphonsus, at that time neither canonized nor declared a doctor of the Church.[18] To a long-standing controversy about sacramental practice, Bruno offered a practical solution: since Rome has declared Alphonsus's writings—including his *Moral Theology* with its guidance for confessors—free of anything worthy of censure, priests may follow this teaching with peace of heart. "His reasoning," the same historian writes, "which simply draws a logical conclusion from the decrees of the Holy See, is of such simplicity that it seems evident at first sight."[19] But this simplicity, "characteristic of many fruitful intuitions," was by no means evident in Bruno's day.[20] His insight, tirelessly repeated, would persuade many and contribute powerfully to the acceptance of Alphonsian moral theology among priests.[21]

The same writer continues: "A historian has defined the author of the *Reflections* as 'the principal promoter of Alphonsian ideas in Italy.' Everything leads us to believe that he was likewise the one principally responsible for their penetration into France."[22] Within ten years of the publication of the *Reflections*, acceptance of Alphonsian moral theology was widespread among French clergy.[23] As French and Italian priests adopted that teaching, confessional practice in both nations grew gentler and more welcoming.[24]

BRUNO WAS NOW SIXTY-FIVE YEARS OLD and forty-two years a priest. Schooling under Fr. Diessbach and long experience had developed in him a love for works he believed critically important: promotion of the Spiritual Exercises, formation of young priests, diffusion of the printed word, defense of Christian truth against current errors, confessions and spiritual direction with emphasis on the message of mercy and encouragement to begin again.

Earlier settings for these works—the *Amicizia Sacerdotale* and the Pious Union of St. Paul—no longer existed. Laity rather than priests directed the *Amicizia Cattolica*, successor to the *Amicizia Cristiana*.[25] The Oblates of Mary had dispersed four years earlier, and former members had found new settings. Some continued to give retreats under Bruno's direction, but years were passing and the future remained unclear. Bruno himself struggled physically and did not expect to live much longer.[26]

In that year 1824, Bruno faced the question of his own future: Was God asking him to continue his present work in Turin until his death? Or did God desire something different during his final years? In 1821, four former Oblates had sought entrance among the Jesuits; a conviction now grew in Bruno that God was asking the same of him.[27]

Bruno had once described himself as feeling "the greatest affection for the Company of Jesus."[28] To one joining the Jesuits he wrote: "I have always considered it a duty to esteem and love all religious orders and to promote these sentiments in others, finding vocations for them when the opportunity presented itself. But I have always had a special predilection for the Company, for which I am ready to make any sacrifice, and I would wish to possess its spirit well so as to communicate it fully to others."[29] In one who so esteemed religious life, so desired to serve God fully in his declining years, and so loved the Society of Jesus in particular, a decision to join the Jesuits was readily comprehensible. At age sixty-five, he who had taught so many to begin again, himself chose a new beginning.

Bruno was already known both to the local Jesuit superior, the future general of the Company and Servant of God Johann Roothaan, and to the general in Rome, Luigi Fortis.[30] In the early fall of 1824, Bruno made the eight-day Spiritual Exercises. By October, his decision to join the Jesuits had matured and was communicated to Fr. Roothaan.[31]

Roothaan informed the general, who responded positively. On October 20, Roothaan shared Bruno's reply with the general: "The good Theologian Lanteri rejoices from his heart at Your Paternity's favorable and gracious response to him, and does not cease giving thanks for so great a favor, first to the Lord, and then to Your Paternity, through whom so many blessings come to him from the Lord."[32] By October 20, both Jesuits and Bruno had made their decision: Bruno had requested and had been granted entrance among the Jesuits. Sentiments of joy and gratitude filled his heart; now only the practical steps remained to be decided.

Admission among the Jesuits required, after a brief probation, two years of novitiate, a time of intense spiritual training for Jesuit life. On that October 20, Roothaan outlined for the general a possible approach to Bruno's novitiate. His letter provides a commentary on Bruno's life, valuable both because of the stature of the writer and because of the firsthand knowledge from which he wrote.

Roothaan described his proposal: "Now, with regard to the first steps to be taken, personally his one desire is to enter the novitiate community as soon as possible, or any other house to which Your Paternity might wish to assign him. But resolving his affairs, which are many, and his relationships, which are very many, and all of them directed solely to the greater glory of the Lord, will take time, and consequently his entrance would be delayed too long. I would propose to Your Paternity, therefore, that the Theologian be numbered among our members while still living at home, undertaking certain exercises of prayer and maintaining frequent contact with me or with whomever Your Paternity may wish to assign him."[33]

Roothaan noted Bruno's familiarity with Jesuit practices: "In the first place, he has always lived the life of a Jesuit; in addition, he already knows many of our things since he was always occupied, as long as his health permitted, in giving the Spiritual Exercises, in which he is most skilled, and he learned this from our Fr. Diessbach, 'whose memory is blessed' [Sir 45:1]." Roothaan continued: "He has lived a truly apostolic life and has trained many priests, excellent men and unshakeable in their calling."[34] With respect to Jesuit exercises of prayer, Roothaan wrote, "I believe he will not have much to add to what he was already doing."[35]

In this planning, Bruno's health emerged as a consideration: "It will be necessary, however, to take great care of his health which is very weak. But in these days I have heard that he was able to accomplish, for the glory of God, a thing that, in view of his condition and the brief time in which he did it, rightly may seem a miracle."[36] Roothaan's observation encapsulated Bruno's entire life: the ongoing "miracle" of persevering application and apostolic fruitfulness in conditions of great physical weakness. Finally, Roothaan highlighted Bruno's impact in Turin: "I will also note that his presence here is of great value for the glory of God and of great importance for us [the Jesuits]."[37]

On November 9, the general replied expressing his desire that Bruno enter the Jesuit house in Chieri, near Turin.[38] After a brief first probation in Chieri, Bruno was to begin two years of novitiate in Turin under Roothaan's guidance. The general wished Bruno to adopt Jesuit dress in public during his first year, and also, during that year, to enter the Jesuit community of San Francesco di Paola, in Turin.[39] Aware of Bruno's particular circumstances, the general added: "If there are any difficulties in fulfilling what I desire, I ask Your Reverence to write to me, and we will find a way to ease everything."[40]

Complications did in fact exist as Roothaan informed the general on November 17: "With regard to the Theologian Lanteri, he raises two difficulties with going to our house for the first probation. The first is the weather which is already severe in this area, though most likely we could find a way to provide for this in our house in Chieri. The second is that were he to go to Chieri at this time of year, others would immediately suspect his purpose and rumors would circulate. It would be better that this not happen so soon."[41] Consequently, Roothaan told the general, "he humbly asks Your Paternity that if possible, he begin the two years here at home and delay his trip to Chieri until the spring."[42] For the rest, "he is very open to whatever you ask and thanks Your Paternity profoundly for the favor that, with such charity, you show him. San Francesco di Paola would be very fortunate to acquire such a person."[43]

The general did not accept the proposal, and on December 7, Roothaan resumed the correspondence: "As concerns our beloved Theologian, I fear, from Your Paternity's most recent letter, that matters will be delayed, and may be deferred indefinitely."[44] Roothaan explained: "His health is poor. In San Francesco di Paola he certainly could help with spiritual guidance and confessions; beyond this, I do not know what he could do. Already for many years he has not been able to preach or give the Exercises. Then too he has a great number of relationships and affairs to arrange; and, finally, how to find a way to present his entrance among us publicly!"[45]

At this point, Roothaan and Bruno met to discuss these issues. In that same letter of December 7, Roothaan shared their conversation with the general: "I have seen the Theologian Lanteri. The poor man does not see clearly how he can accomplish what Your Paternity proposes as quickly as Your Paternity asks. The need to discharge an infinite number of affairs, and the cold weather of this season, will not permit him to benefit soon from the offer you make him."[46] In their conversation, Bruno expressed a desire: "Since Your Paternity insists on the need *of an entire year* of novitiate, he would hope to be able to do that *entire year* after a year.

Would it not be possible that, beginning the two years now, the *entire year* were the second rather than the first? In this way the fulfillment of his ardent desires would not be deferred so long."[47] Three months of inconclusive dialogue had not diminished Bruno's "ardent desires" to enter the Jesuits, and, in communication with Roothaan, he continued to seek a way forward.

This time the general, recommending that Bruno care for his health and conclude his affairs so as to "make his year with true holy liberty and spiritual profit," accepted Bruno's proposal.[48] On January 26, 1825, he wrote to Roothaan: "Provided that he not take vows, not even devotional or secret vows, after the first year, but that he take these after the second year of true novitiate, and that during this first year he live under obedience, and that everything possible be done, I think in this way we might permit this manner of proceeding."[49] Ten days later, on February 5, Roothaan replied to the general: "Our beloved Theologian Lanteri thanks Your Paternity from his heart. Now we will coordinate the manner of his beginning with us. When we have found the best arrangement, I will inform Your Paternity of everything."[50]

In three months all was prepared, and on May 14, 1825, Roothaan notified the general: "Our Theologian Lanteri has gone to Chieri to make the Spiritual Exercises of eight days. In doing so, he is fulfilling Your Paternity's desire that, wishing to join us, he begin in Chieri, and that his stay there serve as a first probation."[51]

The procedural difficulties were now resolved and the first step taken. No trace of hesitation in Bruno regarding his Jesuit vocation transpires from this correspondence. On the contrary, he rejoiced at the general's acceptance and saw in Jesuit life the "fulfillment of his ardent desires." Bruno went to Chieri, Roothaan related, "wishing to join us," convinced that this was his calling.

But others were less sure. Luigi Guala voiced his reservations, as Roothaan observed to the general that same May 14: "With regard to him and his vocation, the Theologian Guala expressed a doubt whether, in view of his circumstances, it be for God's greater glory that the Theologian Lanteri remain as he is, or that he do what he so ardently desires?"[52]

A first misgiving arose from Bruno's infirmities: "His health is very weak, and he needs special care. Though he is only sixty-five, he has little physical strength, and often so little that he is unable to do anything."[53] A second concerned the value of Bruno's existing work in Turin: "His presence here is of great advantage because of his extensive knowledge of the errors of the day and of the maneuvers of the party [those hostile to the Holy See], which has done great harm here as elsewhere, and never ceases to conspire toward its ends, and for his knowledge of good books and of the replies to be given to false reasoning."[54] A final question regarded Bruno's life itself: "Who can say whether the change of life might not hasten the end of his life, certainly precious, indeed of inestimable value?"[55]

On the other hand, Roothaan noted, "Who can say whether this change of life might not be advantageous for his health as well? I hear that now at Chieri he is well, and yet he was very weak the day before he left Turin."[56] And again: "He needs special care, but this can be given in the Company [of Jesus], nor would a man like this be assigned tasks incompatible with health like his." Further, "It may be that his knowledge would be of greater value in the Company, for example, in Rome, where the climate might be favorable to him, as is generally true with the elderly. I see that the Theologian Lanteri would very willingly move to Rome."[57] Roothaan concluded: "I do not believe that he would be well here at San Francesco di Paola because this area is unhealthy, most unhealthy in fact, especially in winter. We would like to know what Your Paternity thinks of all this."[58]

In Guala's doubt, as Roothaan referred it, Bruno's vocational choices were two: to continue his existing ministry in Turin, clearly of value for the Church, or to pass his final years as a Jesuit, possibly in Rome, serving through spiritual counsel, confessions, and his extensive theological knowledge. Roothaan considered that Bruno's Jesuit vocation might well prove for God's greater glory. Guala was less sure. To Bruno himself, his Jesuit calling was clear. For all three, Bruno, Guala, and Roothaan, a surprise lay in store.

As Bruno explored his vocation, future agents in his life were assuming their roles. On September 28, 1823, Cardinal Annibale della Genga was elected pope with the name Leo XII. He and Bruno would meet twice in coming years.

That same May when Bruno went to Chieri to join the Jesuits, his friend Bishop Bigex transferred from Pinerolo to Chambéry as its new archbishop.[59] On the day of his transferal, Rome confirmed Pierre-Joseph Rey as bishop of Pinerolo in his place.[60] Rey, too, would play a significant role in Bruno's remaining years.

An anecdote of 1824 survives in the reminiscences of Felice Giordano, whose father, Giovanni Battista, Bruno guided spiritually for thirty-five years.[61] Giovanni Battista frequently brought Felice and his brother Gioacchino to visit Bruno. Decades later, Felice recalled one such visit when he was ten and Gioacchino fourteen: "Lanteri, noting the age and dispositions of both, soon found a way to render them the greatest service he could in that moment. He turned to the older of the two, and said: 'You, Gioacchino, must begin to prepare yourself to choose well your state in life. Try to live according to the model you will find in this book.' And he gave him those two volumes first published by Marietti, *The Lives of Some Young Men,* etc. Then, to me, who was ten years old: 'For you it is enough to assist at Mass with devotion, to go to confession well, and to receive Communion well.' He gave me a copy of the little book *A Practical Way,* not without some envy on my part when I compared my little book with the two volumes he had given my older brother."[62]

Both Gioacchino and Felice later became priests.[63] In a letter informing Bruno of Gioacchino's vocation, their father wrote: "I will end here so as not to burden you further. Your goodness, and your affectionate heart which, beyond compare, listens to all, counsels all, and consoles all, gave me the freedom to share with you this lengthy account of what has happened to me. And I am sure that you will receive it with the same sentiments of goodness with which, in spite of my ingratitude, you have treated me for thirty-five consecutive years."[64] His heart which *listens to all, counsels all, and consoles all*: it was a fitting summary of Bruno's priestly life.

Chapter Sixteen

Beginning Again

*All our hope rests in Mary, to whom
we are fully dedicated, and in whose
hands this entire matter lies.*
—Bruno Lanteri, of the Oblates

In Chieri, Bruno pursued his Jesuit calling. Day followed upon day in the retreat that served as his first probation. In those hours of prayer, however, an entirely new perspective opened for Bruno, and at last he understood God's call for his remaining years. On June 8, 1825, Roothaan informed the general: ". . . Here things have changed. While [Lanteri] was considering in Chieri in his spiritual exercises how, in his circumstances of health, he might best serve the glory of God, since in the Company he would be more, as it seems to him, and perhaps is true, of a burden than otherwise; it came into his mind to form a house as it were of *Oblates*, who would dedicate themselves to giving parish missions and to giving the spiritual exercises in the Jesuit manner. He is pursuing this idea now, and he hopes to accomplish this goal. It certainly would be a great good, and, *presuming he is able to accomplish it,* which however I doubt, but, *presuming he is able to accomplish it,* I too would believe it a greater good *ad maiorem Dei gloriam* [for the greater glory of God], than entering at such an age and in such health, in the Company."[1]

Prior to Bruno's retreat, Guala had questioned whether God was calling a man of sixty-five and in poor health to the Jesuits. Now, alone with God in prayer, Bruno pondered the same question. Would entrance among the Jesuits in such physical conditions truly be for God's greater glory? With new clarity, Bruno grasped the weight of this consideration: "In the Company he would be more, as it seems to him . . . of a burden than otherwise."

What then did God want? According to Guala, if Bruno did not join the Jesuits, he would remain in Turin and continue his existing ministry. As Bruno prayed, however, a third and different choice emerged: "It came into his mind to form a house as it were of *Oblates." It came into his mind:* Roothaan's simple phrase discloses a work of grace—the Spirit speaking to Bruno's heart, lifting doubts, granting certainty, opening a new path.

God was not calling him to be a Jesuit, but rather to *begin again* the project of the Oblates dispersed five years earlier. This "house as it were of *Oblates"* would dedicate itself "to giving parish missions and to giving the spiritual exercises in the Jesuit manner." Roothaan, though doubting the undertaking would succeed—in fact the ecclesiastical hurdles and political obstacles to its accomplishment were significant—concurred that this congregation would better serve God's glory than Bruno's entrance "at such an age and in such health" among the Jesuits.

Bruno's confessor, Antonio Ferrero, also testified to this moment of grace: "Finally, in the spiritual exercises he made in Chieri with the Jesuits to resolve the more perfect election [discernment] of his state of life, having weighed before the Lord how much his own and others' sanctification would benefit from a Congregation that occupied itself directly and only, with preparing to give and then preaching everywhere the Exercises of St. Ignatius, that directed its energies against the destructive errors of Jansenius, Febronius, and Richer, and against all the errors appearing in our day, and therefore would know and disseminate good books chosen according to the various needs of different persons, with many sacrifices he dedicated himself energetically to this task."[2] Giving Spiritual Exercises, opposing the errors of the day, spreading good books: the Oblates would perpetuate Bruno's lifelong work.

After the Oblates' dispersal in 1820, various bishops in Piedmont had invited them to their dioceses: Novara, Alba, Alessandria, Cuneo, Pinerolo, and others.[3] Bruno's retreat in Chieri now led him to reconsider this possibility, and in particular, the willingness of Pierre-Joseph Rey, the newly appointed bishop of Pinerolo and recipient of Bruno's aid in former years, to welcome the Oblates into his diocese.[4] The retreat concluded and his discernment clear, Bruno approached Bishop Rey.

From this moment, Bruno would never hesitate. Faithful to the grace of those days in Chieri, he unwaveringly pursued the rebirth of the Oblates. He did so well aware of the cost to himself. His choice signified renunciation of peaceful old age with the Jesuits in Rome, cared for in his needs, a confessor and spiritual guide. It required the sacrifice of places, friendships, and occupations cherished throughout forty-eight years in Turin. It demanded the exhausting task of founding a new religious institute, with few human resources, in poor health, in a different city, without support from the archbishop of Turin, in the face of relentless governmental hostility to religious life, and with no guarantee, as Roothaan noted, of success. Some months after that retreat in Chieri, Bruno wrote to Bishop Rey: "My health also constantly declines. I am prepared, however, to sacrifice it without reserve, placing all my hope in the Blessed Virgin, Foundress and Superior of this Congregation."[5]

IN MAY 1825, Bishop Rey enthusiastically invited the Oblates to Pinerolo. This small city of 14,000 inhabitants lay at the base of the Alps, forty kilometers southwest of Turin.[6] Bruno's friend and *Amicizia* member Luigi Provana di Collegno first contacted Rey regarding this possibility. On June 1, Collegno transmitted the bishop's reply to Bruno: "The divine inspiration that you [Collegno] shared with me regarding the project of these zealous priests dedicated to parish missions and retreats is of greater value than we can imagine, and is beyond all doubt from heaven. Yes, certainly! My deeply respected and Christian friend, I open my arms and my residence, and above all my heart to welcome these men of God.... This poor bishop thrilled with joy and wept for consolation after reading your letter. He went immediately to celebrate Holy Mass and I saw him [Rey himself] at Communion, palpitating and sighing

The city of Pinerolo with the Alps in the background.

The city of Pinerolo with the old city in the foreground.

from his heart to thank the adorable Evangelizer whom the eternal Father sent to men, and to bless him for the cherished hope of seeing faithful imitators of this divine model establish themselves in his diocese."[7] One week later, on June 8, Roothaan informed his general that Bruno "is pursuing this idea now."[8]

A sense of urgency marked Bruno's activity in the following months. He wrote letters, prepared documents, traveled, held meetings . . . did all in his power to hasten the approval of the Oblates. The "miracle" Roothaan had noted—Bruno's capacity to accomplish major tasks in conditions of impaired health—was again evident as the next months unfolded. His letters suggest that he knew his time was limited, believed that God had entrusted him this final charge, was willing to fulfill it, and accepted the physical price he inevitably would pay for its accomplishment.

Formal documents were needed for the process, chief among them a new rule, and that summer Bruno undertook the task of preparing them. On July 10, 1825, Bishop Rey encouraged him: "I have asked our good God, my deeply respected Abbè Lanteri, to bless our projects for his glory and for the honor of his holy religion, for the benefit of my diocese and my own consolation as well. Make haste, then, to do and write all that is necessary to prepare a successful outcome."[9]

In July, Reynaudi preached retreats to both priests and laity at the Shrine of St. Ignatius in Lanzo, the first with Guala and the second with Loggero.[10] Bruno did not await his return, but traveled to the shrine, where they conferred regarding the reestablishment of the Oblates. Later that month, Bruno told Bishop Rey that "I have been to [the Shrine of] St. Ignatius, as I wrote Your Excellency earlier, to arrange everything with Don Reynaudi regarding our project."[11]

In the same letter, Bruno continued: "We are sending you the documents we think it well to present to the Holy Father for the approval we so desire and so need for the Institute. We ask Your Excellency to examine them before God and to send us your observations when you have time. If you judge it suitable to send them to Rome, or that one of us go to Rome in person to promote this cause, we ask of you the goodness to add your own decree of approval to them, and some words of recommendation to the Holy Father. We would be deeply grateful for this favor because, if our Congregation can begin again in the Holy Year [Jubilee of 1825], this would serve all the more for the salvation of souls."[12]

On September 10, Bishop Rey responded favorably: "When I returned from pastoral visitations, my dear and respected Abbè Lanteri, I hastened with great attention to read, or reread, the precious documents that our esteemed Monsieur Loggero brought me from you. They are exactly what I desired, and with God's help, they will serve perfectly to fulfill my hopes."[13] In his accompanying letter to the Holy Father, the bishop employed the title "Oblates of the Most Holy Virgin Mary," and described its members as *vere viri misericordiae*: truly men of mercy.[14] Bishop Rey urged Bruno: "Let us not lose a moment, my worthy and respected friend, and above all let us win the support of heaven for our task by fervent prayer that the Vicar of Jesus Christ welcome our aspirations and fulfill my desires."[15]

Four days later, the bishop sent Bruno his formal approval of the new rule, dated September 17, 1825.[16] On that date, the Oblates were reborn as a congregation of diocesan right.[17] In the rule approved that day, Bruno gave definitive expression to the Oblates' apostolic charism—the mission they would fulfill in the Church.[18]

The Oblates, he wrote, "consecrate themselves particularly to giving the Holy Exercises" and "to promoting their use as much as possible, both as parish missions and as retreats."[19] Bruno explained that "to give these Exercises with greater fruit, they have chosen to follow the spirit and method proposed by St. Ignatius."[20] This is "a method approved by the Holy See, and known by experience to be highly efficacious," that contains "a series of truths so well ordered that it serves effectively to impress them deeply on people's hearts."[21]

The Oblates further seek "to assist in the formation of good parish priests, and laborers in the vineyard of the Lord," and consequently "welcome boarders in the Congregation, that is to say, those priests who desire a time of quiet to make the spiritual exercises, or to prepare to give the spiritual exercises, or to study moral theology, or to prepare for parish ministry, and other ecclesiastical tasks to which their respective bishops may assign them."[22] During their stay in the community, the Oblates supply these priests with means for these formative tasks and guidance in their use.[23]

The Oblates also strive "to combat the errors of the day, especially of those unbelievers who attack the faith, and of those who propose erroneous teachings in dogmatic and moral theology."[24] Two practices assist the Oblates in this endeavor: they "recommend themselves often and from the heart to Mary Most Holy, their principal Foundress and Teacher," and they "profess an entire, sincere, and inviolable obedience to the authority of the Holy See, and a complete adherence to its teaching ... professing in addition full uniformity with the mind of the Church in questions regarding which the Church permits a diversity of opinions."[25]

The Oblates, finally, endeavor "to cause good books to be known and spread."[26] As unwholesome books have wrought harm to the Church and spread error, "so good books must also serve as a special antidote to preserve or undeceive those in need of this remedy, and also to promote devotion among the faithful."[27] Later in the rule, Bruno added that "the Oblates attend tirelessly to hearing confessions, ready to welcome all at any time, especially those most in need, with a joyful and willing spirit."[28]

Through this rule, Bruno transmitted to the Oblates the ministries learned from Fr. Diessbach decades earlier and faithfully exercised in a lifetime of priestly service.[29] "This Congregation that is of such value for the salvation of souls," as Bruno would describe it to Bishop Rey, was to preserve that mission in the Church.[30]

For the more juridical details of administration and vows, Bruno adopted St. Alphonsus's rule for his Redemptorists. In a later text, Bruno explained why he chose the rule of St. Alphonsus rather than that of St. Ignatius: "Several considerations led us to take from Blessed Liguori the form of government for our Congregation, and the substance of our rules concerning the vows. We had always professed a special devotion for Blessed Liguori, and,

even more, we saw clearly the need to promulgate sound principles of moral theology in our districts. We adhered to the teaching
of Blessed Alphonsus not only because he is Blessed, but because,
by decree of the Holy See, his teaching contains nothing worthy of
censure. We chose his rule for our government and vows so that
those who would join our Congregation might grow in affection
for the teaching of Blessed Liguori."[31]

DURING THESE MONTHS OF PREPARATION, Bruno traveled to Genoa
to ask the help of Archbishop Luigi Lambruschini.[32] After his
return, Bruno thanked the archbishop: "I cannot express, nor can I
manifest sufficiently to Your Excellency my deep and sincere sentiments of gratitude for the thoughtful kindness you showed me
during my stay there, and which I will remember forever."[33]

In his memoirs, Lambruschini also recalled that visit. He
described Bruno as "a priest of evangelical simplicity, learned,
and highly versed in the science of the saints," and told of Bruno's
decision to establish the Oblates "after he had consulted at length
with God in prayer."[34] Lambruschini wrote: "The Abate Lanteri had
come to Genoa some months earlier specifically to consult with
me, and hear from me what he would need to do for the establishment of this holy work. At that time, he could count only on
three priests, but had found a home for the institute in the Diocese of Pinerolo, offered him by Bishop Rey, the dedicated prel-
ate of that city. When I had examined the matter well, it seemed
to me that this design was of God, and I encouraged the devout
priest to present himself to the King, to ask his protection, and to
travel to Rome where he could present the entire project to His
Holiness and learn his judgment in its regard."[35] Lambruschini's support would be invaluable to Bruno in the dark days that
lay ahead.

On October 6, 1825, at ten in the morning, eight priests gathered in Bruno's home. They had come to elect the first superior
of the renewed congregation: he would be called their "Rector
Major." Like Bruno, three had deep Oblate roots: Reynaudi, Loggero, and Craveri. Four others were new: Ignazio Carrera,

Pietro Vigo Pallavicini, Giovanni Antonio Ferrero, and Francesco Biagio Botto.

The appropriate documents were read, among them the new rule. Then, having "recited the *Veni Creator* [prayer to the Holy Spirit], and recommended themselves to Mary Most Holy, to St. Peter, and to Blessed Alphonsus Liguori," the eight priests pronounced a formal declaration of adherence to the new congregation, testifying that "this is my will, and the firm purpose of my heart . . . to remain until the end of my life in the Congregation of her [Mary's] Oblates."[36] Each appended his signature to the formula of declaration.

These steps completed, "by unanimous vote they elected the Theologian Pio Bruno Lanteri as their Rector Major."[37] The meeting concluded "with the recitation of the hymn *Te Deum* [prayer of thanksgiving], with the verse, and prayers, and an embrace *in Domino* [in the Lord] as to their most loving father."[38]

It was a morning of hope and fresh beginnings. Yet a shadow, perhaps unnoticed that day, lay over the meeting. Craveri, who had arrived late, pronounced the declaration with the others, but would later assert that he did so "explicitly excluding any vow, and restricting it to a simple promise. The . . . Theologian Lanteri agreed that in my case the declaration would be understood in these terms."[39] Craveri would further attest: "I think that Fr. Pallavicini also stated that he did not pronounce this declaration as a vow."[40] In fact, of the eight who gathered that morning, one would die fifteen months later, two would never join, and one, after joining, would quickly leave.

Yet the cause progressed, and by November 1825, the king had been informed and had approved. The file was sent to Nicolò Crosa di Vergagni, Piedmontese chargé d'affaires with the Holy See, who transmitted it to the papal secretary of state, Cardinal Giulio Maria della Somaglia.[41] In his letter of presentation, Crosa affirmed that "the excellent qualities with which the deserving Signor Theologian Lanteri is abundantly endowed are manifest and widely known, and the other priests who at present compose the Congregation are most worthy to be associated with him."[42]

The secretariat of state referred the documents to the Sacred Congregation of Bishops and Regulars, and the process of their examination began.[43]

ON NOVEMBER 7, 1825, the Abbè Eugene de Mazenod, a future canonized saint, arrived in Turin.[44] De Mazenod had come from France, and was on his way to Rome where he sought papal approval of his *Oblats de Saint-Charles*, a congregation dedicated to preaching parish missions in Provence, France.[45] During his stay in Turin, Bruno asked to meet him. On November 16, de Mazenod wrote from Genoa to his assistant, Fr. Tempier: "I had no time to finish my letter in Turin because the great Theologian Lanteri had arrived. He asked of me the favor of giving him all the free time I would have before my departure. So much was to be gained in every way from conversation with him, that I had no difficulty in granting him a favor from which I would draw more profit than he."[46]

De Mazenod described the encounter: "This eminent, holy, good, and wise man is the master, friend, and superior of that other Theologian Guala, of whom I spoke to you in my other letters. From the very start of our first meeting, I inspired in him as much affection and confidence as I felt veneration for him. It was, so to speak, a repetition of what happened with Don Guala, with this difference, that because he is the head and the master, he set no limits to the testimonies of confidence he gave me."[47] The two spoke of a matter of significance, as de Mazenod recounted: "If I had come to Turin only to see these two men, my time and the money of my uncle [bishop of Marseilles] would have been well spent. We spent ten or twelve hours in conversation. I cannot tell you in writing the subject of our discussion; it merited the time dedicated to it. I will have to reserve something for when we speak in person."[48]

What did these two men discuss in that long and engaging conversation? Neither left an explicit record in writing. One scholar suggests that Bruno proposed the union of the two congregations, de Mazenod's *Oblats de Saint-Charles*—later named the Oblates of Mary Immaculate—and the Oblates of the Virgin Mary.[49] Both congregations preached parish missions, and both sought papal approval in 1825. The union of Lanteri's group with de Mazenod's would increase de Mazenod's numbers, and expand his congregation into the kingdom of Piedmont; it would likewise spare Bruno an arduous—and uncertain—pursuit of papal approval and governmental authorization for the Oblates of the Virgin Mary. If such union was indeed discussed, subsequent months would reveal complexities not apparent that November day.[50]

On November 20, Archbishop Lambruschini wrote to Bruno from Genoa: "I thank you from my heart for the gift [books], and even more for your remembrance of me. It is all the more precious to me because of the profound esteem and veneration I have long had for the special qualities that distinguish your worthy person. May the Lord conserve you at length, and bless the exemplary zeal Your Reverence shows so effectively for the cause of the Church, our most holy and most beloved Mother."[51] In the year about to begin, that zeal would be put to the test.

CHAPTER SEVENTEEN

Sojourn in Rome

*All of these great trials give us hope
that God wishes to work great
good through our Congregation.*
—Bruno Lanteri

AS BRUNO PURSUED the foundation of the Oblates, the parish missions and retreats continued. On December 26, 1825, Bruno wrote to Loggero: "After your departure, I examined the list of your spiritual exercises and found that in five months, that is, in 150 days, you gave the exercises eleven times, that is, 110 days. To these must be added twenty-two days for travel to and from the place of the exercises, and four more days for the trip to Genoa, all of which totals 136 days. This leaves only fourteen days. In regard to these, you know that the first day after the exercises it is impossible to sleep because of the agitation the person still feels. That leaves only three days to rest and a little time for hearing confessions as well."[1]

Bruno then counseled Loggero: "The conclusion would be that if you could cancel two retreats and distribute the others better so that you have suitable intervals between one retreat and the other, and thereby ensure at least the necessary rest, you would do a very holy thing. I ask you to consider this."[2] Bruno likewise expressed his concern to Bishop Rey: "What weighs on my heart is to see our good priests killing themselves because of the number of exhausting parish missions and retreats their zeal has led them to accept. In the past six months, they have not had even the time absolutely necessary to rest body and spirit."[3] Rey, himself experienced in retreat ministry, replied: "Alas, yes, our good preachers are killing themselves. But the greatest saints dedicated to such preaching are *suicides* of this kind. Poor sinner that I am, I too have had the good fortune of killing myself many times in this same way, and, after many such deaths, I am still in good health. Let us hope that our worthy Oblates will also find it so."[4] With few Oblates and many requests, Bruno's call for moderation was clearly opportune.

Bruno continued also to make his own annual retreat. On February 10, 1826, Giuseppe Bellotti, the Jesuit superior in Chieri, invited Bruno to return for that purpose: "I beg you also to remember to come to Chieri to make the holy exercises. . . . Your days with us would give great pleasure to me and to all in this novitiate. I would willingly have extended this invitation in Turin when I was there on the first day of Lent, but time simply did not permit it."[5] A month later, on March 16, Bellotti renewed the invitation: "I hope Your Reverence will prepare to visit us in this novitiate for your usual spiritual exercises, and that you will give both me and all my novices the great consolation of spending those days with us."[6] In the latter months of 1826, Bruno would explain that he had not replied earlier to a letter of Bishop Rey "because it arrived in Bardassano [the Grangia] while I was making my spiritual exercises."[7]

IN ROME, THE EXAMINATION of the Oblates' request for papal approval began. On January 20, 1826, the cardinals of the Sacred Congregation of Bishops and Regulars met and discussed the matter. The cardinals responded favorably, but also raised questions: Could the Oblates explain the variations made to the rules of St. Alphonsus regarding the vows? And, above all, since the Church did not approve institutes that had no house and only a brief history, and since in their rule the Oblates had adopted much from St. Alphonsus, would they consider approval as a branch of his Redemptorists? This would resolve the existing difficulties and allow the Oblates to serve the Diocese of Pinerolo without delay.[8]

On February 10, Cardinal Bartolomeo Pacca—companion to Pius VII in his abduction from Rome under Napoleon—transmitted these questions to Bishop Rey, who, on March 9, referred them to Bruno.[9] Five days later, Bruno replied: the Oblates were grateful

The bishop of Pinerolo, Pierre-Joseph Rey.

for the cardinals' positive reply; at the same time, they courteously declined union with the Redemptorists because they understood themselves to be a different community with a different mission.[10] As letters passed between Rome and Pinerolo, Bishop Rey exclaimed to Bruno, "Oh, that you were in Rome! Then the explanations would be given quickly!"[11] Within a month, Bruno would undertake that journey.

In those same days, Eugene de Mazenod obtained papal approval for his Oblates of Mary Immaculate.[12] From Rome, he expressed his joy to Bruno: "I will tell you about it in full detail when we meet because I could not describe it in writing without filling a volume. I beg you and the venerable Monsieur Guala to help me thank the Lord for this."[13] De Mazenod continued: "I have taken care, in the course of proceedings here, to keep informed about your project. The Marchese Crosa told me that it is completed, and I congratulate you with all my heart."[14] As coming months would show, de Mazenod's felicitations were premature.

In a probable reference to their conversation the preceding November, de Mazenod added: "But I continue to believe that it would be opportune to examine before God whether the project you considered for a short time might not be more advantageous for the good of souls."[15] If Bruno had in fact contemplated uniting his Oblates with those of de Mazenod, he apparently did so no longer.[16] The two founders would meet again in Rome.[17]

Already in the summer of 1825, Bruno had spoken of travel to Rome for the Oblates' cause.[18] Both Lambruschini and Rey encouraged him to make the trip, and now Bruno prepared.[19] His departure was set for April 7, 1826. Loggero would accompany him on the trip and during his stay in Rome.

On April 6, Bruno made his will. Aware of his physical infirmities and of the demands of travel by coach and sea, Bruno prepared for a possible failure to return. In that will he wrote: "I commend my soul to the Most Holy Trinity, to Mary Most Holy, my beloved Mother, to St. Joseph, St. Michael, my Guardian Angel, St. Ignatius, Blessed Alphonsus Liguori, and all the Saints and Angels of Heaven, and to the prayers of my heir, of my friends, and of the whole Roman, apostolic, and Catholic Church, in whose embrace I have always desired, and do desire, to live, and to die."[20] Bruno's choice of an heir reveals his closeness to Loggero: "I establish and name as my universal heir, the priest Don Giuseppe Loggero . . . for the great services, the companionship, and the assistance he has constantly shown me, certain that he will fulfill my intentions exactly."[21]

On April 7, Bruno and Loggero took the coach for Genoa, where they arrived the evening of the following day.[22] After six days in Genoa, during which they conferred with Archbishop Lambruschini, the travelers set sail for Rome.[23] The king, Carlo Felice, had obtained them passage on a frigate of the Piedmontese navy bound for Rome.[24] Their voyage by sea lasted five days, the one recorded instance of travel by water in Bruno's life. From Rome, Bruno described the trip to Lambruschini: "After two days of calm . . . we had a favorable wind so that we arrived at Civitavecchia [port city near Rome] on the morning of April 19. Due to Your Excellency's special recommendation, we were welcomed and treated with the greatest courtesy and with special regard by the Signor Captain Olzati. I had no physical difficulty and had a good appetite throughout the days at sea. Don Loggero suffered a little from an upset stomach."[25] The following morning, April 20, the two travelers reached Rome.[26]

In Rome, Bruno visited the appropriate offices and supplied the requisite information. The issues raised in January were discussed, and the process advanced.[27] Bruno's own person, known and respected by the Holy See he had so long defended, assisted the cause. In a letter of April 12 to the Roman secretary of state, papal chargé d'affaires in Turin Antonio Tosti, described Bruno as "a true model of the Piedmontese clergy in learning and holiness, and widely known in Turin as a defender of the rights of the Church and the Holy See."[28] On June 26, Cardinal Pacca replied to a letter from Archbishop Lambruschini: "The Signor Abate Theologian Lanteri brought me the esteemed letter you were pleased to provide him for his trip. I already knew well the piety and the learning of this priest, and your confirmation of the admirable qualities that distinguish him brought me no little pleasure."[29] On April 27, a week after his arrival in Rome, Bruno wrote to Bishop Rey: "Thus far our hopes are good, and all our trust is in Mary Most Holy, to whom we are completely dedicated, and in whose hands our whole endeavor lies. Thus far I have not suffered at all from the trip; on the contrary, my health has improved."[30]

On June 9, the Holy Father created a commission of four prelates to examine the Oblates' request: Cardinals Bartolomeo Pacca, Carlo Maria Pedicini, Antonio Pallotta, and Archbishop Giovanni Marchetti.[31] Archbishop Marchetti, whose writings Bruno had long propagated, would cause him profound anguish in weeks to come.

In June, Bruno's infirmities worsened. On June 11, he told Bishop Rey that "I suffer more than ever from my health."[32] In early July, his friend Luigi Provana di Collegno urged Bruno to care for his health "which I hear suffered somewhat last month."[33] Already the brief springtime of beginnings in Rome had ended.

A consolation awaited Bruno, however, on June 19, when Pope Leo XII received him and Loggero in personal audience. Loggero recorded the event in his diary: "We were admitted to the presence of His Holiness. . . . The Signor Theologian [Lanteri] thanked His Holiness for the special commission he had formed to examine our petition. His Holiness benevolently replied that he had chosen this way as the quickest, that these affairs tended by their nature to take much time, and that he himself would expedite its conclusion as much as possible."[34]

Bruno then spoke of the University of Turin, most probably of concerns with respect to its theological teaching, and of calumnies against the *Amicizia Cattolica*. He told the Holy Father of his plan "to compile an anthology of papal Bulls and the retractions of those in error during the past 200 years."[35] Bruno shared his lifelong conviction regarding "the good wrought by the Exercises, the need to make good books known, and to form good priests"—the apostolic mission now entrusted to the Oblates.[36] The pope's reply suggests that Bruno spoke compellingly: "He told us that we might have left another here in our place, without leaving so great a work in Piedmont unattended. When we replied that we had no one else, he said that this too was a good work and for the glory of God, and that therefore we should remain in Rome until the matter was concluded."[37]

The two priests voiced a request: "We told him that approval as a religious order was necessary, and he said that he hoped to be able to console us, and that God would bless his own work."[38] As the audience concluded, Bruno professed his vows as an Oblate. Loggero recorded that "the Holy Father received his vows, and bade us farewell, leaving us deeply consoled."[39]

On July 15, the commission met, reviewed the Oblates' rule, and approved both the rule and the institute.[40] Bruno shared the glad news with his *Amicizia* friend Cesare d'Azeglio: "On the fifteenth of this month, the special commission of three cardinals, Pacca, Pedicini, and Pallotta, and Archbishop Marchetti ... held its meeting. They unanimously approved our request. Last evening, Archbishop Marchetti brought the commission's decision to the Holy Father, who approved it fully, and confirmed it. Now only the formal proclamation remains."[41] Bruno soon would learn that the most painful struggles were just beginning.

THE CAUSE OF HIS ORDEAL was Archbishop Giovanni Marchetti, the secretary of the commission, a celebrated author and preacher, and a man who loved and had courageously defended the Church under the French occupation. He was called "the hammer of Jansenism."[42] Even to the best of causes Marchetti brought an abrasive approach. Contemporaries judged that Marchetti's strange behavior in the summer of 1826 arose from declining mental health as well.[43]

Marchetti had long sought papal condemnation of the four Gallican propositions of 1682.[44] These propositions limited papal authority in France, proclaimed the superiority of a general council over the pope, and taught that the pope was not infallible in matters of faith without the consent of the Church.[45] The propositions reinforced, therefore, the efforts of European governments to wrest control of the Church away from Rome. Rome had reproved these propositions in the past, but judged renewed pronouncements imprudent; to do so could only exacerbate already tense relations with civil authority.[46] Marchetti thought otherwise, and determined, if possible, to force the issue.

Noting the Oblates' adherence to papal authority, Marchetti believed his opportunity had come. Each year on June 29, the feast of St. Peter and St. Paul, the Oblates renewed their profession of faith according to a formula prescribed by Pius IV.[47] Marchetti now imposed a different formula containing a text he understood as a condemnation of the Gallican propositions.[48] The archbishop falsely assured Bruno that this was the Holy Father's wish. Bruno, understandably, accepted the word of an official who had direct access to the pope.

In the text of a decree of approval he drafted, Marchetti wrote that the Oblates would adopt this new formula.[49] As Bruno later affirmed, "the archbishop's purpose was to persuade the Oblates . . . that the formula of profession of faith now included in the decree would be a definitive condemnation of the four Gallican Propositions, and a decision regarding faith itself."[50] In Marchetti's contorted thinking, therefore, this decree, by which the pope approved the Oblates as a congregation, would constitute a definition of faith condemning the Gallican propositions.[51] Bruno subsequently commented to the Oblates' friend Rodolfo de Maistre: "This man burned with desire to procure a papal condemnation of the Gallican propositions, and judged that our Congregation provided a favorable opportunity for his purpose."[52]

Never imagining the archbishop might so grossly misrepresent the pope, Bruno accepted the modification as the Holy Father's will. He would also relate to de Maistre, however, that "we foresaw the tribulations that would derive from this."[53] Nor did these long delay. Word reached foreign ambassadors in Rome that the pope planned to condemn the Gallican propositions through the approval of a new congregation.[54] The ambassadors considered this a direct challenge to the authority their governments claimed over the Church. A more sensitive nerve in church-state relations could not have been touched.

In his diary for August 15, Loggero recorded that an unidentified person "had cried alarm to the ministers of foreign powers, such that in a dinner where all were Protestants except the ambassador of France, they resolved to unite and collectively express their opposition to this papal Brief [the document approving the Oblates] to His Eminence, the Cardinal Secretary of State. They had been told that His Holiness wanted to condemn the four propositions in a papal Brief, and establish a Congregation for the express purpose of combatting them, and that would serve as an instrument to gain adherents to the Holy See."[55] Suddenly, a handful of Piedmontese Oblates had become the object of international indignation.

Confusion over Marchetti's decree now threatened the approval itself. In their tribulation, Bruno and Loggero turned to Mary. Loggero wrote in his diary: "On the evening of the tenth [of August], we promised Mary with a vow, that one or the other of us would go to Loreto [Marian shrine] and celebrate two Masses for the shrine, or that we would celebrate, or have others celebrate, thirty Masses in another church."

Two days later, on August 12, Loggero observed that he and Bruno "left unhappy" from a meeting with Marchetti, and that "the Signor Theologian Lanteri was deeply afflicted" by the turn of events.[56] In conversation with Cardinal Pacca the following day, Bruno learned that Marchetti—from misguided zeal or mental disturbance or both—had misrepresented the Holy Father's will. Pacca told Bruno that the pope did not wish to condemn the Gallican propositions, had no intention of including such condemnation in the decree approving the Oblates, and that all was a fabrication of Marchetti himself.[57] The cardinal outlined the steps to be taken, and assured Bruno that all would be well. Loggero wrote: "From our hearts we thanked Mary Most Holy, who does not fail to console the afflicted, and we found peace."[58]

A difficult meeting with Marchetti now lay ahead. Loggero described the emotional tumult of that August 14: "We went to St. Peter's and prayed for his help (the Signor Theologian went to confession to a Franciscan confessor). Then we went home trembling because we would have to visit Archbishop Marchetti during the day and get the decree [withdraw Marchetti's text]. Since we had not gone during the morning, the Archbishop sent word that we were to come. Don Loggero went trembling, and saying Hail Marys, because he had to tell him what Cardinal Pacca had said: that this decree was not to be printed. (The Signor Theologian was so disconcerted that he felt unable to go.)"[59] Remarkably, Bruno, courageous throughout twenty years of French occupation, appeared overwhelmed that August 14 in Rome.

But things were different the following day. Loggero wrote: "On the evening of the fifteenth, we went to see Archbishop Marchetti, who persisted in his claim that the decree [his text] could not be annulled or changed, because it was a definition of faith, etc., as he had said earlier. This caused the Signor Theologian to grow very angry, and after an hour of heated argument without being able to persuade him [Marchetti] differently (because of his fixation), protesting throughout that we wished to obey the Holy Father, and he insisting that this was the Holy Father's will as expressed to him when he spoke with him officially in audience, we took our leave."[60]

This caused the Signor Theologian to grow very angry. For weeks Marchetti had betrayed the trust of the two Piedmontese priests. He had consistently misrepresented the Holy Father, whom Bruno revered, and for whose office he had risked his life.[61] He had attempted to exploit Bruno and the Oblates for a personal end. His interference had raised international tensions and threatened to obstruct approval of the Oblates. Marchetti's "fixation" had caused Bruno himself weeks of deep affliction. Perhaps, too, Bruno's weakened health and his expenditure of energy in preceding weeks contributed to the emotions of those two days: the agitation of the one day, and the anger of the next.

Marchetti's machinations had now been exposed and disavowed by higher authority. When, on that August 15, Marchetti incredibly *still* pursued his project, Bruno's Piedmontese restraint collapsed and his anger emerged.

When the pope learned what had occurred, his regard for the Oblates grew. On August 17, Cardinal Pacca told Bruno and Loggero that "far from losing the Holy Father's esteem, his regard for us had increased when he saw that we submitted to the [Marchetti's] formula of profession of faith believing it to be his will, and immediately rejected it once we learned the contrary to be true. From this we had gained, rather than lost, esteem in His Holiness's eyes."[62] On August 22, Pacca repeated that "His Holiness's esteem for us had grown, and he had great hopes for our Congregation."[63]

In September, Marchetti presented his resignation to the Holy Father. His request was granted, and Marchetti returned to his native Empoli, near Florence, where he passed his remaining three years.[64] Before their departure from Rome, Bruno and Loggero asked to meet Marchetti and offer final salutations. Marchetti wrote in reply "that he had not the strength to meet with us in person, but that he would always accompany us in his heart."[65] Loggero commented: "The goodness of his heart is evident in his words."[66]

Bruno's response is conserved in the Vatican file: "I cannot sufficiently express to Your Excellency the profound sorrow we have felt and continue to feel for the events that took place in the matter of the Congregation of the Oblates of Mary Most Holy, and that caused Your Excellency such grave affliction, certainly very much against our wishes, since we would have suffered anything that might have saved you this. . . . In our tribulations, however, it is of some comfort to see that Your Excellency is not offended with us, and was pleased to tell us that 'you will always accompany us with all your heart.' Your words reveal your great goodness, and we cannot fail to render you our sincere thanks for this."[67]

Bruno concluded his letter: "We cannot sufficiently express to Your Excellency our gratitude for the interest you took in our regard, and because we cannot repay you in any other way, we certainly will always keep you without fail in our humble prayers before the Lord, that he fill you with every heavenly blessing. We truly regret that it will not be possible to visit you before our approaching departure for Turin. We hope, however, that you will not fail to honor us with any commissions you may have for our region."[68] Bruno signed the letter, "with sentiments of the greatest respect and greatest veneration."[69]

A painful hurdle had been overcome in Rome. A greater awaited Bruno's return to Turin.

CHAPTER EIGHTEEN

"We Hope, and We Fear"

Our affliction is greater than ever.
The storm is so severe that we
can only "hope against hope."
—Bruno Lanteri

WITH MARCHETTI'S INTERFERENCE removed, the cause progressed rapidly. On August 22, 1826, Cardinal Pacca presented the revised decree to the Holy Father, who fully approved it.[1] The final step would be composition of the papal brief that would formally express this approval.

Loggero recounted that Pacca, pleased with Bruno's loyalty to the pope as shown in the Marchetti episode, gave orders that this document be drafted "in ample form and with wording that would do us much honor."[2] Also on August 22, Loggero, serving as Bruno's secretary, met with the official responsible for the text. In his diary, Loggero noted: "I gave him in writing the name of the Theologian Lanteri as founder and superior, and that of Don Reynaudi as cofounder of the Congregation, so that they would be included in the Brief."[3]

On September 1, 1826, Leo XII approved *Etsi Dei Filius*, the document that constituted the Oblates as an institute of pontifical right. On that day, the "Congregation of the Oblates of the Blessed Virgin Mary," as the brief officially named them, began to exist in the universal Church.[4]

The papal text described the Church's trials and affirmed that God always inspires zealous laborers to meet her needs. The brief applied this truth: "It appears that among these are to be numbered our beloved sons Pio Bruno Lanteri and Giovanni Reynaudi,

priests of Piedmont, who, together with their companions, have
dedicated themselves for many years to the fruitful ministry of promoting the formation of the clergy and the evangelization of the
faithful."[5] The abundance of this fruit, and the desire of many bishops for their ministry, have led to the present request: "Finally, the
same beloved son, Pio Bruno Lanteri, accompanied by the priest
Giuseppe Loggero, came to Rome to ask of this Apostolic See, in
his name and in that of the other founder, Giovanni Reynaudi, and
the other members, confirmation of the Rules and Constitutions
that they have given the new Congregation."[6]

The brief summarized the rule, reviewed the process of
approval, and concluded in a Marian key: "Finally, we exhort the
above-named men, Pio Bruno Lanteri and Giovanni Reynaudi,
and their companions, that, as they have desired to form one body
under the protection of the Blessed Virgin Mary, so they never
leave the blessed feet of the same Mary. Thus we may have greater
hope that, sustained by her aid, they will bear much fruit."[7]

Ten days later, on September 11, Bruno and Loggero met for
a second and final time with Pope Leo XII. Loggero recorded
the event: "Our audience began at two in the afternoon.... We
were deeply consoled and the Holy Father granted us all we
asked.... His Holiness tenderly and warmly recommended that
we pray for the Church in America."[8] That day, Bruno's five months
in Rome concluded with consolation of heart.

Departure from Rome now approached. The trip northward,
this time by land, would last two weeks. Bruno and his spiritual
son Leopoldo Ricasoli had hoped to meet in Florence along the
way. Delays in Rome, however, and Bruno's declining health compelled him to renounce this hope. From Rome, he notified Ricasoli:
"I have waited until now to reply to your gracious letter, hoping
daily to be able to let you know the date of my departure, and so
that I would have the consolation of seeing you again, but it was
in vain. My task is done only now, and I must remain several days
yet to obtain some important documents. This long delay, together
with problems of health that continue to increase, compels me to
hasten my return as much as possible. As a result, with my deepest

regret, I can no longer stop in Florence on my return. We will both have to make this sacrifice to God, which, I confess, is not little for me."[9] The sacrifice of that encounter, accepted as unavoidable, would indeed not have been little. Bruno must have known that further opportunities to meet Ricasoli would arise infrequently if at all.

Earlier in Rome, Bruno had attempted to visit Ricasoli's Jesuit son, Luigi. His efforts had been unavailing, as Bruno explained: "I also depart with the regret of not having been able to meet your son, the Jesuit novice. I went to the novitiate several times, but was not able to see him. I could not go more often because of the distance from my lodgings [two kilometers] and my problems of health."[10] Bruno concluded with the words of one ever close to his heart: "This life is destined for offering continual sacrifices to the Lord, and Fr. Diessbach used to say that paradise pays for all."[11] It was almost a summary of Bruno's life: readiness to accept physical and emotional sacrifice when the Lord asked, and persevering service in the hope of eternal blessedness.

God, however, did not ask Bruno and Ricasoli to sacrifice their meeting. On September 16, shortly after midday, Bruno and Loggero left Rome for Turin.[12] Some fifty kilometers from Florence, in Poggibonsi, Bruno and Ricasoli met for several hours. Ricasoli later recalled the "miracle" of that brief encounter: "Oh, how much I regretted that you did not spend at least a day with me! But I thank God that I saw you again, and this was a true miracle."[13] It was, very likely, the last meeting of the two.

Pursuing their journey, the travelers halted in Genoa where Bruno stayed with Archbishop Lambruschini and shared the glad news from Rome. On September 30, they reached Turin.[14]

ROME'S APPROVAL HAD BEEN GRANTED, and the congregation now existed juridically. The time had come to gather in community, and preparations began immediately. Three days after Bruno's return, the Oblates acquired a residence: the former monastery of St. Clare, in Pinerolo. The official acts of the congregation record the purchase: "The above-named Father Rector Major Lanteri, and the Local Rector, Father Reynaudi, in the name of and on behalf of the Congregation, acquired the Monastery of St. Clare from the Signor Claudio Calligaris. The acquisition was registered in a document dated October 3 of the same year 1826, in this city of Pinerolo."[15]

The residence suited the new congregation well. A friend of the Oblates, Francesco Gonella, a banker in Turin and a dedicated Catholic, described the purchase: "At their own expense they bought an old and large monastery with a beautiful church, situated in one of the most advantageous locations in all Piedmont. The air is excellent, and the buildings are secluded, but near the center of the city of Pinerolo. The site is elevated, overlooking the city, and at the same time peaceful and solitary."[16] Once adjusted, the house provided space for the Oblates community and rooms for forty retreatants.[17]

In fact, the property served the Oblates' mission admirably. From it, they could travel throughout Piedmont for parish missions and retreats. When they returned, the house offered quiet for prayer, study, and rest. Its closeness to the center of the city afforded the people ready access to confession, another key element of the Oblates' ministry. The many rooms permitted hospitality for priests who sought further formation, and for retreatants, both individuals and groups.

To help finance the purchase, Bruno sold the Grangia.[18] It was a first surrender of things long cherished for the sake of the Oblates in Pinerolo. The Grangia, loved as a place of peace, as the site of countless retreats, and as "my cherished solitude" during exile under Napoleon, was lost to him. Disciple Luigi Craveri would testify that Bruno "established the Congregation with the sacrifice of the things that he possessed and were dear to him."[19] By the end of October, the first Oblate had arrived at St. Clare's.[20]

Now, however, a grave obstacle arose. The Piedmontese government had long claimed the right to grant or deny civil effect within its territory to papal decisions. In 1719, the Piedmontese senate had decreed that "no one who has obtained . . . [papal]

St. Clare's (upper left) in Pinerolo, first house of the Oblates after papal approval in 1826.

Street in Pinerolo leading up the hill toward St. Clare's.

Street in the old city of Pinerolo.

bulls, briefs, rescripts, or other provisions emanating from outside the State . . . may put them into effect unless they are first presented to the Senate, and this body has declared that it has nothing contrary to them."[21] Piedmont, therefore, unilaterally subjugated papal authority to civil within its borders. The Holy See never accepted this claim; but papal objections notwithstanding, the practice remained law in Piedmont.

As a result, the papal brief *Etsi Dei Filius* that approved the Oblates had no legal weight until sanctioned by the Piedmontese senate—and influential members of the government were determined that this should not occur. Hostility to Rome and religious life underlay this opposition, and pointedly toward an institute that aimed to combat the very "current errors" such men espoused. King Carlo Felice, more receptive to Rome, had power to order authorization of the brief, but wished to avoid political tensions.

On November 3, 1826, Bishop Rey told Bruno of his conversation with Roget de Cholex, minister of the interior and one adamantly opposed to *Etsi Dei Filius*.[22] The bishop rightly foresaw that this would be "one of the greatest storms" the Oblates would face in their beginnings.[23] If the senate did not sanction *Etsi Dei Filius*, the Oblates could not exist.

Bruno's reply expressed both pain and hope: "Yesterday I received your esteemed letter, and felt great sorrow for the deep affliction you have endured for our Congregation. But because this whole matter lies in Mary's hands, the reward you will receive will be great and worthy of a Queen. I have no doubt that she will once again crush the head of the serpent, who does all he can to hinder the good for souls that he foresees will come from our Institute."[24] Bruno's words manifest his conviction of the spiritual fruitfulness of the new congregation.

Bruno then shared his personal response: "I confess that when I first read your esteemed letter, I was downcast and disheartened. But rereading it attentively, I found that the case is not as desperate as I thought."[25] Bruno proposed answers to the minister's objections, planned to enlist Archbishop Lambruschini's help, and concluded: "In the meantime, we can only pray without ceasing to the

Lord and to Mary Most Holy, that they help us more than ever, and this we are striving to do."[26]

On that same day, Bruno wrote to Archbishop Lambruschini: "Finding myself immersed for some days in the most serious trouble concerning our new Congregation, I am making bold to share my afflictions with Your Excellency's paternal heart, and to tell you everything, hoping from the goodness you have shown us and the great interest you have always taken in our cause, that you will be willing to continue your protection and assistance to us in this critical and difficult time."[27] Lambruschini's support would be invaluable in the months that lay ahead.

In January 1827, both Bishop Rey and Archbishop Lambruschini met with Carlo Felice on behalf of the Oblates.[28] To both, the king promised that the Oblates would be granted legal status. Caught, however, between desire to assist the Oblates and unwillingness to antagonize his government, the king hesitated, and took no action.

Months of hope and fear passed, and the impasse persisted. Bruno remained in Turin with Loggero, laboring for the legal sanction of the brief. On February 1, 1827, Reynaudi wrote from Pinerolo to Carlo Daverio, Bruno's friend and a dedicated Oblate supporter in Turin. Reynaudi appealed to Daverio: "I beg you to give our respects and to comfort our deeply beloved and deeply afflicted father, and to recommend us to his prayers."[29] Two days later, Reynaudi enjoined Loggero: "Present my respects to our deeply beloved father, and take care of him in every way: our whole Institute and all the good that God will choose to work through it depend on him."[30] Humanly speaking, the Oblates did depend entirely on Bruno, the recipient of their love and protagonist of their cause.

In February, Bruno informed Cardinal della Somaglia in Rome of the delay and the harm it caused: "We do not know yet whether the Brief of His Holiness for the Oblates will be authorized. We hope, and we fear, and I have considered it best to remain in Turin so that we may not be exposed to greater attacks. In this state of affairs, I cannot tell you how greatly God's work suffers, and . . . it is painful to see the Congregation of the Oblates delayed in beginning its life together, which alone can permit acceptance and formation of new members."[31]

In March, Bruno himself met with the king to seek legal approval for the Oblates. Before the meeting, he shared his anticipation with Archbishop Lambruschini: "I will soon have an audience with His Majesty, and I am given hope that in that encounter we will be consoled."[32] But three weeks later, Bruno wrote to Bishop Rey: "Some time ago I had asked for an audience with His Majesty, and was told that I would be given it during Lent. Two days before the King left [for Genoa], I had the opportunity to present myself at the time indicated. I was given a few minutes only, because it was close to the end of the time reserved for audiences. His Majesty had the goodness to reply that he was pleased with the good we were doing, and that he recommended his person and the queen to our prayers. Our sovereign later left for Genoa, and I hear that the Brief has not yet been sent to the senate."[33] The king had offered expressions of esteem and had requested prayers, but had done nothing more.

The legal impasse eroded the energy of the beginnings, as Bruno related to Bishop Rey on May 21: "In the meantime, it is undeniable that this delay of seven months has harmed us greatly because it has caused us to lose many valuable new members."[34] How could new candidates join a community that lacked civil status, and whose future was uncertain? Growth would be impossible until the stalemate resolved.

EVEN AS PROSPECTIVE MEMBERS turned elsewhere, the existing membership declined. In November 1826, Pietro Pallavicini, one of the original eight, suddenly announced his entrance among the Jesuits.[35] Pallavicini's departure afflicted Bruno not only because the Oblates lost a valuable member, but also because Pallavicini had not shared his vocational doubts. The first drafts of Bruno's reply reveal his hurt, laboriously mastered in his final letter.[36] On December 9, Bruno told Luigi Craveri: "I will reply [to Pallavicini] that I am consoled that he has overcome every difficulty in following the will of God now seen more clearly, that this is our only rule, without which we can have no peace of heart; that I thank him for what he has done for us, and ask that he keep me and the Congregation in his prayers when he celebrates Mass."[37] His loss was a blow to Bruno and to the struggling congregation.

Two months later, Ignazio Carrera, another of the initial eight, died in Turin. On his return from a strenuous parish mission, he fell ill in the home of benefactor Francesco Gonella. He died in Gonella's home on January 29, 1827. That day, Bruno informed Loggero: "I had told you just a short time ago of the danger of losing our beloved Theologian Carrera. Today, with deep pain in my heart and tears in my eyes, I must tell you that we lost him this past midnight. He was assisted by the good Theologian Simonino. He was conscious almost throughout, and accompanied the prayers with fervor, when suddenly he was taken by a convulsion and surrendered his soul to the Lord. I hope from my heart that this victim we offer him will draw special blessings on our small Congregation."[38] The following day, Reynaudi shared his tribulation with Bruno: "What will become of us! One leaves us, another dies. . . . There is no assurance that can comfort us even a little, but the hope against hope of Abraham."[39]

In May 1827, a third of the eight, Francesco Botto, departed for reasons of health. Bruno learned of Botto's decision "with the greatest sorrow."[40] More grievous still was the decision of a fourth, Luigi Craveri, to remain in his parish. Two factors contributed to this choice: the unrelenting resistance of Colombano Chiaveroti, Craveri's bishop, to his entrance among the Oblates, and the great affection of his parishioners for a deeply loved pastor. After prolonged hesitation, and with subsequent turmoil of heart, Craveri renounced his Oblate vocation.[41]

His decision gave joy to his parish and pain to Bruno and the Oblates. Years later, Craveri would write that "the suffering he [Bruno] underwent on account of the trials I caused him would itself suffice to hold his name in honor."[42] That suffering was personal, because Craveri's decision broke a decades-long bond between spiritual father and son. It was also institutional, because the talented Craveri might have served as leader in a fledgling congregation greatly in need of his abilities.[43] In fact, Craveri would later be named vicar general of the diocese of Fossano and rector of its seminary. Twice he would decline nomination as bishop.

For the Oblates the loss was great. Bruno pressed Craveri to "reflect, also, that since others have already left, if you do not come, it is very possible that the whole edifice may crumble."[44] Earlier that same 1827, when severe winds damaged the Oblates' residence in Pinerolo, Reynaudi wrote to Bruno that he remained "battling with the night, with every wind and storm, simply crying out, 'Save us, Lord, we are perishing.' God certainly must love us greatly, because he scourges us unto death. . . . We have no hope but in the infinite power of God."[45]

A further disappointment awaited Bruno in Antonio Biancotti's decision, after long hesitation, to remain with the Jesuits.[46] Biancotti, whom Bruno called "one of the first and most fervent founders of the Congregation in Carignano," had given Bruno hope of his return to the Oblates. Bruno explained to Cardinal Pacca: "In the six years he has spent in the Company of Jesus, he has acquired all the necessary learning; he is practiced in observance of the Rule, and has the experience to organize the Congregation immediately and well. Further, he has the full esteem, regard, and confidence of his first companions, who would consider themselves fortunate to have him among them once more for this purpose."[47]

Another consideration also moved Bruno to desire Biancotti's return: his own sense of inadequacy as leader. Bruno told Biancotti that "the one at the head [Bruno himself] is totally other than holy, as all founders generally are, and should be. On the contrary, he is sinful, utterly incapable of anything, without breath, blind, deaf, mute, unable to say even a few words. But perhaps this is necessary so that the Congregation may not seem a human work, but of the Virgin Mary, who is its one Foundress and Superior, and so that we will put our confidence in the teachings of the Gospel alone."[48]

These were humble words from a man of Bruno's spiritual stature—one whose virtue, learning, skill as spiritual guide, and ability in training priests were widely recognized. Among those who had benefitted from Bruno's guidance was the very Biancotti to whom Bruno wrote these words.

But if humble, Bruno was also realistic. He was elderly and physically worn. The task of establishing a new institute and guiding its first steps would be arduous. An experienced religious among the Oblates, a "founder" from the beginnings in Carignano and esteemed by all, appeared a welcome provision for many needs.

Yet this hope, too, would be deceived. Biancotti's initial enthusiasm waned, and he felt his Jesuit calling reaffirmed. In conversation with Fr. Johann Roothaan, now general of the Society, Biancotti declared his desire to remain a Jesuit. On September 10, 1829, Roothaan informed Bruno of Biancotti's decision, and, after three years of discussion, the matter closed.[49]

In the midst of trials, the Oblates pursued their course. Benefactor Francesco Gonella described those troubled days: "Of eight priests who gave their name for this foundation, the death of one and change of resolution of three others left only four remaining as solid and unshakeable pillars on which the building would be established and sustained, and these are the Reverend Father Rector Major Lanteri, the Father Rector Reynaudi, Father Loggero, and Father Ferrero."[50] These four would be enough.

CHAPTER NINETEEN

Pinerolo

> *We can never hope too much;*
> *the one who hopes for every-*
> *thing, obtains everything.*
> —Bruno Lanteri

FRIENDLIER FORCES, HOWEVER, were also at work. In January 1827, Archbishop Lambruschini met with the king to urge approval of the Oblates. He recalled the encounter in his memoirs: "When I reached Turin . . . I shared my thoughts about this matter openly with the King. I showed him that the opposition was not based on reasonable motives, but on frivolous pretexts raised to obstruct a work of the Lord. . . . I added that the King should not deprive himself of the merit he would gain before God by protecting a new Congregation of great spiritual advantage for souls. Finally, I concluded by noting that, after his gracious support of Lanteri before the Pope, the honor itself of His Majesty would be compromised if he did not order quick authorization of the papal bull."[1]

Lambruschini's plea impressed the King: "My words produced a happy effect on the religious heart of the august Monarch. He promised me that he would give, and indeed did give, precise orders in favor of the founder of the Oblates of Mary."[2] In fact, Carlo Felice would direct the senate to sanction *Etsi Dei Filius*, but only months later and after repeated pressure from the Holy See.[3] On June 12, 1827, the senate at last granted legal existence to the Oblates.[4] Nine months had passed since papal approval in Rome, and the final obstacle, it seemed, was overcome.

Yet the senate added a sting to the authorization. It placed two significant restrictions upon the Oblates: they were granted legal residence only within the diocese of Pinerolo, and individual Oblates were prohibited from possessing property.[5] The first condition limited Oblate houses to the small diocese of Pinerolo; the second signified that should a member depart, or should the congregation be legally suppressed—no idle threat, as future decades would reveal—that member would be destitute.

In personal notes, Loggero recorded a conversation regarding this last restriction: "On June 2, the Signor Marquis Massimino . . . said that the Signor Count Gattinara had confided to him that our affair was completed, that is, was entirely approved by the Senate. Lest, however, the Oblates should imagine that they would divide the goods of the Congregation among themselves if it were suppressed, or that they would resume possession of their personal goods were they to leave the Congregation, the Senate made this impossible, so that the government would not be defrauded of its justifiable rights over the goods of the Congregation. He added that this would at least diminish the enthusiasm, and hold back many who otherwise would flock to join the Oblates of the Virgin Mary."[6] The Oblates would soon feel the truth of this prediction.

The granting of legal status in June 1827 was a bittersweet victory. The main point was gained: the Oblates at last could begin life and ministry together. But the constraints were troubling, though Bruno sought to view them with hope. On June 19, he wrote to Archbishop Lambruschini: "In the legal approval there is a restriction to the Diocese of Pinerolo alone, but this can help us to establish the Congregation well in observance of the rule, and to form good members, before expanding to other places. With time, it will be possible to obtain the requisite permissions from our good Sovereign."[7] Bruno recognized that the second restriction "may keep some from entering, in case they should leave [and so remain without financial means]."[8] The only remedy was trust in God: "We will bear this too, and for now adapt ourselves to this as well. As regards the future, God will provide."[9] "In the meantime," Bruno continued, "our consolation could not be greater. . . . At present we are all preparing to gather immediately in Pinerolo."[10]

Now, at sixty-eight, Bruno *began again* for the final time. On July 6, 1827, six Oblates formally entered the congregation in St. Clare's: Bruno, Reynaudi, Loggero, Ferrero, and two religious brothers, Teodoro Romano and Luigi Calosso.[11] The preceding day, Bishop Rey had come to bless a bell donated by Francesco Gonella.[12] On July 6, Rey returned for the formal installation of the Oblates and the blessing of their church. Rey's biographer described the arrival of the bishop at St. Clare's: "The Rector Major (this is the title of the superior of these religious), the Abbé Lanteri, wearing a surplice and accompanied by the members of the community, came before the bishop. When the bishop saw him, he hastened toward him, and, without giving him time to kneel, embraced him tenderly, and with great tenderness spoke to him in words of great devotion and kindness."[13]

The bishop celebrated a solemn Mass in the Oblates' church, "pronouncing during the Mass an eloquent and energetic discourse suited to the occasion."[14] The function concluded with the *Te Deum*, the Church's hymn of thanksgiving, and a blessing with the Holy Eucharist. Oblate life in St. Clare's had begun.

For Bruno, that beginning in Pinerolo also signified the definitive end of his former life. Two years earlier, Roothaan had told the Jesuit general that Bruno's entrance in the Society would require "resolving his affairs, which are many, and his relationships, which are very many."[15] At that time, Bruno was spared a painful parting; this time, he was not. Pinerolo, accessible only by coach and imperfect roads, was far removed from Turin. Relocation to that small city demanded the surrender of all Bruno had cherished in Turin: home, ministry in the nation's capital, deep bonds with friends, places familiar and loved. . . .

That sacrifice, accepted as God's will, gave life to the institution that would transmit his heritage to future generations. Bruno's name and his person, even in old age and infirmity, lent credibility to the Oblates, and won them friends and support. The reverence of all for their rector major strengthened the entire community. Years earlier, Bruno had written that we meditate upon the passion of Jesus "so that when we find ourselves in such circumstances, we may learn and resolve, in imitation of our Divine Master, to gain every victory over ourselves, to sacrifice to God, if necessary, comforts, goods, honors, friends, even life itself."[16] Now Bruno lived what he had written.

SHORTLY AFTER JULY 6, the Oblates made the spiritual exercises as a community.[17] Two months later, at the request of Bishop Rey, they offered the spiritual exercises for priests in St. Clare's. Thirty-four priests, twenty-eight from the diocese of Pinerolo and six from the Archdiocese of Turin, entered the Oblate house on September 12 to begin the days of retreat.[18] As so often, Reynaudi and Loggero preached the exercises.[19] The following spring, in April 1828, the Oblates offered a first retreat for laity in St. Clare's; again Reynaudi and Loggero preached.[20] The congregation continued this practice in subsequent years: each fall, it offered a retreat for priests in St. Clare's, and, each spring, another for laity.[21]

After a halt of four months, travels throughout Piedmont for parish missions and retreats now resumed. Reynaudi and Loggero preached to the priests of Mondovì in August, and to the Ursuline sisters of Alessandria in September. In October, Reynaudi and Ferrero conducted a retreat for the priests of Alexandria, and a parish mission for laity in the cathedral of the same city. Together they preached a parish mission in Monforte in November . . . and the rhythm of parish missions and retreats continued.[22] During the last five months of 1827, the Oblates gave eight parish missions and retreats; in 1828, nineteen; and in 1829, twenty-five.[23]

Their intense labor elicited a counsel from Bruno's friend, Carlo Daverio: "I am happy to hear that Fr. Loggero has recovered his health. Forgive me if I beg you to recommend, on my behalf as well, both to him and to the others, a great moderation in their labors at least in the first years, so that the Congregation may gain new members and set down solid roots. Such overwork can *give scandal*, that is, it may also cause those who might have wished to enter to feel apprehensive and intimidated, fearing that they will be obliged to undertake such grueling labors."[24]

The Oblates welcomed individual retreatants in St. Clare's, and guided their prayer. In August 1828, layman Count Massa di San Biagio, unable to attend a retreat near Turin, asked his pastor where he might make the exercises. The priest "encouraged me to approach Your Reverence [Bruno], assuring me that I might make my retreat at any time, individually, in the house of these Oblate religious."[25]

In reply, Bruno told Massa di San Biagio of the group retreats in St. Clare's, and added: "With regard, then, to particular individuals who desire to make the exercises in other times of the year, at present we do not have enough members to give talks to each individual, because we are few, and generally those few are traveling constantly for the exercises in parishes or retreat houses in different cities when we are invited."[26] "Consequently," Bruno wrote, "if anyone is willing to make the retreat privately with the help of books we supply for this purpose, and under the direction of one of the priests, we willingly welcome such persons into our house for retreats of this kind."[27] Should this be acceptable, "you could arrive at our residence on the morning of the 16th, and begin in the evening. I would ask only that you let us know beforehand if you wish such a retreat. Ordinarily the exercises last for ten days."[28] On August 11, Massa di San Biagio replied that he very willingly accepted the offer.[29]

Constance de Maistre, laywoman and daughter of Joseph de Maistre, likewise made an individual retreat in St. Clare's. On January 23, 1827, Reynaudi notified Bruno that "Mademoiselle [de] Maistre has begun her exercises."[30] Five days later, Reynaudi wrote of "the work begun with Mademoiselle [de] Maistre who is most edifying," and who "is peaceful."[31] Finally, on January 30, as the retreat was concluding: "Every day I visit Mademoiselle [de] Maistre, who is about to finish her exercises. She is well, and seems tranquil in spirit. She profits from every moment in which she is free to enjoy the solitude, and the presence of God. I find her very edifying. I will see her after lunch today, as I hope."[32]

The Oblates labored in Pinerolo and beyond, as Bishop Rey's biographer attested: "At his [Rey's] invitation, they opened their

Constance de Maistre, daughter of Joseph de Maistre.

house to laymen who desired to make retreats. They went into the prisons to console, instruct, and bring back to God the unhappy persons whom crime had brought to those places; and they evangelized the rural areas."[33] Bishop Rey thanked God for "these tireless laborers whose devotion and charity know no bounds."[34]

In May 1829, friend of the Oblates Francesco Gonella wrote to Cardinal Pacca: "As the work of the Congregation advances, and the prudence, selflessness, and tireless zeal of the Oblates of the Virgin Mary are increasingly revealed, there is none who does not admire the immense labors of these priests who are accustomed, during the Holy Exercises, to spend fifteen and even sixteen hours between the day and part of the night, in preaching and hearing confessions. Preconceived prejudices against them disappear, and many calumniators of their [Alphonsian] moral theology grow silent as they see before their eyes the fruitfulness of the loving and tender welcome they offer sinners, to win their conversion. This approach works marvels among the people who, at their arrival, flock in great numbers to hear their preaching."[35] Initial trials and limited numbers did not diminish the Oblates' ardor, and their apostolic impact widened.

A PAGE COMPOSED IN 1827 manifests Bruno's unceasing application to the spiritual life.[36] To the end, Bruno sought spiritual growth, and did so in the manner long practiced: concrete proposals, some focused on personal progress and others on his new service as superior.

Bruno sought "exactness with respect to the Rule," and primarily in his meditation and spiritual reading.[37] For both practices, Bruno chose the writings of classic Jesuit authors: Huby, Bellecio, Pinamonti, Rodriguez, and Hayneuve.[38] After decades of faithful and deepening prayer, Bruno continued to *prepare* that prayer with texts of substance.

He planned to reserve "a half-hour every day before the Blessed Sacrament to consider my own spiritual growth, the greater good of the Congregation, and of each member."[39] The Eucharist remained the center, and daily reflection before the Blessed Sacrament would assist his key tasks: personal spiritual progress, care for the congregation, and attention to each member. Thirty years earlier, Bruno had dedicated one morning each week "to reflecting on how to promote the cause of God, of my soul, and of my neighbor."[40] A similar reflection was now to accompany his role as superior.

In all things, Bruno desired to seek Jesus: "Whatever happens independently of my doing, I will accept from the paternal hand of my Jesus as permitted for my good. Everything that does depend on my own will, which can accomplish nothing without the help of God, I will do together with my good Jesus, profiting from his help not only in the order of nature, but also of grace."[41]

Bruno named the virtues he would pursue: humility, gentleness, and confidence. In the new setting of community life, Bruno's quest for gentleness continued. His remaining years would witness the struggles and fruit of that quest. Bruno then summarized these three virtues in two simple words, "Love. Love."[42] In a final resolution, he proposed a monthly day of retreat and a monthly "conference on promoting the good of the Congregation."[43]

Such notes testify to Bruno's persevering search for spiritual growth, and his lifelong commitment to prayer. They highlight unchanging characteristics of his spiritual life: preparation, method, fidelity, reflection, unwavering pursuit of progress, and, above all, desire for Jesus. If he was "a watchdog in the flock of the Lord who cries out to his last breath," he was also a disciple of Jesus who sought the Lord he loved until his physical energy failed.

IN THE FALL OF 1827, Bruno returned briefly to Turin.[44] As the visit was ending, he met for a final time with his spiritual son and collaborator Luigi Guala. Sorrow filled the parting of these two, who for decades had worked so closely together. Bruno's departure from Turin left Guala, as he would later recount, feeling alone and afraid.[45] The two entered into conversation. As they spoke, suddenly, to their mutual surprise and dismay, a sharp dispute arose between them.[46]

Two months earlier, a certain Teresa Quey had died, and had willed her estate to the Oblates.[47] She had asked that her two servants, Giuseppina and Catarina, be assisted according to their needs. Giuseppina was now seriously ill.[48] As Bruno and Guala spoke, Guala mentioned various details of the will, supposing them unknown to Bruno.[49] In Guala's words, however, Bruno perceived a doubt that he intended to fulfill Quey's requests.[50] The conversation disturbed both, and burdened an already sorrowful parting.

After his return to Pinerolo, Bruno wrote to Guala about the dispute. Pain and desire to reaffirm his affection for Guala led Bruno to unusual self-revelation. Bruno first defended his fidelity to Quey's wishes: "I left Turin deeply afflicted and with much pain on account of the struggle between us, the basis of which I do not know, since I think I have always sufficiently shown that I had, and will always have, full readiness to assist the two servants. In confirmation of this, I think you know that when Giuseppina fell ill, I sent them 100 Lire [the sum requested for the significant expenses involved] without even asking whether there was any need, and without desiring any receipt. In addition, I had given the Signor Advocate Rossi freedom to give them as much as they requested, and I never asked any account of this, or anything in writing."[51] Bruno drew the conclusion: "It seems to me that this is the only matter about which any dispute was possible, and I see nothing in it for which I might blame myself."[52]

Bruno welcomed Guala's further observations: "Still, I beg that you be willing to continue to offer me your suggestions, since I am ready to accept anything that is just, reasonable, and fitting. May God keep me from opposing in the slightest detail the intentions of the poor deceased woman."[53]

Bruno then addressed what he considered the root of their struggle: "If, however, I am to say what I think, the true cause of a dispute of such energy between us was sorrow at the parting that was to take place that day, because I know your great affection for me, and especially because a deep melancholy suddenly came upon you in that moment."[54] A personal observation followed:

"Dearly beloved, the heartfelt affection I have and have always had for you, is indeed very great, and certainly does not leave me indifferent to this separation. But because God's greater glory and the salvation of souls must be our one concern, for this we must always be ready to sacrifice to God even the things most dear."[55]

Conscious of Guala's sorrow, Bruno opened his heart to his spiritual son: "I assure you that, in addition to the sacrifices I too must make, the task alone that I am undertaking fills me with fear, and sometimes oppresses me so much that I am forced to beg from my heart for the help of the Lord and Mary Most Holy, in order not to succumb, and I must exercise [Abraham's] hope against hope. But since God's will in this seems clear, I can only bow my head and try not to resist him, but rather give him what he asks with a good heart, and with more of my heart in the measure that it costs me more, and even to give this with good grace, since God loves a cheerful giver [2 Cor 9:7]."[56] The cost of Bruno's role as founder and superior, his firm conviction that God willed this of him, his fear, his struggle, and his "hope against hope" emerge in this uncharacteristically personal passage.

Bruno offered heartfelt counsel to Guala: "I beg you, then, from my heart, to be careful not to give in to melancholy, which the enemy always seeks to insinuate, confident that the Lord does not let himself be outdone in generosity."[57] Bruno then concluded: "Let us always remain closely united in the Lord. I do not doubt that you will continue to give me your affection, and I assure you that I too will always hold you in my heart. Pray much for me, and I embrace you warmly in the Sacred Heart of Jesus."[58] In this letter, Bruno wrote to Guala as his collaborator, but more as his spiritual son, affirming his integrity regarding Quey's will, sharing his understanding of Guala's melancholy, revealing his personal burdens, calling Guala to a vision of faith, and declaring his unshakeable affection.

Four days later, Guala replied. After the salutation, "Most Reverend and most gracious Father in Jesus Christ," Guala expressed his view of the dispute: "I never thought that Your Most Beloved Reverence would fail to fulfill the will of the deceased. I only wished to inform you of the promises made, and because I thought that not all of this was known to you. To doubt your readiness to fulfill her requests would be to do Your Reverence an unquestionable and serious wrong. To hear myself suddenly accused of this was troubling for me, especially in such circumstances, and as we were about to part: a parting deeply painful in itself and for various reasons, seeing myself left alone, and because of the fear that accompanies this parting, made more bitter by a coldness I had done nothing to merit. This is what I recall."[59]

Guala, too, shared his heart: "It seems to me, however, that the Lord is glorified by this, because I constantly remember to pray for the Congregation, and especially for Your Reverence, whose situation causes me great pain. I feel this deeply not only in my heart, but also in my imagination, and this disturbs me greatly when I celebrate Mass and hear confessions. I continue to ask the Lord to enlighten you and strengthen you, and I am offering Masses for Your Reverence. After your departure, my melancholy indeed did grow, and your words, that you will always keep me in your heart, were a timely balm; you were already always held in mine. These words remain warmly engraved in my heart, and I thank you sincerely for them."[60]

The sorrow of separation and mutual misunderstanding led two friends to a painful dispute. Each felt wrongly accused by the other, and the parting left both troubled. Bruno communicated quickly to resolve the discord. He defended his integrity regarding Quey's will, and assured Guala of his continuing affection. To help Guala cope with the grief of separation, Bruno shared his own struggles, and offered spiritual counsel. In reply, Guala too defended his good intentions, and reaffirmed his regard for Bruno.

Both continued to express affection in subsequent communication. Two months later, on December 13, 1827, Carlo Daverio wrote to Bruno from Turin: "The Theologian Guala ... was deeply touched by Your Paternity's heartfelt words in his regard, and he asked me most sincerely to express the same sentiments to you."[61] In December 1829, Guala concluded a letter to Bruno with a request: "Please continue to ask others to pray for me, that all these things be for the glory of the Lord, and, in the chapel near your room, remember me often before the Lord. I think of you with the greatest affection, and renew my best wishes in the Sacred Hearts of Jesus and Mary."[62] Guala signed himself Bruno's "servant and son in Jesus Christ."[63]

For Bruno, such trips to Turin were rare. His life now centered on the Oblates in Pinerolo and their mission. For them and for that mission, he would spend his remaining strength.

CHAPTER TWENTY

"His Shadow Is Enough"

Of myself I can do nothing good,
but I can do all things in God.
—Bruno Lanteri

NEW MEMBERS NOW JOINED Bruno and his first companions. Though not all remained, the community grew steadily. Among the fresh arrivals was Michele Valmino, who entered in December 1827.[1] Valmino was from Carignano, a former soldier who, after losing his faith, had reembraced it through the Oblates' ministry. He would be a faithful Oblate and key witness to Bruno's final days.

That same December, twenty-year-old Giovanni Battista Isnardi entered; he would serve as fourth rector major of the congregation.[2] In June 1829, twenty-one-year-old Pietro Gardetti joined the Oblates as a religious brother.[3] Gardetti would assist Bruno in his last months and, with singular efficacy, transmit the memory of those days. The following year, Giovanni Battista Biancotti, nephew of the Antonio Biancotti whose choice to remain a Jesuit had saddened Bruno, entered the community.[4] He would succeed Isnardi as fifth rector major of the Oblates.

On February 2, 1828, the feast of the Purification of Mary, Bruno and six others formally vested the Oblate habit.[5] The following August 15, the feast of the Assumption of Mary, Bruno pronounced his vows as an Oblate, and received those of Reynaudi, Loggero, and Ferrero.[6] One further Oblate professed vows in 1828, and seven in 1829.[7]

Two years after the beginnings in St. Clare's, Oblate friend Francesco Gonella wrote to Cardinal Pacca: "The Lord . . . has raised up . . . men of merit, of virtue, and of great promise, who

213

Fr. Giovanni Battista Reynaudi.

have asked to join. In addition to the four founders named above [Bruno, Reynaudi, Loggero, Ferrero], there are at present in the Congregation another six members in vows, four novices, and six brothers, a total of twenty members, whose perfect community life, fervor in the observance of the rule, commitment to study to obtain the goal of the institute, and loving brotherly union, edify and awaken the admiration of all who come to know this Congregation."[8] The Oblates were establishing roots and growing.

BRUNO'S ENERGIES, HOWEVER, were waning. During his two-year quest for papal and civil approval, Bruno had traveled, consulted, written, and acted with remarkable energy and decision. Now that activity diminished. Bruno remained the moral leader of the Oblates and their rector major, esteemed and consulted by all. For administration, however, he increasingly depended on Loggero as secretary, and on supporters in Turin, in particular Carlo Daverio and Francesco Gonella. Bruno was aging and growing weaker.[9]

Friends repeatedly expressed their concern. On February 10, 1828, Bishop Rey wrote emphatically: "Take care of your health, *I order you*. This is the one serious command I wish to give you."[10] In December of that year, Carlo Daverio urged Bruno to "take care of your health, and dismiss any scruples that would hinder you from doing this."[11] On December 28, reversing their habitual roles, Sr. Crocifissa wrote from Genoa: "Please give me news of your health, and try to use all the means that can help you. I heard from Fr. Loggero that you are very weak. Try to take some substantial broth with contents that will give you a bit of strength and fortify you. . . . Do not observe community life in everything because your age does not permit it, and in all communities there are always exceptions for those who are older, and those who are physically weak. And so, try to use the helps that you need, so that you can set the new Congregation solidly on its path, and guide it safely to its port. If the Congregation is established well, it will give great glory to God and work great good for souls."[12]

Luisa di Baldissero, whom Bruno had guided spiritually for years, expressed similar sentiments: "It troubles me greatly to learn that your health is continually weak, and also, if I may dare to say it, that you do not take proper care of it at all. Consider, Monsieur, that your life is necessary both to your new Congregation and to many other persons who, though they live at a distance, find peace in knowing they can consult you, and have recourse to you. If you hasten so to enter *in Patria* [into the eternal fatherland], you abandon your spiritual children, and, forgive me the expression, this would be a kind of selfishness."[13]

Though physically weakened, Bruno continued to serve as the center and inspiring force of the new congregation. On May 23, 1829, Francesco Gonella advised Cardinal Pacca that "the Father Rector Major Lanteri's health is very weak, and he is burdened by a most painful oppression [of the chest]. That is why he has not written in his own hand to Your Eminence, and why he asked me to beg you to accept his excuses. His shadow, however, is enough for the Congregation, which hopes and prays that so zealous, learned, and devout a founder be conserved for it at length."[14] Two years earlier, Roothaan had characterized the elderly Bruno's life as "precious, indeed of inestimable value." His aging presence remained incalculably precious for his Oblates and for others in the Church.

Many continued to ask Bruno's aid. Some wrote for spiritual or material assistance. Others requested retreats. Still others sought counsel regarding books, or assistance in promoting Alphonsian moral teaching.[15] Bruno's response grew slow and labored. Yet the ministry progressed, no longer simply his, but now of an institute founded to promote these works.

On June 19, 1827, the French priest Félicité de Lamennais, of European-wide fame, visited Bruno in Pinerolo. The following day, Bruno related the encounter to Loggero: "Yesterday morning we had a visit from the Signor Abbé Lamennais. The Reverend Signor Canon Vicar General chose to come with him, and remained with him throughout. They were here more than two hours. He had to leave again yesterday after lunch for Turin, where he said he would remain another two weeks, and did not plan to return here."[16] It was a sober account of a meeting with one whose then brilliant career would end unhappily.[17]

Letters from Constance de Maistre reveal the continuing concern and affection for Bruno of the de Maistre family. On March 12, 1828, rejoicing in the growth of the Oblates, Constance wrote to Bruno: "Nothing less than the sight of your fruitful fatherhood [in Pinerolo] can console us for the emptiness you left behind you in Turin. My family feels your absence in a special way, and we miss you greatly for our mother's sake; you were the only one who could curb her penances, and since your departure she sets no limits to them."[18] Elsewhere Constance described Bruno's guidance of her mother, Francesca: "The Signora, my mother, was a holy woman, and given to rigorous penance. No one could restrain her on this path except the Abate Lanteri, founder of the Oblates of the Virgin Mary. That holy man had full authority over her, and, with regard to penances, kept her firmly within limits. But when the Theologian [Bruno] died . . . my mother followed her impulse to do great penances, and continued doing them to the end of her life."[19]

Two months later, on May 10, Constance replied to a letter from Bruno: "You caused me much pain, my Reverend Father, when you told me in your last letter that your health was poor during the winter. I am afraid that the climate of Pinerolo is not good for you. Should we lose you, we would experience a double sorrow [loss of Bruno's presence in Turin, loss of his life]. Let me hope that the better weather will permit you to make a brief trip to Turin. We would rejoice greatly to see you again, and would express to you in person a great truth: that nothing can add to the sentiments of veneration and affection for you of each member of this family."[20]

Bruno did not visit Turin, however, and, on December 1, Constance gently questioned him: "Summer has given way to autumn, and autumn to winter, without seeing you appear in the capital [Turin], my Reverend Father. Now the cold and bad weather are here, and we must renounce the hope of a visit from you until the birds return. Is it courage you lack, or is it physical strength? I would prefer it were courage, so that instead of being afflicted by the weakening of your precious health, I would have only to reproach you for a little too much love of your cherished solitude."[21]

Constance concluded her letter: "Mother and all the others in the family ask you to remember them, and present their respects."[22]

In 1829 Turinese publisher Giacinto Marietti issued a work entitled *The Spiritual Exercises of St. Ignatius of Loyola with a Directory for a Fruitful Use of These Exercises, and Several Annotations Regarding Them*. The book did not name its author. The inclusion in it of Bruno's *Directory for the Exercises of St. Ignatius* confirms his at least partial role in producing this volume.[23]

Decades earlier, Bruno had composed this directory as a guide for those preparing to give the Exercises.[24] Now, as his end drew near, Bruno offered his directory to a wider public. The Spiritual Exercises are, Bruno wrote, "*in general*, a most powerful instrument of Divine Grace for the reform of the entire world, and, *in particular*, a sure method for all to become saints, great saints, and quickly."[25] Well made, the Exercises awaken solid dispositions of holiness; one need only persevere on this path.

As BRUNO SETTLED in Pinerolo, change continued in the Church and Europe. On February 10, 1829, Pope Leo XII died. From Turin, where travels for retreats had taken him, Reynaudi informed Bruno: "Although it is with great sorrow, I believe it my duty to announce to you the death of the Holy Father, Leo XII, which occurred last Tuesday. I was told that the news was brought here by the special coach for Paris."[26] On March 31, Cardinal Francesco Saverio Castiglioni was elected pope and took the name Pius VIII. He would reign only twenty-one months, the last pope during Bruno's lifetime.

On July 9, Johann Roothaan was elected general of the Jesuits. Bruno and Roothaan exchanged letters a final time in September. Bruno asked the new general that he "continue to show to me and to the Congregation the affection and protection we so greatly value."[27]

In France, resistance to King Charles X intensified. Revolution and the end of centuries-old Bourbon rule were nearing. As so often in his lifetime, Bruno's final days too would witness political turmoil in Europe.

BECAUSE HE WAS NOW LIVING IN COMMUNITY, Bruno's personal life was more visible than before. The Oblates witnessed his words and actions, and recorded them. Among these witnesses was Michele Valmino, who entered St. Clare's in 1827 at the age of forty-four.[28]

Asked in subsequent years to relate his memories of Bruno, Valmino told of Bruno's prayer before the Eucharist: "The Reverend Father Lanteri was deeply devoted to the Blessed Sacrament, and therefore desired that it always be reserved in the internal chapel of this house in Pinerolo. The chapel was adjacent to his room, and, that he might adore the Lord more frequently, especially in time of illness, he had a small window made in his room through which he could see the altar of this chapel. Through that window, he adored the Lord almost continually in his last illness, since the window was situated directly in front of his bed."[29]

Valmino continued: "During his last illness, as long as he was able, he received the Eucharist daily, and with great consolation. As regards Holy Mass, he celebrated it daily with much devotion, and I do not recall that he ever failed to celebrate it unless he was gravely ill. Rather, one morning, some time before his last illness, though he was so ill that he could hardly stand, he wanted nevertheless to celebrate Mass. But when he reached the epistle [first reading], he collapsed, and it was necessary to divest him of the sacred vestments, and take him back to his room."[30]

Valmino related a personal experience: "He liked very much to hear others speak to him about this adorable Mystery [the Eucharist]. In this regard, I remember that once I was in his room, and he was seated at a small table. He had me read aloud various passages from St. Thomas [Aquinas] concerning this Mystery. After I had read for some time, I turned toward where he was seated to ask him something, and I saw the joy in his face, lit with a lively reddish color. It made a great impression on me because I had never seen him like this before."[31]

Others, too, witnessed Bruno's love for the Eucharist. Twenty-one-year-old Pietro Gardetti, a lay brother, later recounted: "Before going to bed I would pass by his room to ask him if he wanted anything. At times he would ask for some help, at times for nothing, telling me that he was greatly consoled because the Holy Father had granted him the grace [given canonical permission] of having the Blessed Sacrament close to him."[32]

Antonio Ferrero, one of the original eight and Bruno's confessor in his last months, described the brief prayers that Bruno frequently directed to Jesus in the Eucharist: *Jesu Bone sitio te* (Good Jesus, I thirst for you), or, more succinctly, *Sitio, sitio* (I thirst, I thirst).[33] Bruno turned to Mary with a similar prayer: *Beatissima Virgo Maria satia me* (Most Blessed Virgin, satisfy my heart).[34]

Ferrero testified to Bruno's lifelong devotion to Mary. As noted earlier in this account, Bruno, bereft of his mother when four years old, one day told Ferrero that "I have hardly known any other mother than her [the Virgin Mary]."[35] Ferrero wrote: "He loved the Virgin Mary deeply, and surrounded himself with images of her. He kept a precious collection of books that speak of her, and read from them for a few hours every week. He celebrated her novenas [in preparation for the principal Marian feasts], and spoke very often about her. He said that it was not enough simply to inspire devotion for her in others, but that it was necessary to lead them to a great confidence in her. Whenever the Exercises were given, he wanted a talk preached on her. He spoke of her as his mother, as the one who nurtured him, and as his paradise."[36]

In Mary, Bruno found the feminine tenderness taken too soon from him as a child. In her, he found warmth, gentleness, and hope. Mary was his mother, his lady, his model, the teacher and principal foundress of the Oblates.[37] Bruno told Ferrero that "in all my life, I have never received anything but caresses from this mother so filled with goodness."[38] One secret, perhaps, of Bruno's remarkable ability to persevere in pain and darkness is found in the Marian "caresses" which eased the pain and lightened the darkness.

In addition to the Eucharist, Valmino related, "he also spoke with great pleasure about other spiritual things. At times, when he was too weak to walk as much as his health required, if one of us began a conversation about such things, he would gain strength a little at a time, and be able to continue the walk."[39] Bruno, Valmino recorded, "did not speak of these things to show his learning, or to be thought a spiritual person, but rather because he spoke of that which formed the principal object of his thoughts, and was, in short, the treasure on which his heart was set."[40]

Valmino described a trait of Bruno's conversation that he admired. Much younger than Bruno, a former soldier and once a non-practicing Catholic, Valmino personally experienced this quality in Bruno: "I remember having observed many times, both when he was healthy and when he was ill, that he not only tolerated that I, who knew nothing and was not spiritual at all, should speak to him of spiritual things, or try with some spiritual maxim to help him accept God's will, but even showed a true and cordial pleasure in this. And when I sometimes recognized my temerity, and asked him to bear with me if I presumed to instruct Minerva [Roman goddess of wisdom], he replied with goodness, 'It is true that these are things we know, but it is always good and useful to have them called to mind.'"[41]

Valmino added a personal reflection: "This is one of the things that has always given me great esteem for the virtue of that holy man, since we generally listen to others speak of spiritual things, and accept exhortations to bear what God wills, and to live virtuously, if those who speak are learned or holy persons; but to listen patiently and with pleasure to such words and exhortations from ignorant or unspiritual persons, can only be done by those who are rooted in virtue."[42]

Valmino recalled a teaching Bruno frequently repeated: "Regarding the spiritual maxims most familiar to him, I only remember one that he repeated to me often. It concerned God's presence, and is this: that in every action we perform or every difficulty we encounter, it is very helpful to imagine God present to us, 1. observing how we conduct ourselves in that action or in that difficulty; 2. assisting us with his grace; 3. preparing a reward for us in proportion to the merit we will have gained. *Spectator est. Adiutor est. Remunerator est* [God sees. God assists. God rewards]."[43] In fact, Bruno proposed these words of St. Augustine to his Oblates as an aid to remembering God throughout the day.[44] Clearly, in repeating them to Valmino, Bruno was reflecting his own effort to live constantly in God's presence.[45]

THE YEAR 1829 also brought Bruno times of consolation. In July, his friend Bishop Carlo Sappa de' Milanesi came to visit. In their conversation, the subject of Alphonsus Liguori, whom the bishop also esteemed highly, arose. Gardetti recalled that day and Bruno's joy in the hope that Blessed Alphonsus Liguori might soon be canonized: "He often said, 'Oh, how happy I am that this great saint may well be canonized soon.' "[46] Gardetti continued: "I know that one time Bishop Sappa, the bishop of Acqui, came to visit Fr. Lanteri in Pinerolo, and stayed for lunch with the community. After lunch, they went walking together in the interior garden, and spoke at length about this canonization of Blessed Alphonsus. Fr. Lanteri showed extraordinary consolation in the hope that a time he so desired might come soon."[47]

In all likelihood, Sappa de' Milanesi's visit was to be the final meeting of the two friends. Pope Gregory XVI would canonize St. Alphonsus ten years later, in 1839, an act that would sanction Bruno's lifelong promotion of Alphonsus's teaching. Further confirmation would be added in 1871, when Pius IX declared St. Alphonsus a doctor of the Church.

On October 6, 1829, the Oblate community celebrated Bruno's saint's day. The event strikingly manifested the veneration of both the Oblates and Bishop Rey for Bruno. Without word to Bruno, Bishop Rey had been invited to the celebration. Gardetti recalled that festive occasion: "On the day of St. Bruno in 1829, Bishop Rey was invited to dinner without informing Fr. Lanteri. At that time, there was only one table in the refectory because the family was still small, with only twenty-two members, including the religious brothers. The bishop and the whole family were in the refectory waiting for Fr. Lanteri to arrive, and the bishop bent down behind the large chair so that Fr. Lanteri would not see him. When Fr. Lanteri began the blessing, the bishop stood up and embraced Fr. Lanteri. It was for Lanteri a moment of inexpressible consolation. The bishop said the rest of the blessing, and we shared the

Bruno Lanteri, Rector Major of the Oblates of the Virgin Mary (painting by Amedeo Augero).

meal with great consolation for the entire little family. I, as the least of the brothers and of the family, sat at the base of the table, almost facing the bishop."[48]

That same day, Ferrero wrote to Loggero, absent preaching a retreat: "Oh, what a wonderful celebration this was for us today!"[49] Bruno, he told Loggero, "is very happy. . . . We are well, happy, and healthy, and we have everything except paradise and the eternal enjoyment of God."[50] It was a day of great consolation for Bruno and joy for the bishop and Oblates united around him. It was the last saint's day Bruno would celebrate.

CHAPTER TWENTY-ONE

"The Lamp Is Going Out"

> Our Father who art in heaven,
> *see before you one of your sons,*
> *who places himself in your hands,*
> *and gives you his heart.*
>
> —Bruno Lanteri

TWO LETTERS OF A LAYMAN to his wife offer a privileged window into Bruno's final active months. The writer was Michele di Cavour, father of renowned Italian statesman Camillo di Cavour. On February 24, 1829, Michele wrote to Bruno and asked admission to the spring retreat for laity in St. Clare's.[1] He was accepted, one of thirty-six laymen who lodged in the Oblate residence during the Spiritual Exercises.[2] External retreatants, both men and women, joined them in church for the talks. On this occasion, too, Reynaudi and Loggero preached.[3] The Exercises lasted eight full days, opening the evening of Saturday, April 18, and closing on the morning of Monday, April 27.

At 5:30 in the morning on the second day, Michele wrote to his wife, Adèle: "My room looks out on the side of Superga [near Turin], and, at this hour, after having thought about God, I think of you. This life of retreat seems to suit me in everything. In the first place, by inclination I prefer to obey rather than command; here the obedience is to a man who is most gentle [Bruno]. The body receives all it needs; I feel better here than at Vaudier [France], and I sense that the time here will do me more good than that spent in Vaudier. There is also physical exercise, since we go to the church ten times during the day; ten times, therefore, that I think more especially of all of you."[4]

Michele expressed his esteem of Reynaudi as a preacher: "We have one of the most distinguished orators I have heard, Don Reynaudi. He is recovering from a congestion of the chest, and preaches three extended meditations every day."[5] Michele likewise shared his impressions of Bruno: "The superior, Father Lanteri, is very gentle. His health could not be worse, but I prefer to speak with him because he assisted grandmother, whose final moments are constantly present to my memory. My room is next to his, and I talk with him during the two hours of recreation after lunch and after supper. The rest of the time we are in silence, and I continue to welcome it."[6] That Cavour, in choosing a single quality to characterize Bruno, should highlight his gentleness, suggests that Bruno's lifelong quest for this virtue was not in vain.

Cavour concluded: "Goodbye, my tender Adèle, my good mother, my dear Franquin, and my children. I will pray for you, and will contribute to your happiness by gaining interior peace. I embrace you all."[7]

Two days later, Michele again wrote to Adèle: "I received your letter. It is the rule that during these ten days we should suspend all correspondence foreign to the great work with which we are to occupy ourselves. For that very reason, the superiors permit letters that, rather than distract from that purpose, reinforce, fortify, and encourage it. I have not replied to you with my pen, because I had more important occupations; but I have replied to you with my heart, because God does not forbid that I join to the idea to drawing close to him, that of being united with you in an eternity of glorifying, blessing, and thanking him for having created us."[8] The impact of talks on St. Ignatius's Principle and Foundation—the eternal purpose for which God created human beings—is evident in Michele's words.[9]

Bishop Rey, too, participated in the retreat: "The bishop attends some of the meditations. He has preached a little, but it is not at all necessary, because Don Reynaudi is as eloquent as he, in my view. He [Rey] is a well-educated man, who has traveled a great deal."[10] Michele then described his hosts: "The Oblates are a branch of the Jesuits; they follow St. Ignatius. They hold that benign doctrine that allows us to hope that God in his mercy will receive the people of all religions who have served him according to the natural law and with great love for what is good."[11] And his further impressions of Bruno: "For myself, I can tell you that I am very happy with the Abbé Lanteri. I have spent much time with him. I find him gentle, persuasive, and, above all, most considerate. God gives him much light to understand and explain things very well."[12] A lifetime of prayer, study, ministry, and pursuit of spiritual growth had shaped Bruno as a man of warmth, alive to God's inspirations and proficient as a spiritual guide.

The following morning, Michele added a postscript: "I received your letter, and mother's. I have a chance now to reply, and am sending what I had already written. I shed tears this morning. The meditation last evening inspired fear: eternity. That of this morning was most warm: the prodigal son, the return of the soul to God."[13]

Then, with respect to Bruno: "I was deeply stirred when I received your letter. I had gone to the Abbé Lanteri to ask permission to read it. I found him physically worse than other days. He said, 'Read as much as you wish, the sentiments of the heart are pleasing to God'; but tears were falling from his eyes, he could scarcely breathe. 'The lamp is going out,' he said. His whole being was at peace. He looks to heaven during his attacks and pronounces the word 'paradise' with so much faith, that it stirs everything within me."[14] Bruno had long prepared for death, and had long desired eternal union with God. Now his heart turned increasingly to that release from pain and that unending blessedness in which he firmly believed, and for which he greatly hoped.

Michele continued: "He did not wish to have any other penitent than me. One of the priests brought him a note from a person who asked to speak with him. Looking at me, he replied, 'I have only a little breath, I am reserving it for you.' The priest replied in a firm and half-severe voice: 'If God has permitted that a second soul should ask for you, he has also chosen to give you enough breath to lead that soul to himself.' It is blessed, my Adèle, to shed such tears! I shed many at those words. I do not believe that the

Abbé Lanteri is so close to his end."[15] At such cost to himself, Bruno continued to serve.

The memory of those days endured in Cavour's heart. Two weeks after the retreat, he wrote to Bruno: "I have delayed too long in thanking Your Reverence for your many courtesies toward me when I made the exercises. . . . I cannot find words for the good I received from these holy exercises. I will remember them forever."[16] In January of the following year, Cavour expressed similar sentiments: "The memory of those days spent in solitude has not disappeared from my thoughts. To them I owe a great sense of peace, and I hope to return for more like them."[17]

On Christmas 1829, Bruno celebrated the three Masses permitted to a priest.[18] Cavour learned of this and rejoiced: "How happy I was to hear that Your Reverence was able to celebrate your three Masses on the most holy day of Christmas. May heaven conserve you for an Institute of such great spiritual value as is yours, and for us all."[19] With the opening of the new year, however, Bruno's capacity for even limited activity declined.

In early January 1830, Bruno sent New Year's greetings to several Oblate benefactors. More than greetings, his letters seemed almost a final sharing of the heart, and the warmth of his words moved the recipients. On January 10, Carlo Daverio replied: "You cannot imagine the great consolation your last letter gave me, both because of the heartfelt sentiments you expressed toward me, which I have never doubted, and of which I have always been fully convinced; and because of the assurance you give me that you know the deeply tender affection with which I return your own, and will always return it, and that you know my unshakeable readiness to assist the Congregation."[20]

Three days later, Archbishop Lambruschini likewise answered: "The deeply affectionate and warm letter Your Reverence wrote on January 3, expressing such goodness and love for me, could not have been more appreciated and welcome to my heart. I thank you from the depths of my heart for this."[21] On January 19, Cardinal Pacca replied from Rome: "I know that the good wishes you extended to me for the New Year are not a mere formality, but come from a sincere heart that bears me affection."[22] Pacca signed his letter, "With great affection and readiness to serve you, your friend, Bartolomeo Cardinal Pacca."[23]

In February 1830, Bruno's health worsened, and then improved. On February 21, Loggero informed diocesan priest Carlo Calosso: "The Theologian Lanteri today began to rise a little from bed."[24] Two days later, Don Agostino Golzio asked Loggero to share with Bruno "my most sincere rejoicing for the recovery of his precious health."[25] Throughout his illness, Bruno's many friends in Turin and the clergy of the Priestly Residence prayed for his recovery.[26]

On March 19, the feast of St. Joseph, Bruno celebrated Mass. Novice Pietro Gardetti remembered that day: "For some time, he had not been able to celebrate Holy Mass because of his great weakness. One day he told me that he hoped to celebrate it on the day of St. Joseph. On the day of St. Joseph, he began the Mass and continued until he read the Gospel. After that, he rested for a short while seated on a chair. Then he continued to the end, and told me that St. Joseph had given him the grace he desired."[27]

Nine days later, Ferrero wrote to Loggero, absent with Reynaudi for a parish mission: "The Reverend Father Rector Major continues to say Mass daily and to come to dinner in the refectory. He asks for your prayers."[28] Before sending the letter, however, Ferrero added more sobering news: "The Reverend Father Rector Major has not been well since this morning. He was seized by a tremor throughout his whole body. He came to dinner, but with very great difficulty, and, with extreme difficulty, was almost carried back to his room. They think he is having contractions. If things worsen, I will let you know immediately."[29]

On March 30, Ferrero again wrote to Loggero: "The Reverend Father Rector Major is no longer in any danger. He rises for a few hours every day. For the rest, he desires to see you both, so that, once the exercises have finished, you would do well to return straight to Pinerolo."[30]

In early April, Holy Week arrived. Gardetti recalled two events of those special days. "On Palm Sunday," he wrote, "Fr. Valmino celebrated Holy Mass in his [Bruno's] chapel [next to his room]. Opening the little window, from his bed he could easily see the priest who celebrated. He had the Passion read to him by the seminarian Maglia, who stood at his side."[31]

And five days later: "On Good Friday, our church in Pinerolo was completely filled with people who awaited the sermon to be given on the Passion. We [Bruno and Gardetti] were in the interior garden and were walking together, when Fr. Lanteri remembered that he had not yet made his adoration of the Cross. He told me to accompany him and support him so that he would not fall. When we entered the church and reached the altar of Blessed Alphonsus, where the Cross was, he had me help him remove his shoes. He made his adoration a short distance before the altar, then approached the Crucifix and kissed it, to the wonderment of all who saw him. As we left the church, he expressed great satisfaction at having made his act of worship."[32]

BROTHER PIETRO GARDETTI had entered the Oblates in June 1829, at the age of twenty-one.[33] He had been a tailor's apprentice, a young man of good life though limited education.[34] Gardetti would remain a faithful Oblate until his death in 1883, at the age of seventy-five. As a novice, he assisted Bruno in many concrete ways, and daily during his last illness. Gardetti's simple and unstudied testimony offers unique access to Bruno's joys and struggles in his final days.[35]

This was a time of both blessing and trial for Gardetti. Difficult experiences mingled with warm interactions between novice and superior, and Gardetti recorded both. Years later, he related: "What I am able to recall at present of Fr. Lanteri is that, at times, to exercise my patience, he would have me go to the room above where laundry was kept, to crush the breadsticks into crumbs so that he could take them in a broth. This was the breakfast he ordinarily took in his last months."[36] Gardetti understood that Bruno's purpose in so directing was *to exercise my patience.*

And again: "During his last days, on several occasions he changed the brother who was assisting him. He assigned me to

Sketch of Bruno Lanteri.

work as a tailor for the community, saying that he no longer had any use for me. I stopped assisting him. A few days later, he called me back and I continued with him until his death."[37]

Gardetti recalled a further experience: "He kept in his room a little liquor that he would take at times. Once he accused me of having drunk some of it. I said that I had not, but he continued in his opinion. Seeing this, I went to the balcony in the church and poured out my heart to the Lord, in tears. Afterward, I returned to ask him if he had any tasks for me, and found him completely different, almost wanting to ask my forgiveness."[38] And yet again: "As I rarely left the house, at times he sent me with my hat to the garden to get some fresh air. If he saw that I did not have my hat, he grew red of face, seeing that I had not done exactly as he had said."[39]

How is Bruno's treatment of Gardetti to be understood? Why send him elsewhere in the house to prepare the bread for broth? Why dismiss him as a useless assistant, and then recall him? Why accuse him of what he did not do? Why the silent expression of displeasure?[40]

One key to the answer is found in Gardetti's words: *to exercise my patience.* In Bruno's day, "a certain paternal severity in the formation of novices" was considered necessary to prepare them for the crosses of life.[41] Superiors, therefore, would consciously *exercise the patience* of novices to this end.

An eyewitness narrates of St. Ignatius of Loyola that a Jesuit brother "was much loved by our Father [Ignatius] and therefore treated in accordance with this love. . . . He trained him in every kind of mortification and penance. . . . He did not permit any fault of his to pass without reprimand, and he never praised him in his presence for the good things he was doing."[42] The same witness described Ignatius's gentleness with the weak, and his harsher treatment of the strong, that they might grow in strength.[43]

Gardetti recognized this motive in some, at least, of Bruno's behavior. Such awareness most likely contributed to the serene tone of his testimony years later. Nothing in his narrative suggests that these experiences diminished the relationship between novice and superior. In fact, his novitiate concluded, Gardetti lived a long and faithful religious life. One who conversed often with him in Gardetti's last years testified to Gardetti's "special veneration" for Bruno.[44]

Yet questions may be raised: Does the above completely explain these incidents? Was desire to train a novice the *single* motivation of Bruno's austerity? Might increasing infirmity and pain have rendered him more easily impatient? Diminished his hold on a laboriously acquired gentleness? Did Bruno struggle to exercise a "paternal severity" without some admixture of a more human severity?

Gardetti noted Bruno's uneasiness after accusing him of a fault not committed. Elsewhere in his testimony, Gardetti added: "When he reproved anyone, even a priest, if he saw that person somewhat despondent because of the reproof, he immediately wanted to get down on his knees and ask that person's forgiveness."[45]

Was such uneasiness discomfort with a superior's role that required Bruno, against his own inclinations, to address his Oblates' shortcomings with severity? Was it recognition of something too human in his conduct? Was it a varying mixture of both? How do such actions harmonize with the great gentleness, for example, shown Cavour in his retreat? Or with the witness of Luigi Craveri that "I admired in him the great gentleness of his gaze, his words, and his external appearance, even when occasions arose that could have caused him to grow angry"?[46]

Both factors—a formative "paternal severity" and human limitations—may have shaped Bruno's interaction with Gardetti. Paternal and human severity may have mingled, the latter less easily restrained as physical weakness increased. If so, Bruno's desire for forgiveness testifies that he lived *to the end* the proposal adopted decades earlier, and taught to so many: "If I should fail, were it even a thousand times, I will not lose heart, I will not be disturbed, but will always immediately say, with peace, *now I begin*."[47]

AS THE SUMMER OF 1830 approached, Luigi Craveri and the de Maistre family visited Bruno in Pinerolo. Years later, Craveri recalled that encounter: "It was around the year 1830 that I went with the de Maistre family to visit him in Pinerolo. I felt a sense of veneration when I saw him, and I was struck by the way he seemed to foresee his imminent death. When I told him I hoped to return to visit him again, I saw him indicate with his hand that he would be beneath the earth."[48] In fact, it was the final meeting of the two.

In June, Bruno again fell ill. On June 18, Loggero relayed the news to Gonella, who replied the following day that "I learned with true sorrow that his condition is worsening."[49] Four days later, Gonella again wrote to Loggero: "Last evening, I heard from the Signor Doctor Capello that the threat to the precious life of the Reverend Rector Major is serious. A holy triduum of prayer for him, in honor of St. Aloysius, will begin today in the church of St. Joseph."[50]

Bruno's condition improved and, on June 26, Gonella manifested his consolation to Loggero: "I rejoice to hear of the improvement in the Reverend Father Rector Major's condition. You did well to give me this news in some detail; that has allowed me to make copies and send the news . . . to those who were impatiently awaiting it."[51] Bruno's struggles persisted, however, as Gonella's words to Loggero four days later attested: "I am replying to your letters of June 27 and 29, and I share with you my sadness at hearing that the Reverend Rector Major is in the condition you describe."[52]

In Genoa, Sr. Crocifissa learned of Bruno's illness, and, on July 9, expressed her concern: "I hear that the Lord has visited you with illness, and I know that these are difficult and painful visitations. I can tell you from my heart that your situation afflicts me deeply, and causes me sorrow, the more because I can do nothing to help ease your pain, in spite of the great desire I have to do so. I do not fail to use the one means I do have, which is to pray for Your Reverence."[53]

By mid-July, Bruno's condition had worsened, and he was unable to rise from bed.[54] On July 17, his friend Carlo Daverio, himself gravely ill, sent word to Bruno: "I am unable to read or write because of an oppression of the chest . . . and have asked our beloved Fr. Loggero to write for me these sentiments of my heart. . . . Your condition of health causes me great pain, and I certainly will not fail to recommend you continually to the Lord, to Mary Most Holy, and to Blessed Liguori, that you be granted health, and all those abundant graces that may serve for the greater glory of God, for your good, and for that of the Congregation."[55]

Daverio had learned of Bruno's concern that the intentions of deceased benefactress Teresa Quey be fulfilled. As the administrator of her will, he assured Bruno that all was in order, and added: "Beloved Father, if you have any confidence in me, which I do not doubt, dismiss all anxiety about this."[56] Daverio concluded: "The hour is late and I must go. I leave the sentiments of my heart deposited in yours. I ask that you remember me briefly in prayer when you can, and, from my heart, I embrace you in the Lord."[57] *The hour is late and I must go*: with these words, Bruno's correspondence—forty-nine years of letters written and received—concluded.

Hope of Bruno's recovery waned, and on July 19, his confessor, Antonio Ferrero, administered the extreme unction.[58] Bruno's witness, however, was not yet complete.

CHAPTER TWENTY-TWO

Last Days

*I am created by God for this single
purpose, that is, that I may praise
him and serve him, and, in the
end, gain my eternal salvation.*

—Bruno Lanteri

AS BRUNO GREW MORE physically dependent, his personal life, concealed for so long, could be hidden no more. The Oblates saw and recorded the words and actions of his final days. Among these witnesses, novice Pietro Gardetti held a privileged place through his daily contact with Bruno.

Bruno, who had always sought fidelity to daily prayer, strove to maintain that commitment in his last weeks. Gardetti remembered those days: "In his illness, he always wished to keep his times of prayer, even when he was very weak. The two of us would say the prayers together, and the rosary. When he drifted into sleep, I would not disturb him, and continued by myself. When he realized this, he would reprimand me for not waking him. When I read the *Visits to the Most Blessed Sacrament* of Blessed Liguori at 11:45 in the morning, he always tried, as much as he could, to listen, saying to me, 'This is worth more than all the rest.' "[1] Years later, Gardetti would speak of "the attitude almost of contemplation" that Bruno maintained during this illness.[2]

On one occasion, Bruno recommended specific reading to Gardetti: "He told me once that I should read often and well *The Practice of the Love of Jesus Christ* by St. Alphonsus, that I would gain much fruit from it, because it was an excellent book."[3] Gardetti recalled a further interaction with Bruno: "During his illness he had me put several things precious to him in various places for safekeeping, especially the relics of the saints. It was then that he found the zucchetto [skullcap] of St. Francis Xavier and was very happy to have found it. I, seeing a relic of St. Aloysius Gonzaga, asked him for it. He told me that he was reluctant to give it to me because it was precious and I was too young, that I would not treat it with the great reverence suitable to it. I promised him that I would take great care of it. A few days later, he gave it to me, placing it around my neck, and, at the same time, he blessed me, promising that in heaven he would pray for me."[4]

Years before, Bruno had counseled another to prepare regularly for death. He had proposed monthly preparation, named spiritual writings that assist such preparation, and had added: "In the meantime, begin immediately to desire it often; this practice will greatly ease and assure willing acceptance of death when it draws near."[5] He had taught that such preparation "also helps us greatly to accept willingly, even with joy, death itself when it approaches, since this is the most important time of all."[6] When exiled by Napoleon eighteen years earlier, Bruno had awaited "my departure from this unhappy world, and the union for which I long with my gentle Jesus."[7] For years, the words of his beloved Fr. Diessbach had never been far from his heart: "Paradise pays for all."[8]

As his last hour drew near, Bruno intensified that preparation. Too weak to celebrate Mass, he received Communion almost daily, as often as his illness permitted.[9] Gardetti recounted that "in the final days of his illness, he went to confession almost every evening."[10] As he prepared, Bruno experienced moments of anxiety. Gardetti related: "At times, Fr. Valmino and I would hear him exclaim, 'Who can say whether I will go to heaven?' One time Fr. Valmino said to him, 'Father Rector Major, why do you have so much fear of not going to heaven? If you have so much fear of not going there, what should I, who have been a sinner, think? But you have always worked for the Lord.' Fr. Valmino said this to him, and Fr. Lanteri said nothing more."[11]

Medical efforts to assist Bruno were unavailing. On one occasion, local doctors, and two sent from Turin by Bruno's friends, visited him. Gardetti recalled the incident: "In 1830, I think in the month of June, doctors came to examine him in his illness. Doctor Riberi came from Turin, Doctor Agliardi was there, and Doctor Grossi, and, if I remember well, also Doctor Martini. These doctors were all from Pinerolo. After they had examined him together for almost two hours, they came to no clear conclusion, but recommended that he anoint his stomach with olive oil. Fr. Lanteri waited until they had left the room, and, turning to me, said, 'Brother Pietro, there are three "M's" that no one understands.' I did not grasp what he was saying. Then he began to laugh, and said, 'Matto, medico, e musico' [Mentally disabled, medical doctors, and musicians.]."[12] Reserved Piedmontese that he was, Bruno could laugh even in his last days.

Nor was he a passive patient. As Gardetti noted, Bruno refused to endure another such consultation: "A few days later, he told Fr. Valmino that he wanted no doctor other than Doctor Martini, and that, in his [Bruno's] name, he [Valmino] should dismiss Doctors Grossi and Agliardi. He said this with some energy so that Fr. Valmino would understand clearly, since Fr. Valmino was a good friend of Doctor Grossi."[13]

Ferrero wrote of Bruno that "during his lifetime, he never wished his portrait painted."[14] Now the Oblates made final attempts. Gardetti told of their outcome: "The painter Comandis came several times to paint his portrait. In order that Fr. Lanteri not be aware of this, he went into the chapel where the small window looked directly on to the bed. But it was never possible. Once he came with Doctor Martini, brought by Martini himself as a medical intern, and Fr. Lanteri asked Martini who the person with him was. Martini answered that he was an acquaintance of his. 'Well,' said Comandis, somewhat irritated as they left the room, 'it seems impossible! His aspect changes almost constantly.' He was not able to paint his portrait until after his death, when he came immediately."[15]

In the dawn of his life, Bruno had turned to Mary. Brief remarks to Gardetti and Ferrero appear to indicate her presence in the eve of his life as well. Gardetti recounted: "One evening, as dusk was falling, we were saying the rosary together. He was seated on his small chair, and I was next to him, kneeling on the floor. He interrupted me, and asked me who that Lady was who had come to visit them. I replied that I had not seen any Lady, because this was a cloistered area. Then we resumed the rosary to its end."[16]

Ferrero, too, remembered Bruno's words to him: "In his last illness, he told me several times that he had a beautiful Lady with a lovely child in her arms who never left him, but would say no more."[17] The Marian meaning of these words seems evident; so Bruno must have intended them, and so his Oblates understood them.[18] Mary, then, continued to the end her unchanging role in Bruno's life: she was the tenderness, the warmth, and the love that eased his fear and instilled hope, now as death approached.

Mary was also central to an experience of prayer regarding the Oblates' future. On an undated page, most likely from his final years, Bruno wrote: "The Lord also gave me to understand that I should make known to the beloved sons of Mary, the Oblates, that this great Queen had obtained for them the spirit of fortitude, and they will be invincible to their enemies; they will triumph in their sufferings, and many of them will have the blessed lot of shedding their blood, and giving their lives for their faith in Jesus Christ; that they should not fear the devices of perverse men, ministers of the Demon, but should stand firm in their vocation: being faithful to God, God will be faithful to them."[19]

In no other surviving text did Bruno speak so openly of personal communication with the Lord. His words, "The Lord *also* gave me to understand," suggest that this page is a partial description of a more complete experience of prayer.[20] This page, then, may offer a privileged glimpse of a level of prayer that Bruno otherwise concealed. It bequeathed to his Oblates a Marian encouragement, and a call to persevere in their Oblate vocation.

Bruno's final illness was a time of *faith*. After Bruno's death, Ferrero observed: "His faith? He lived only of faith; he spoke of it with such intimate persuasion and with such richness of thought, that he reawakened or increased it in all who listened to him. He kept himself, therefore, constantly in the presence of God. He frequently reread those books that speak of faith most effectively; in all things he worked for God. His one fear, even in his last illness, was that he might not act for a supernatural purpose, for the greater glory of God alone."[21] With such "fear" and such desire, Bruno approached his end.

IN THOSE FINAL WEEKS, Bruno sought the aid of friends. Reynaudi wrote to Bishop Rey, absent in Savoy for reasons of health, informing him of Bruno's illness and transmitting Bruno's request for his blessing. On July 17, the bishop replied: "What joy it would be to hear from you, my very dear friend, were it not clouded by the danger to the health of our venerable Rector Major! Oh, how I suffer in being so far from him! Gathered with all of you around his bed, I too would consider myself one of his sons."[22] The bishop then granted his blessing: "Because he desires it, with all my heart I raise my hands to heaven and extend them to bless in the name of the Father, the Son, and the Holy Spirit, the worthy father of a family that I honor and love with my whole being, and with all the ardor God has given my heart."[23]

Bruno also asked his Jesuit friend Giovanni Antonio Grassi to visit from Turin.[24] Grassi later informed Roothaan of that encounter: "The Abate Lanteri is rapidly approaching the end of his life. He sent word, asking me to visit him in Pinerolo. I did as he requested, and, among other things, he enjoined me to find means to let His Holiness [Pius VIII] know that he has always upheld the infallibility of the Holy Father.[25] He also asked me to send many greetings to Your Paternity."[26]

Bruno now desired Gardetti's presence constantly throughout the day. Gardetti related: "Except for the little time I took for lunch, he did not want me to abandon him during the day. This was when he asked me if I would be there at his death. I answered that if he died during the day, I would be there, because he did not want me to remain in his room at night."[27] In fact, Bruno would die in mid-morning.

On July 27, the Oblates gathered around Bruno's bed to ask his blessing. Bruno gave both a blessing and an exhortation: "Since the condition of our above-mentioned Father grew constantly worse, he gave his blessing to his sons, prostrate around his bed, and recommended to them charity, the observance of the Rule and Constitutions, and devotion to Mary Most Holy."[28] As his end drew near, Bruno urged his Oblates to treasure three things: mutual charity, faithful following of their rule, and closeness to Mary. It was almost a last testament to his spiritual sons.

As BRUNO'S FINAL MOMENT approached, discontent in France exploded into revolution. Violence erupted in the streets of Paris on July 27, as the city rose against King Charles X and his troops. Fighting escalated, and the capital once again witnessed mobs, death, and pillaging. In three days, the king was defeated; he abdicated and fled the country. On August 9, Louis Philippe, the "Citizen King," was proclaimed sovereign of the French in his place: the centuries-old rule of the Bourbons in France had ended, and a new era was beginning.

In Paris, the mob sacked the archbishop's residence, the Jesuit novitiate, and a center dedicated to foreign missions.[29] The archbishop was threatened with death and went into hiding. Priests who wore the cassock in public were mistreated. Churches were locked to save them from profanation, and, not without risk, opened on Sundays. Bishops were forced to emigrate; parish priests were insulted and evicted from their rectories. Anticlerical newspapers, pamphlets, and plays denounced "the men in black."[30]

That same August, revolution spread to Belgium, and later to Germany, Italy, and Poland. Revolutionary fever stirred in Piedmont as well, though attempts to incite an uprising failed.[31] Bruno had repeatedly witnessed political turmoil in his life; as he lay dying, revolution once more swept across Europe and into Italy.

Did Bruno, now gravely ill and close to death, know of the revolution in France and its impact on Europe? An interaction with visitors suggests this may have been so. Gardetti recounted: "During the time of his illness, which lasted somewhat more than a month without his rising from bed, three Jesuits came from Turin to visit him. They spent a long time around his bed, and then went to lunch in the refectory with the Oblates. They returned again after lunch to visit Fr. Lanteri a last time. Fr. Lanteri looked at them and said, 'What? Are you in Turin with all this turbulence of which they speak?' A Jesuit father answered him, 'Fr. Lanteri, as long as the Jesuits do good work, they will always be persecuted.' And saying this, they took leave of him, and departed for Turin."[32]

Was the turbulence in Turin sparked by that in France? Was it of different origin? If Bruno did know of renewed revolution in Europe, it must have saddened his final days: his part was ending, but the struggle of the Church he loved continued.

JULY PASSED, AND AUGUST BEGAN. Local doctors and another from Turin visited Bruno, and his condition appeared to improve.[33] Loggero would later remember those first days of August and write that "We were all deeply consoled."[34]

But their hopes would be deceived. Bruno's "long and painful career," as a lay friend would term it, now swiftly approached its end.[35] He had lived seventy-one years, three months, and twenty-two days, a life that began in Cuneo, led to Turin, and now was ending in Pinerolo.[36]

In Cuneo, Bruno had experienced love and sorrow. From deeply Christian parents, he had received a faith he never doubted, and that guided his entire life. The death of his mother had opened his heart to Mary; in her, he found the tenderness denied him through loss of his own mother. During those seventeen years, Bruno grew in love of prayer and study, and the desire for religious life awakened within him. When health forbade a Carthusian calling, Bruno sought diocesan priesthood.

Contact with Fr. Diessbach shaped in Bruno an enduring identity: adherence to the Holy Father, mastery of the Spiritual Exercises, esteem for St. Alphonsus, formation of priests and laity, promotion of good books, and defense of Catholic teaching against current errors. Already in his early twenties, Bruno's lasting theological and pastoral identity was forged. Subsequent searching in his life would concern not his identity but the structures in which that identity could best be lived.

These structures would change with the vicissitudes of troubled times: *Amicizia Cristiana, Amicizia Sacerdotale, Aa,* Pious Union of St. Paul, Priestly Residence, *Amicizia Cattolica,* and Oblates of the Virgin Mary—changing institutions that supplied a setting for unchanging dedication to his chosen ministry. The last of these, the Oblates, would perpetuate Bruno's mission in centuries to come.

Bruno was fully a Piedmontese, sharing a character described as "tenacious, of few words, well-organized, measured, and realistic."[37] His spiritual guidance was direct and encouraging, and his quest for gentleness, though the struggle remained, bore fruit. Bruno's courage appeared in the dangerous days of French domination, when loyalty to the Holy Father placed his life at risk. A similar courage was evident in Bruno's refusal to surrender to ill health, and his remarkable activity in spite of it—the ongoing "miracle" of his life, as Roothaan termed it.

Bruno was a man of study who "continually studied theology, and only theology."[38] His knowledge of theology was profound, and rendered him a sure guide for many; his interest in literature and the arts, apart from their impact on faith—which concerned him deeply—was, at most, relative.[39] He was, as one scholar writes, "not a theologian, nor an original thinker, but rather an excellent defender of doctrine."[40] Thousands of manuscript pages reveal the endless study that made Bruno, indeed, an excellent defender of doctrine in confusing times.[41] A further scholar adds that Bruno "was always more concerned with efficacy on a deep level than with sensational results."[42] His work remained largely in the background: the spiritual and pastoral *formation* of priests and laity who, as devout and capable apostles of Christ, served his Church with abundant fruit. Future decades would reveal the magnitude of their contribution.

Native intelligence, constant study, and faithful prayer formed Bruno as a man of wisdom and clear vision, who counseled others with a "surety of judgment, rarely at fault."[43] Personal study, coupled with an open mind, enabled Bruno to maintain ecclesiological balance in ever-changing times. Craveri attested: "I frequently saw him exercise humility, especially when I saw him ask advice, and submit his writings and his opinions to various persons toward whom, from every point of view, he could have taken the role of master."[44] Bruno's theological choices—the teaching of Rome, Alphonsian moral theology, God's mercy as a sure road to conversion, papal infallibility, the Immaculate Conception, and the rest—would be vindicated in future years and prove inexhaustibly fruitful in the Church.

Until his final three years as superior of the Oblates, Bruno never held positions of canonical authority: he was not pastor of a parish, not a bishop, not a professor of theology, not rector of a seminary. His authority arose from his person alone: his spiritual depth, mastery of theology, love for the Church, wisdom, and experience as guide drew priests, religious, and laity to him in search of assistance.

Bruno, however, was above all a man *who loved Christ*. Of his Oblates he would say: "In every action, therefore, they keep Jesus constantly before their eyes. Jesus is always their companion and their model, and they strive to imitate him as perfectly as they can, both in their inner thoughts and sentiments, and in their exterior actions."[45] "In short," Bruno continued, "they live constantly in the company of Jesus, they always converse with Jesus, they are always united with Jesus in their intentions and their actions; in this way, they become a living copy of Jesus."[46]

As a consequence, "Jesus becomes the one treasure of their hearts; thus, Jesus lives in their hearts, and they live in the Heart of Jesus. Is there anything greater and more consoling than this?"[47] *Is there anything greater and more consoling than this?* Bruno's words partially lift the veil that shrouds the deep center of his "long and painful career": the hidden joy, the companionship, the consolation, and the love of Jesus that gladdened his heart and motivated his every choice.

BUT NOW THAT "career" was complete. Loggero would later write to Bruno's cousin Agostino Eula that in those final days of hope and fear for Bruno's life, he "was strengthened by receiving all the holy Sacraments."[48] Everything was ready; the end would come quickly.

CHAPTER TWENTY-THREE

Final Passage

O good Jesus, I thirst for you.
—prayer of Bruno Lanteri

DURING THE NIGHT OF AUGUST 4, Bruno's condition appeared stable. At 8:00 in the morning on August 5, Antonio Ferrero was reading a letter from Giovanni Battista Rubino, a priest acquainted with Bruno and long associated with the Oblates.[1] Suddenly, Ferrero was advised that Bruno had entered his final agony, and ran to Bruno's room where the community was gathering rapidly.[2]

Bruno's death agony, Loggero would write, was "most gentle."[3] He "followed the prayers commending his soul to God with deep devotion."[4] Tears fell from the eyes of the Oblates gathered around his bed and expressed their sense of loss.[5] Bruno, Ferrero recounted, "wished a large Crucifix hung around his neck, and a pouch completely filled with relics."[6] He remained "perfectly aware and in peace until his last breath."[7]

Prayers and scriptural texts were read aloud at Bruno's bedside and, Ferrero continued, "he smiled at every thought that expressed sentiments of confidence and outpourings of love."[8] Moments before he died, "he blessed us all once more," and enjoined his Oblates "that we love one another, and that we remain always united in heart and at the cost of any sacrifice, in Jesus and Mary."[9] Bruno "asked our forgiveness if he had ever hurt us."[10]

Loggero described Bruno's final request: "When the words of the Gospel of St. John were read, 'Holy Father, keep them in your name, which you have given me, that they may be one, even as we are one,' he told Fr. Ferrero who was assisting him, to repeat those words."[11]

As Ferrero reread the Gospel text, the culminating moment arrived. Loggero continued: "When he heard those words, he raised his eyes to heaven with a warm smile. Then he lowered them, and entered Paradise."[12] Ferrero added: "When the words of the Gospel, 'Keep them, that they may be one as I am in you,' were read to him, he lowered his eyes, and was no longer among us."[13] It was 9:05 in the morning, August 5, 1830.[14]

Though all were watching him, Ferrero wrote, Bruno's breathing ceased so gently "that none realized it."[15] In fact, "I thought he was alive and said the *Proficiscere* [prayer for the dying], but he was already with God."[16] Loggero would speak of Bruno's death as a "happy passage to eternal rest," and Ferrero would write that Bruno "died the death of a just man, in keeping with the way he had always lived."[17]

In the moments after death, Bruno "retained his color and a peaceful countenance."[18] The Oblates immediately offered Mass for Bruno, and the painter Comandis was called; what Bruno had not allowed in life could now be done, Ferrero recounted, "so that we would have a likeness of him."[19] The Oblates lingered at Bruno's bedside: "Those of the family [the Oblates] were unwilling to separate themselves from him, and felt something of heaven in remaining close to him. They cut his hair and nails to have relics."[20]

Bruno had died, but Oblate life continued, and a new superior was needed. Bruno's papers were examined to see if he had named a vicar to govern until a new rector major could be elected.[21] A diligent search found nothing, and, two hours after Bruno's death, his councilors, Fathers Reynaudi, Loggero, Ferrero, and Valmino, gathered in the chapel adjacent to Bruno's room. Reynaudi was unanimously voted as vicar.[22] Two months later, on October 2, he would be elected second rector major of the Oblates.[23]

The day after his death, Bruno's body was placed for viewing in the Oblate church. That August 6, Ferrero described the scene to Rubino: "As I write, his body is displayed in the church, and the people continue to look upon him without ceasing. Last evening, when we came to dress him in priestly garments, his members were flexible."[24]

In his last will, Bruno had asked that "Mass be celebrated with the body present, and that my burial be without pomp."[25] The funeral was held, and, according to the custom for persons of special regard, Bruno was buried in the Oblate church, behind the main altar.[26] Preparations began for the solemn Mass of remembrance to be celebrated thirty days later.

Word of Bruno's death spread, and friends shared the Oblates' sorrow. On August 6, Rodolfo de Maistre, son of Joseph de Maistre and brother of Constance, wrote to Loggero: "We received with the greatest sorrow the sad news Your Reverence sent us in your letter of the fifth of this month, regarding the loss of our dearly beloved and deeply venerated Father Lanteri. We cannot doubt that, having concluded his long and painful career, he has received from God the reward *magna nimis* [very great] promised to his faithful servants; but we sorrow for the true friendship that united us with him here on earth. His sons should console themselves with the thought that, his youth now renewed like the eagle's [Ps 103:5], he will defend and protect them with much greater strength and efficacy than he could before, and will obtain from Mary, whose devotion he upheld and promoted, graces and blessings for the Order in its beginnings."[27] His youth now renewed like the eagle's: Bruno's physical struggles—his exhaustion, labored breathing, weakened eyes, and painful efforts to serve—belonged forever to the past.

Rodolfo concluded: "In the choice made [of Reynaudi as vicar], and in the unanimity with which it was made, we already see the blessed spirit of justice and Christian harmony that, from their holy founder, has descended on his beloved sons. I speak for my whole family when I express our sorrow, and I beg you not to forget in your prayers the friends of your founder, and particularly me, who, more than any other, needs special graces and divine assistance."[28]

Two days later, the bishop of Mondovì, Francesco Gaetano Buglione, likewise wrote to Loggero: "A mixture of anguished sorrow and warm hope filled my heart when I learned from Your Reverence's esteemed letter of the sixth of this month, about the truly painful loss of its worthy superior, Fr. Lanteri, sustained by your venerable Congregation: a loss that all those who were blessed with the precious gift of knowing the illustrious deceased will certainly share with the Congregation, as indeed will all those who esteem true virtue and the good of souls."[29]

The bishop expressed a conviction: "The fervent zeal that shone in his whole being and that was his single motivation, and his eminent virtue, the more admirable as he earnestly strove to hide it, persuade me that God has not taken him from this Congregation, and from the many who desire his aid, except to crown with heavenly glory the sublime gifts with which he so abundantly adorned him, and to provide the same Congregation, and all those who seek God, a new and deeply dedicated protector in heaven."[30]

On September 6, thirty days after Bruno's death, the Oblates celebrated a "solemn funeral" for Bruno in their church.[31] Bishop Rey and other priests of the Diocese attended. After the Gospel, Giovanni Battista Rubino preached the eulogy in formal oratorical style, reviewing Bruno's life and virtues.[32] The day would come when the cause of canonization of both orator and deceased would be introduced in Rome.

SO BRUNO'S EARTHLY LIFE CONCLUDED. In forty-nine years of priesthood, he had guided countless priests and laity, distributed tens of thousands of books, given and trained others to give innumerable retreats and parish missions, heard endless confessions, ceaselessly defended Church teaching as "a watchdog who cries out to his last breath," founded a new congregation, and proclaimed to burdened hearts a message of mercy, hope, and new beginnings.[33] Bruno's life had ended, but the seeds sown in his lifetime bore lasting fruit.

One scholar writes that Bruno "justly may be considered the prime mover of Catholic resistance in one of the most crucial periods [the French occupation] in the religious history of Piedmont."[34] Another notes that Bruno was "one of the principal authors of the victory of benign moral theology," terminating the two-centuries-long rule of rigorism in sacramental practice.[35] Yet another describes Bruno as "one of the most zealous and active apostles who appeared in Piedmont at the end of the eighteenth century and beginning of the nineteenth."[36]

In the decades following Bruno's death, the Piedmontese clergy shed its rigorism and diffidence toward Rome, adopted Alphonsian moral teaching, and embraced the authority of the Holy Father with new conviction. The Priestly Residence, ably directed by Luigi Guala and his inspiring successor, St. Joseph Cafasso, would play a major role in this transformation.[37]

Those same years witnessed a new phenomenon in Italy: the emergence of "a Catholic laity, active and operative in widely diverse branches of thought and action."[38] This occurrence "can be considered one of the principal characteristics of Catholic life in the nineteenth century, with decisive influence on events in the life of the Church in the twentieth century as well."[39] Catholic journalism increased, congresses were held, and Catholic associations with apostolic aims were formed.[40] Diessbach's *Amicizia Cristiana*, which Bruno guided for so many years, and Bruno's own work with so many lay men and women, contributed to that renewal.[41]

As Bruno lay dying, Piedmont was entering a unique age of sanctity. One scholar comments of Bruno: "For fifty years he had spent himself in the struggle, often in the midst of contradictions, and the outcome in Piedmont had seemed a defeat; it was, however, the dawn of a new solidity of doctrine, accompanied by a blossoming of Christian life and holiness."[42]

The nineteenth century witnessed an expansion of sanctity in Piedmont with few parallels in Church history.[43] An author notes that "so extraordinary a flowering was not only without precedent in earlier centuries in Piedmont, but perhaps in no other place on earth as well."[44]

In 1966, a study of holiness in Piedmont in the nineteenth and early twentieth centuries found fifty-eight men and woman whose causes of canonization had been introduced in Rome.[45] A further study in 2001 named sixty in the nineteenth century alone, and the number is likely to grow as more causes are introduced in future years.[46]

Of the fifty-eight identified in 1966, thirty lived and labored in the city of Turin. The same author comments: "Seeds of sanctity were sown by the hand of God in great abundance in Piedmont, and especially among the clergy, religious, and laity of the city and Archdiocese of Turin."[47] Another historian notes that Turin "presents itself in these decades as a stronghold of charity."[48]

Some of these figures are internationally renowned: St. John Bosco, St. Joseph Cafasso, St. Joseph Cottolengo, and St. Dominic Savio. Others are remembered more locally: St. Leonard Murialdo, St. Joseph Marello, St. Maria Domenica Mazzarrello, Blessed Francis Faà di Bruno, Blessed Michael Rua, Blessed Frederick Albert, Blessed Joseph Allamano, Blessed Clement Marchisio, and many others.[49]

Historians highlight a particular quality of Piedmontese sanctity in the nineteenth century: the link that binds these holy persons in a progressive "chain." Repeatedly in these decades, contact with one saint fostered holiness in another, who in turn awakened thirst for God in another. And of this chain, Bruno was an essential link.

A writer describes "the chain of exceptional persons, linked among themselves by common desire for spiritual growth, in a century of particular importance for Piedmont."[50] The same author comments: "The remote origin may be found in Blessed Sebastian Valfrè. The proximate and concrete foundations of this holiness, however, are Lanteri, Cottolengo, and Cafasso. From these, others go forth and become, in their own right, centers of irradiation."[51]

In chronologically reverse order, another scholar outlines "a chain . . . whose principal links were: St. John Bosco, a disciple of Cafasso; St. Joseph Cafasso, a disciple of Guala; Guala, a disciple of Lanteri; the Venerable Pio Bruno Lanteri, a disciple of Diessbach, of the Company of Jesus."[52] As so often, Diessbach lay at the origin. Bruno, however, was an indispensable link in this extraordinary chain of sanctity. His quiet labor of spiritual formation would bear fruit beyond imagining, and for decades to come.

AFTER BRUNO'S DEATH, the Oblates continued to grow. Four years later, in 1834, they opened a second community at Our Lady of

Consolation in Turin, and, the following year, a priestly residence in Nice.[53] As numbers increased, Oblate ministry expanded geographically, including labors in Burma (Myanmar).

In 1855, the Piedmontese government passed a law suppressing religious institutes, and a time of trial began for the Oblates. After thirty years in St. Clare's, they were evicted by governmental order in 1857. The Oblates returned to Pinerolo in 1885, in their new church of the Sacred Heart.

Subsequent decades would see the Oblates spread throughout Italy and into France, Austria, Argentina, Brazil, the United States, Canada, Nigeria, and the Philippines. Men of holiness would arise among them, notably the Venerable Felice Prinetti and the Servant of God Raffaele Melis.[54] Through the Oblates, Bruno's spirit and mission remain operative in the Church and world.[55]

ONCE RETURNED TO PINEROLO, the Oblates obtained permission to transfer Bruno's body from St. Clare's to their church of the Sacred Heart. On March 11, 1901, in the presence of witnesses, the tomb was opened.[56] In 1939, Oblate Fr. Domenico Pechenino recalled that day: "I am the last surviving member of the small group present when his [Bruno's] tomb was opened, and his remains transported from the church of St. Clare's to its present burial site in our church of the Sacred Heart in Pinerolo. I remember as if it were today, that when the worker—in the presence of a delegate of the Curia, of Doctor Fer, and of Fr. Gastaldi, who had indicated the exact place of the tomb as he remembered it—opened the tomb and lifted the cover of the wooden casket, with these eyes I saw Fr. Lanteri, dressed in the habit of the Oblates, with his biretta on his head, his hands folded, and his thin face with the pallor of the deceased. After a few moments, as it came into contact with the air, that venerable figure, which appeared just as depicted in the painting in Pisa (which was made from his body when he lay on his deathbed), dissolved, disappearing from the gaze of the onlookers, who stood there as if numb."[57] That same day, Bruno's body was reinterred in the church of the Sacred Heart, where it remains at present.[58]

Tomb of Bruno Lanteri, seen from the interior of the church of the Sacred Heart, Pinerolo.

Tomb of Bruno Lanteri, seen from the vestibule of the church of the Sacred Heart, Pinerolo.

The question of a cause of canonization arose from the time of Bruno's death in 1830. In 1919, the General Chapter of the Oblates resolved to undertake the cause.[59] Fr. Tommaso Piatti was named postulator, and the process began in Pinerolo on August 5, 1930, a century after Bruno's death.[60] Four years later, the documents were transferred to Rome. In 1965, after exhaustive examination of Bruno's life and writings, the Church formally recognized his heroic virtue, and he was declared the Venerable Bruno Lanteri.[61]

YEARS AFTER BRUNO'S DEATH, Fr. Enrico Simonino—brother of the Filippo Simonino who had died in Carignano in 1819—prepared a conference for his fellow Oblates. In his talk, he shared a personal remembrance of Bruno: "I also had the fortune of associating with him for some years, and can say confidently that I never received anything from him but [edification]. Many among us were blessed to know him, associate with him, and live with him, and I too was of that number, even before our Congregation was canonically instituted, and for several years. Oh, what an odor of sanctity transpired from his conversation, and from his appearance itself. His words were only of God and to lead others to God. It was not possible to spend time with him without feeling new fervor in the service of God."[62]

It was not possible to spend time with him without feeling new fervor in the service of God. Years earlier, another priest, Jean Baptiste Aubriot de La Palme, had met Bruno and had felt the same. De La Palme had described the ideal member of the *Aa* as one "with whom it is impossible to associate without becoming better."[63] He had added: "Monsieur Lanteri is most likely such a one."[64]

Time has not diminished the power of Bruno's witness. To "spend time with him"—to ponder his life, his goals, his self-sacrificing dedication, his struggles, his faith, and, above all, his love for Christ—is to feel impelled to love and serve the Lord more deeply. That call is Bruno's lasting heritage.

Chronology of
Bruno Lanteri's Life

Indented and italicized entries indicate significant European events during Bruno Lanteri's lifetime.

1732   February 15: Birth of Nikolaus Albert von Diessbach

1759   May 12: Birth of Bruno Lanteri

        October 19: Diessbach enters the Jesuit novitiate

1763   July 19: Margherita Lanteri, Bruno's mother, dies

1772   November 28: Bruno receives the sacrament of Confirmation

        1773, July 21: Pope Clement XIV suppresses the Jesuits

1776   Bruno attempts to enter the Carthusians

1777   September 17: Bruno receives permission to wear clerical garb and goes to Turin to begin studies for priesthood

1779   Bruno and Diessbach meet

1781   August 15: Bruno's pact of slavery to Mary

        September 22: Bruno is ordained subdeacon

        December 22: Bruno is ordained deacon

1782   End of January: Bruno accompanies Diessbach to Vienna

        March 22: Pius VI reaches Vienna to meet with Joseph II

        May 25: Bruno is ordained a priest

        July 13: Bruno receives his doctorate in theology

1784   October 31: Death of Pietro Lanteri, Bruno's father

1787   April–May: Bruno travels to Savoy and Switzerland for the *Amicizie* and *Aa*

        1789, July 14: Storming of the Bastille; French Revolution begins

        1792, September 21: French army invades Savoy

        1793–1795: French army progressively invades Piedmont

        1796, March 27: Napoleon takes command and conquers Piedmont

        May 15: Treaty of Paris and end of Piedmontese independence

255

1798   December 22: Death of Fr. Diessbach

      1800, March 14: Election of Pius VII as pope

      1802, August 31: French suppress religious communities in Piedmont

1803   September–November: Bruno travels to Florence for the
      Amicizie

      1804, December 2: Pius VII crowns Napoleon as emperor

      1808, February 2: French troops occupy Rome

      *1809, June 10: French annex the Papal States; Napoleon
      excommunicated*

      July 6: Pius VII abducted and taken captive to Savona

1811   January 29: Bruno interrogated by French police

      March 25: Bruno departs for exile in the Grangia

      1812, June–December, Napoleon's army destroyed in Russia

      *1814, April 6: Napoleon abdicates and is exiled; end of French
      empire and restoration of independence in Piedmont*

1814   April 20: Bruno returns from exile to Turin

      Summer: Meeting of Reynaudi, Biancotti, and Golzio
      in Carignano

      August 7: Pius VII reestablishes the Jesuits

1815   February 22: Bruno initiates the Pious Union of St. Paul in Turin

1816   Summer: Reynaudi asks Bruno's counsel regarding the
      initiative in Carignano

      November 13: Provisional rule of the Oblates of Mary
      canonically approved

1817   August 12: Definitive rule of the Oblates in Carignano approved

      November: Beginning of the Priestly Residence in Turin

1818   December 21: Colombano Chiaveroti named Archbishop
      of Turin

1820   May: Dispersal of the Oblates of Carignano

      1821, March–April: Revolution in Piedmont

1823   Publication of Bruno's *Reflections on the Holiness and Teaching
      of Blessed Liguori*

1824   Bruno pursues entrance among the Jesuits

1825   May: In Chieri, Bruno hears the call to found the Oblates anew

        September 17: Bishop Rey approves the Rule of the Oblates

        October 6: Bruno is elected Rector Major of the Oblates

1826   April 7: Bruno and Loggero depart for Rome

        September 1: Papal Brief *Etsi Dei Filius*, giving papal approval to the Oblates

1827   June 12: Piedmontese senate grants legal existence to the Oblates

        July 6: Bruno and five other Oblates formally enter St. Clare's in Pinerolo

        1830, July 27–29: Revolution in Paris

1830   August 5: Death of Bruno in the house of St. Clare's

1901   March 11: Bruno's body is moved to the Oblate church of the Sacred Heart in Pinerolo

1919   The Oblate General Chapter resolves to undertake Bruno's cause of canonization

1965   November 23: Heroic nature of Bruno's virtue is recognized by the Church and he is declared "Venerable"

Abbreviations

AOMV	Archive of the Oblates of the Virgin Mary.
ASCR	Archive of the Sacred Congregation for Institutes of Consecrated Life and Societies of Apostolic Life.
ASV	Secret Archive of the Vatican
B	Candido Bona, I.M.C. Le "Amicizie": Società segrete e rinascita religiosa (1770–1830). Turin: Deputazione di storia patria, 1962.
Bi	Nicomede Bianchi. Storia della monarchia piemontese dal 1773 sino al 1861. 4 vols. Rome: Fratelli Bocca, 1877–1885.
C	Paolo Calliari, O.M.V., ed. Carteggio del Venerabile Padre Pio Bruno Lanteri (1759–1830) fondatore della Congregazione degli Oblati di Maria Vergine. 5 vols. Turin: Editrice Lanteriana, 1976.
Co	Tomaso Chiuso. La Chiesa in Piemonte dal 1797 ai giorni nostri. 5 vols. Turin: Tipografia Fratelli Speirani, 1887–1892.
Elenco esercizi	Elenco degli esercizi e tridui dettati dagli Oblati di Maria Vergine e loro aggregati, ecc. Dal maggio 1817 al dicembre 1843. In AOMV, Serie Generali, vol. Elenchi, Registro 1.
Elenco/Nota	Elenco degli esercizi dettati dagli Oblati di Maria Santissima e delle diverse edizioni fatte dai medesimi, with subtitle, Nota degli esercizi dettati dagli Oblati di Maria Santissima di Carignano dopo l'erezione della loro Congregazione. In ASCR, P. 16.
Esp	Timothy Gallagher, O.M.V., ed. Un'esperienza dello Spirito. Pio Bruno Lanteri: Il suo carisma nelle sue parole. Cuneo: AGA, 1989.

259

G	Pietro Gastaldi, O.M.V. *Della vita del Servo di Dio Pio Brunone Lanteri, fondatore della Congregazione degli Oblati di Maria Vergine.* Turin: Marietti, 1870.
loc.	location (page) in Kindle e-book.
OM	Paolo Calliari, O.M.V. *Gli Oblati di Maria. Vol III: Primi quattro anni di vita.* Editrice Lanteriana, 1980.
P	Amato Frutaz, ed. *Pinerolien. Beatificationis et cano- nizationis Servi Dei Pii Brunonis Lanteri fundatoris Congregationis Oblatorum M. V. (1830): Positio su- per introductione causae et super virtutibus ex officio compilata.* Rome: Typis Polyglottis Vaticanis, 1945.
RNAB	Revised New American Bible
RSVCE	Revised Standard Version, Catholic Edition.
S	followed by an *Arabic* numeral signifies "Scritti," that is, one of the four volumes of *Scritti e documenti d'archivio.* Rome: Edizioni Lanteri, 2002. Thus, "S 1" indicates *Scritti*, volume 1; "S 2" indicates *Scritti*, volume 2, etc.
S	followed by a *Roman* numeral signifies "Series" in the Archive of the Oblates of the Virgin Mary (AOMV). Thus, "S I" indicates AOMV, Series I; S II indicates AOMV, Series II, etc.
V	Paolo Calliari, O.M.V. *Il venerabile Pio Bruno Lanteri (1759-1830) fondatore degli Oblati di Maria Vergine nella storia religiosa del suo tempo.* Typescript, 1978-1983.

Notes

Preface

1. Pietro Gastaldi, O.M.V., *Della vita del Servo di Dio Pio Brunone Lanteri, fondatore della Congregazione degli Oblati di Maria Vergine* (Turin: Marietti, 1870). Less complete but valuable biographies followed: Tommaso Piatti, O.M.V., *Un precursore dell'Azione Cattolica: Il Servo di Dio Pio Brunone Lanteri apostolo di Turin fondatore degli Oblati di Maria Vergine* (Turin: Marietti, 1954); Léon Cristiani, *Un Prêtre redouté de Napoléon: P. Bruno Lanteri (1759–1830)* (Nice: Procure des Oblats de la Vierge Marie, 1957). Others were of more popular nature: Icilio Felici, *Una bandiera mai ripiegata: Pio Brunone Lanteri fondatore dei PP. Oblati di M. V. precursore dell'Azione Cattolica* (Pinerolo: Alzani, 1950); Lorenzo Peirone, *Pio Brunone Lanteri: Precursore dell'Azione Cattolica e Fondatore degli Oblati di Maria Vergine* (Bari: Edizioni Paoline, 1958); Alberto Moscatelli, O.M.V., *Il venerabile Padre Pio Brunone Lanteri: un maestro di vita nel mutamento di un'epoca 1759–1830* (Foligno: Edizioni Lanteri, 1996); Michele Babuin, O.M.V., *Dire Cristo al mondo: piccola biografia del venerabile Pio Bruno Lanteri (1759–1830) fondatore degli Oblati di Maria Vergine* (Rome: Provincia italiana degli O.M.V., 2007). The five-volume biography composed by Paolo Calliari, O.M.V., an invaluable resource for this book, remains unpublished: *Il Venerabile Pio Bruno Lanteri (1759–1830) fondatore degli Oblati di Maria Vergine nella storia religiosa del suo tempo,* typescript, 1983. All of these works, with the exception of Cristiani's, were written in Italian. Cristiani's French text was later translated into other languages, among them English: *A Cross for Napoleon: The Life of Father Bruno Lanteri (1759–1830)* (Boston: St. Paul Editions, 1981). For a nuanced assessment of Gastaldi's fine biography, see P, XXXIV–XXXV, 684–687. Fully recognizing the magnitude of Gastaldi's achievement, I have preferred to base my biography on the original documents, and rarely have utilized Gastaldi as a source independently of these documents. Because it is impossible to verify what content in Gastaldi's biography derives from oral sources—he met and lived with several Oblates who had known Bruno personally—I have adopted the safer course and have quoted Bruno's words only as found in the original documents.

2. Housed in the General House of the Oblates, Rome. Bruno's writings (Series I-VIII) have been reproduced digitally.

3. Amato Frutaz, *Pinerolien. Beatificationis et canonizationis Servi Dei Pii Brunonis Lanteri fundatoris Congregationis Oblatorum M. V. (1830): Positio super introductione causae et super virtutibus ex officio compilata* (Rome: Typis Polyglottis Vaticanis, 1945); Candido Bona, I.M.C., *Le "Amicizie": Società segrete e rinascita religiosa (1770–1830)* (Turin: Deputazione subalpina di storia patria, 1962); Paolo Calliari, O.M.V., *Carteggio del Venerabile Pio Bruno Lanteri (1759–1830) fondatore della Congregazione degli Oblati di Maria Vergine* (Turin: Editrice lanteriana, 1976); Vittorio Moscarelli, O.M.V. and Otello Ponzanelli, O.M.V., eds., *Manoscritti del Fondatore Pio Brunone Lanteri* (Rome: Centro Stampa OMV, 1976–1980); Timothy Gallagher, O.M.V., ed., *Un'esperienza dello Spirito. Pio Bruno Lanteri: il suo carisma nelle sue parole* (Cuneo: AGA, 1989); Oblates of the Virgin Mary in collaboration with "Informatique & Bible," Abbey of Maredsous, *Pio Bruno Lanteri: Scritti e documenti d'archivio* (Rome: Edizioni Lanteri, 2002), 4 vols.; Agostino Valentini, ed., *Lanterianum: Rivista di studio dell'Istituto degli Oblati di Maria Vergine*, 1993–2012.

4. Among these: Archive of the Sacred Congregation for Institutes of Consecrated Life and Societies of Apostolic Life (ASCR), and the Secret Archive of the Vatican (ASV); Frutaz, *Positio*, 1945; Bona, *Le "Amicizie,"* 1962; Jean Guerber, S.J., *Le ralliement du clergé français a la morale liguorienne: L'abbé Gousset et ses précurseurs (1785–1832)* (Rome: Università Gregoriana Editrice, 1973); Timothy Gallagher, O.M.V., *Gli esercizi di S. Ignazio nella spiritualità e carisma di fondatore di Pio Bruno Lanteri* (Rome: Typis Pontificiae Universitatis Gregorianae, 1983); *Lanterianum*, 1993–2012; Andrea Brustolon, *L'azione missionaria degli Oblati di Maria Vergine fuori del Piemonte nel quadro storico della Restaurazione e della vita della Congregazione* (Rome: Edizioni Lanteri, 2000); Armando Santoro, O.M.V., *Il cammino spiritual del P. Pio Bruno Lanteri (1759–1830) Fondatore della Congregazione dei Padri Oblati di Maria Vergine* (Rome: Provincia italiana degli O.M.V., 2007).

5. I name these in the Acknowledgments.

6. In translating, I have sought accuracy of content, cultural accessibility, and readability in English. I have tried to render as accurately as possible in English the content of the original in Italian, French, or Latin; to make accessible in our different cultural context the tone of communication (friend to friend, priest to bishop, layman to priest, and so forth) expressed in late eighteenth- and early nineteenth-century Italian usage;

and to render the translations easily readable in English, so that the fact of translation intrudes as little as possible upon the text in English.

7. Examples include the activity of Francesco Antonio Giani in spreading the writings of St. Alphonsus Liguori. Gastaldi, *Della vita del Servo di Dio Pio Brunone Lanteri*, 1870, 119-120, attributes this to Bruno's guidance; Colombero, *Vita del Servo di Dio D. Giuseppe Cafasso*, 1895, 44, however, attributes this to Guala's guidance. The disputed attribution to Bruno of the September 18, 1828, letter to Lamennais offers a further example: see C, 5, 253-254.

8. If, for example, this biography says little about Bruno's mother, or about the death of his father, or about the day of his ordination to the priesthood, and so forth—events about which the reader would wish to know more—it is because in these and other cases the sources conserved say little. I have accepted those limitations and not attempted to amplify the discussion through speculation. My purpose is that everything affirmed in this biography rest upon solid evidence. In each case, I have supplied in the endnotes a reference to the sources.

9. The great difficulty facing any biographer of Bruno Lanteri is his lifelong desire to remain hidden. Bruno's first biographer noted that "what crowns every other attribute and enterprise in his life is that, faced with the great honor that might have been his in the eyes of the world, he so ably hid his works and his entire person." Gastaldi, 9. Several factors combine in this desire: the secrecy inherent, by Diessbach's design, in the *Amicizie*; the similar secrecy of the *Aa*; the extended French occupation (1796-1814) with its rigorous police surveillance of Church activities; and Bruno's Piedmontese and personal reserve. Guerber writes of "the extreme discretion with which he [Bruno] enveloped the greater part of his activities, and that corresponded both to his temperament and to the needs of the times." *Le rôle*, 356. See also Guerber, *Le ralliement*, 113-114. Gastaldi affirms that many of Bruno's manuscripts "perished consumed by flames." With much probability, the texts of greatest interest to the biographer—recordings of intimate spiritual experience, chronicles of hopes and struggles, and the like—were among them. Gastaldi adds that the reserve with which many disciples and close associates spoke of Bruno, "led many to believe that Lanteri himself commanded them, or desired of them a promise not to speak of him in regard to anything that might give him glory or honor from those who would come after." Gastaldi, 9-10. I share that opinion. The silence or fragmentary references to Bruno by many close to him—notably Loggero—is otherwise almost impossible to explain.

Acknowledgments

1. I make my own the words of Oblate Armando Santoro, who wrote of "our deceased confrère, Fr. Paolo Calliari, O.M.V., a great scholar of our Founder, whose writings composed in a lifetime of study, have served as a constant point of reference in the writing of this book": *Il cammino spirituale*, 10 (see Preface, note 4 above). In the introduction to his monumental typewritten biography (3600 pages) of Bruno Lanteri, Paolo Calliari described his intention to include as much as possible "everything that can be said" about Bruno Lanteri. He added: "The method of synthesis will certainly follow the analytical method I have used—a rich synthesis worthy of presentation in elegant literary style. Following this [my] biographical-critical labor, other biographies of Lanteri may be written and published, utilizing what I have done, but without the heavily detailed and documented apparatus I have employed, more accessible to all categories of readers": *Il Venerabile Pio Bruno Lanteri (1759–1830)*, 1, 6 (see Preface, note 1 above). It is my hope that the present biography, deeply indebted to Calliari's, may respond in some measure to his desire.

Chapter 1: Into Exile

1. Antoine Lestra, *Histoire Secrète de la Congrégation de Lyon: De la clandestinité a la fondation de la Propagation de la Foi (1801–1831)* (Paris: Nouvelles éditions latines, 1967), 189.

2. E. E. Y. Hales, *Napoleon and the Pope: The Story of Napoleon and Pius VII* (London: Eyre & Spottiswoode, 1962), 130.

3. A vicar capitular was the administrator of a diocese without a bishop, elected by the canons (body of priests) of the cathedral in the diocese.

4. B, 288.

5. In 1803, Berthaut du Coin had joined the *Congrégation* of Lyon, a group of priests and laity founded in 1801 by Fr. Pierre Alexandre Aimé Roger to create a group of fervent Catholics among young members of the bourgeoisie. Under Napoleon's empire, they were part of the secret chain between France and Italy in support of Pius VII. See B, 284, n. 93; C 2, 380–383.

6. P, 20.

7. P, 45–46. Gastaldi, 357, describes Bruno's eyes as "cilestri," i.e., pale blue. One official document of the Napoleonic government in Piedmont qualifies his eyes as "biggi," i.e., of grayish hue: P, 45. A second

official document of the same government portrays his eyes as "bruns," i.e., brown: P, 46. In my description, I have followed what appears to be the preponderance of the evidence.

8. C 2, 294.

9. P, 629.

10. P, 23.

11. P, 23.

12. P, 21–25.

13. P, 23. Pope Clement XIV, surrendering to pressure from the Catholic monarchs of Europe, suppressed the Jesuits in 1773. See chapter 3, below.

14. P, 24.

15. P, 26–27. The word "grangia" signified a country dwelling with cultivated terrains, with the corresponding buildings. See Brustolon, *Guida*, 282.

16. P, 28.

17. P, 31.

18. B, 293; P, 146–147.

19. P, 41. "Loggero" is pronounced "low-*jeh*-row."

20. C 2, 298.

21. C 2, 299.

22. P, 35–36.

23. C 2, 299–300.

24. P, 682. Phrase used by Vincenzo D'Avino in the *Enciclopedia dell'Ecclesiastico*, vol. 3, Turin, 1865, under the entry "Oblati di Maria Vergine."

25. C 2, 322.

Chapter 2: Beginnings

1. Diessbach, *Disinganni, o sia il Solitario Cristiano Cattolico*, 1778, vol. I, 2–3; B, 9.

2. Diessbach, *Disinganni*, I, 17–18.

3. P, 78.

4. P, 78; B, 10–13.

5. P, 78.

6. B, 16–17.

7. B, 28.

8. P, 79; B, 17.

9. Bi 1, 569.

10. The *Encyclopédie*: 28 volumes, published in France between 1751 and 1772, a main vehicle for the thought of the Enlightenment.

11. Thomas Campbell, S.J., *The Jesuits 1534-1921: A History of the Society of Jesus from Its Foundation to the Present Time* (Boston: Milford House, 1971), 465. Campbell discusses these events on pp. 462–465.

12. P, 598; cf. G, 21.

13. S 1, 563–564.

14. C 5, 411.

15. C 5, 417.

16. Cf. G, 19–20.

17. P, 629.

18. P, 598.

19. V 1, 73–77; P, 598, 642.

20. P, 629.

21. P, 6–7.

22. P, 6. Giovanni Battista Biancotti (1810–1870) recounted that "the Abate Eula, his cousin, who was also from Cuneo and of like age, had frequent and close contact with him [Bruno] in his early years, and affirmed that he had always known him to be pure and exemplary in his conduct, and fervent in his piety." P, 643.

23. P, 598, 645; G, 27–30; V 1, 105–110.

24. B, 21.

25. The Jesuit "tertianship."

26. B, 21–22.

27. B, 22.

28. P, 79; B, 22.

29. *Le Chrétien Catholique inviolablement attaché a sa Religion par la consideration de quelques unes des preuves qui en établissent la certitude*, 3 vols. (Turin: Jean-Baptiste Fontana, 1771).

30. Diessbach, *Le Chrétien*, 370; B, 31–37.

31. B, 31.

32. In Simon Schama, *Citizens: A Chronicle of the French Revolution* (New York: Random House, 1990), 180.

33. www.economist.com, "Coffee Houses: The Internet in a Cup." See also, Maurice Vaussard, *La vie quotidienne en Italie au XVIIIe siècle* (Paris: Hachette, 1959), 129–136.

34. Diessbach, *Le Chrétien*, vol. 3, 370–371.

35. Diessbach, *Le Chrétien*, vol. 3, 371–372.

36. Diessbach, *Le Chrétien*, vol. 3, 372.

37. Diessbach, *Le Chrétien*, vol. 3, 374–375.

38. Diessbach, *Le Chrétien*, vol. 3, 375–376.

39. Diessbach, *Le Chrétien*, vol. 3, 376.

40. Diessbach, *Le Chrétien*, vol. 3, 385.

41. Diessbach, *Le Chrétien*, vol. 3, 388.

42. "Good works of supererogation" are good acts that a person is under no moral obligation to perform, and chooses freely to undertake.

43. Diessbach, *Le Chrétien*, vol. 3, 390.

44. Diessbach, *Il zelo meditativo di un pio Solitario Cristiano e Cattolico espresso in una serie di riflessioni, e di affetti* (Turin: Giambattista Fontana, 1774), 147.

Chapter 3: A Gathering of Friends

1. E. E. Y. Hales, *Revolution and Papacy 1796–1846* (Garden City, N.Y.: Doubleday & Company, Inc., 1960), 40.

2. Hales, *Revolution and Papacy*, 44.

3. B, 24–28.

4. B, 38–40, 47–53.

5. V 1, 121, n. 23.

6. P, 7–8, 646.

7. V 1, 285, n. 11.

8. P, 629, 646.

9. P, 617; V 1, 148.

10. P, 617.

11. See Hubert Jedin and J. Dolan, eds., *History of the Church*, vol. 6, *The Church in the Age of Absolutism and Enlightenment* (New York: Crossroad, 1981), 24–57, 381–428; Karl Bihlmeyer and H. Tüchle, *Church History*, vol. 3, *Modern and Recent Times* (Westminster: Newman Press, 1966), 236–245; C 1, 38–46; Brustolon, *Alle origini*, 25–30; Cristiani, *Un Prêtre redouté de Napoléon,* 15–17.

12. Gregorio Penco, O.S.B., *Storia della Chiesa in Italia. Vol II: Dal Concilio di Trento ai nostri giorni* (Milan: Jaca Book, 1978), 197–200.

13. Penco, *Storia*, 289.

14. B, 27, n. 100.

15. Jedin and Dolan, *The Church in the Age of Absolutism and Enlightenment*, 534–535; Bihlmeyer and Tüchle, *Modern and Recent Times*, 284; Denzinger-Schönmetzer, *Enchiridion Symbolorum* (Fribourg: Herder, 1967), nos. 2634–2639; Hales, *Revolution and Papacy*, 59; V 1, 418–427.

16. C 4, 22, n. 2.

17. C 4, 22, n. 2; cf. Guerber, *Le ralliement,* 84–93.

18. Penco, 196, 203.

19. P, 617.

20. Guerber, *Le ralliement,* 111.

21. P, 559.

22. P, 617.

23. Antonio Tannoia, C.Ss.R., *Vita di S. Alfonso M. De Ligouri,* 762, in B, 225. At this time Alphonsus was still living: he died in 1787.

24. P, 560.

25. P, 81.

26. P, 58.

27. P, 598.

28. P, 599.

29. P, 599.

30. P, 650.

31. C 4, 333, n. 1; cf. Gallagher, *Gli esercizi,* 198–201.

32. C 4, 179.

33. B, 58.

34. B, 57.

35. B, 485.

36. B, 487–488.

37. B, 488.

38. B, 64–65.

39. B, 76–77.

40. P, 9; V 1, 257–258.

41. P, 9; V 1, 257–260. The patrimony consisted of a house in Cuneo with three floors, situated in the parish of St. Ambrose, and valued at 6,000 lire: see V 1, 259.

42. P, 9; V 1, 260.

43. V 1, 260–262.

44. P, 9; S II, 1b.

45. P, 9; V 1, 269–271.

46. B, 104.

47. P, 187.

48. B, 503.

49. P, 187.

50. P, 187.

51. B, 505.

52. B, 505; P, 187.

53. B, 505–506; P, 187.

54. P, 506.

55. B, 109–110, 507.

56. B, 94; C 2, 13.

57. B, 93–94. Others propose *assemblée des associés* (assembly of [those] associated), *association* (with its double use of the letter "a"), *association des amis* (association of friends), or, in later writing and probably by analogy with Diessbach's two "amicizie," *amicizia anonima* (anonymous friendship): B, 93–94; P, 153.

58. B, 94; C 2, 13–14, 57, n. 5.

59. B, 98–99.

60. C 2, 180.

61. Bruno and de La Palme would later engage in literary controversy regarding Alphonsus Liguori. Since both published their works anonymously, neither learned the identity of his literary opponent. See Guerber, *Le ralliement*, 103–110.

62. B, 99–101; C 2, 20–22, n. 4. On Luigi Craveri, see below, chapter 18.

Chapter 4: "Nunc Coepi"

1. S 1, 558.

2. S 1, 553.

3. S 1, 552.

4. S 1, 554.

5. S 1, 561.

6. S 3, 1877.

7. S 1, 571.

8. S 1, 551.

9. S 1, 554.

10. S 1, 560.

11. S 1, 560.

12. S 1, 572.

13. S 1, 560, 567-568, 572.

14. S 1, 558.

15. S 1, 558.

16. S 1, 573.

17. S 1, 576.

18. S 1, 566.

19. S 1, 573.

20. S 1, 562.

21. S 1, 566, 576.

22. S 1, 566.

23. S 1, 574.

24. S 1, 567, 572, 574.

25. S 1, 566.

26. S 1, 568.

27. S 1, 566.

28. S 1, 576.

29. S 1, 565.

30. S 1, 560.

31. S 1, 560; P, 527. For St. Ignatius's teaching, see *The Spiritual Exercises*, nos. 85-86. A cilice is an instrument of penance worn against the skin.

32. P, 605. See also P, 744.

33. S 1, 561.

34. S 1, 563-564.

35. S 1, 564.

36. S 1, 559.

37. P, 9; V 1, 297-298.

38. Hales, *Revolution and Papacy*, 54-55.

39. G, 69.

40. C 2, 204.

41. P, 600; B, 119-121; G, 66-73; V 1, 299-313. The references are to Johann Nikolaus von Hontheim (1701-1790), known as Febronius; Edmond Richer (1559-1631); Joseph Valentin Eybel (1741-1805); and the Synod of Pistoia (1786). See G, 66-70, and Brustolon, *Alle origini*, 21-38.

42. P, 9; V 1, 313-315. I am accepting the limitations of the documentation in presenting Bruno's ordination so succinctly. No surviving document records his experience of what must have been a significant day in the life of one who so esteemed and loved the priestly vocation.

43. P, 10; V 1, 319-323.

44. P, 10-11; V 1, 359-360.

45. S 1, 559.

46. S 1, 566.

47. G, 81; V 1, 405-406, 414, n. 61.

48. P, XIV; V 1, 386; Santoro, *Il cammino*, 138.

49. C 2, 115.

50. C 2, 115.

51. C 2, 117.

52. P, 5; C 2, 119, n. 2; V 1, 368.

53. C 2, 118.

54. P, 648; V 1, 372–375.

55. P, 55; V 1, 407. The Index of Prohibited Books was the list of books that Catholics were forbidden to read by the Church.

56. S I, 142. See V 1, 407.

57. B, 64.

58. P, 630.

59. C 2, 162.

60. P, 618.

61. S 1, 649–70; V 1, 405–407; cf. S 1, 669, n. 1.

62. P, 619.

63. P, 620.

64. P, 11; V 1, 386–389.

65. P, 631.

66. P, 632.

67. P, 619.

68. P, 603.

69. P, 324.

70. P, 324–325.

71. C 2, 122; cf. P, 90–91; B, 511.

72. C 2, 124.

73. P, 166.

74. P, 168.

75. P, 171.

76. S 1, 589.

77. S 1, 589.

78. S 1, 589.

Chapter 5: Spiritual Struggles

1. C 2, 98.

2. The three Estates were formed, respectively, by the clergy, the nobles, and the commoners.

3. Hales, *Revolution and Papacy*, 47–53.

4. Jean Leflon, *La crise révolutionnaire 1789–1846* (Paris: Bloud & Gay, 1951), vol. 20 of the *Histoire de l'Église depuis les origines jusqu'à nos jours*, ed. Augustin Fliche and Victor Martin, 57.

5. Leflon, *La crise*, 67–71.

6. Leflon, *La crise*, 96.

7. S 1, 590–595.

8. Cf. S 1, 644.

9. Cf. S 1, 644.

10. S 1, 590–595. In the Two Standards (*Spiritual Exercises*, 136–147) Ignatius invites a person to consider two contrasting spiritual paths: that of Christ, beginning with love of poverty and leading to humble openness to God; and that of Satan, beginning with coveting of riches and leading to a consuming pride.

11. S 1, 595.

12. S 1, 595.

13. S 1, 596.

14. S 1, 596.

15. S 1, 596.

16. S 1, 596.

17. S 1, 597.

18. S 1, 597.

19. S 1, 597.

20. S 1, 597.

21. S 1, 642.

22. S IV, 432, f. 61.

23. S IV, 432, f. 87.

24. S IV, 432, f. 56. In St. Ignatius of Loyola's teaching, the *general* examination of conscience reviews the entire spiritual experience of the day; the *particular* examination of conscience, on the other hand, reviews a single area of growth, chosen as especially important for the individual. See *Spiritual Exercises*, nos. 24–31, 43.

25. S IV, 432, f. 83.

26. Alonso Rodriguez, S.J. (1526–1616), *The Practice of Christian Perfection.*

27. S IV, 432, f. 74.

28. S IV, 432, f. 115.

29. See Gallagher, *Gli esercizi*, 217, n. 23.

30. S II, 201b.

31. S II, 201b, p. 6.

32. S II, 201b, p. 6.

33. S II, 201b, p. 6.

34. S II, 201b, p. 6.

35. Leflon, *La crise*, 99–100.

36. S II, 201b, p. 6.

37. C 2, 99–102; B, 536, n. 38.

38. C 2, 100.

39. C 2, 100.

40. C 2, 101.

41. C 2, 101.

42. C 2, 102.

43. The arrests occurred on August 12, 1792. See B, 173.

44. B, 173; C 2, 102, n. 9.

45. C 2, 102.

46. William Doyle, *The Oxford History of the French Revolution* (Oxford: Clarendon Press, 1989), 193.

47. Nicomede Bianchi, *Storia della Monarchia piemontese dal 1773 al 1861* (Rome: Fratelli Bocca, 1878), vol. 2, 3.

48. Bi, 2, 27.

49. Cristiani, *Un Prêtre*, 71.

50. Bi, 2, 24.

51. S 1, 632–640; V 1, 534–543.

52. P. 682.

53. S 1, 632–540.

54. S 1, 638–639.

55. S 1, 639.

56. S 1, 639.

57. S 1, 639.

58. S 1, 639.

59. Robert Sobel, *The French Revolution: A Concise History and Interpretation* (Gloucester: Peter Smith, 1974), 110.

60. Leflon, *La crise*, 116–127.

61. Bi, 2, 115ff.

62. S IV, 432, f. 55.

63. Bi, 2, 283.

64. P, 674, n. 1.

65. P, 674; C 2, 353–354.

66. B, 100, and 590, n. 119; P, 615.

67. P, 622.

68. S IV, 432, ff. 27–29; cf. Gallagher, *Gli esercizi,* 217, n. 23.

69. S IV, 432, f. 28.

70. S IV, 432, f. 28.

71. S IV, 432, f. 28.

72. S IV, 432, f. 28.

73. S IV, 432, f. 29.

74. S IV, 432, f. 29.

75. S IV, 432, f. 29.

76. S IV, 432, f. 29.

Chapter 6: "The Calamitous Circumstances of the Times"

1. Tomaso Chiuso, *La Chiesa in Piemonte dal 1797 ai giorni nostri* (Turin: Giulio Speirani e figli, 1887), vol. 2, 31.

2. Bi, 2, 732–733; Co, 2, 31–32. The queen's cause of canonization would be introduced shortly after her death.

3. Co 2, 31.

4. Co 2, 31.

5. B, 214–221; V 1, 650–654.

6. B, 203; V 1, 646–650.

7. B, 475.

8. B, 475.

9. B, 475–476.

10. B, 476. Text of Gal 2:20 from RSVCE.

11. P, 80.

12. B, 222. St. Clement Hofbauer (1751–1820) encountered Diessbach in Vienna.

13. C 4, 181.

14. Bi 3, 355–360.

15. French troops seized Rome in February 1798. The eighty-year-old Pius VI was removed from Rome, and, during eighteen months of captivity, taken to Siena, Florence, Parma, and finally Valence. See Leflon, *La crise,* 156–157; Hales, *Revolution and Papacy,* 128–129.

16. Leflon, *La crise,* 157.

17. Leflon, *La crise,* 157; Hales, *Revolution and Papacy,* 130. The kingdom of Naples governed the southern part of the Italian peninsula.

18. Leflon, *La crise,* 157.

19. Hales, *Revolution and Papacy,* 134; V 2, 43–47.

20. P, 600.

21. P, 600–601.

22. P, 631.

23. This was a practice in the Catholic society of the day.

24. P, 631.

25. P, 619.

26. P, 620. The Civil Constitution of the Church, adopted in revolutionary France in 1790, subjected the Church in France to civil authority.

27. P, 562; S 2, passim; V 2, 310–344; Cristiani, *Un Prêtre*, 76–77.

28. S IV, 432, f. 56; cf. V 2, 64; Gallagher, *Gli esercizi*, 217, n. 23.

29. S IV, 432, f. 56.

30. S IV, 432, f. 56.

31. S IV, 432, f. 56.

32. Co 2, 149.

33. Co 2, 149; V 2, 200.

34. Co 2, 149; V 2, 200.

35. Co 2, 150.

36. P, 600.

37. C 2, 139.

38. C 2, 138–140.

39. C 2, 201.

40. Co 2, 176; V 2, 201.

41. Co 2, 150–151.

42. V 2, 201–203.

43. P, 638–639. Antonio Bresciani, S.J. (1798–1862), a well-known writer, very probably met Bruno in September 1826. See, P, 633–634.

44. G, 467–470; C 2, 125–128.

45. C 2, 126.

46. C 2, 128.

47. C 2, 128–136; P, 533–541.

48. C 2, 129. St. Ignatius discusses these truths in his Principle and Foundation, *Spiritual Exercises*, no. 23.

49. C 2, 130. In Bruno's time, daily Communion was not common among the people, and weekly Communion would have been considered frequent.

50. C 2, 131.

51. C 2, 133–134.

52. C 2, 134–135.

53. Hales, *Revolution and Papacy*, 146. A "concordat" is an agreement between the Holy See and the government of a nation regarding the Catholic Church's presence and activity in that nation.

54. Hales, *Revolution and Papacy*, 139–154.

55. Co, 2, 197. This clause allowed the pope oversight in the choice of new bishops: while named by Napoleon, they required papal confirmation (canonical institution) to exercise their authority.

56. P, 5; V 2, 139–140; cf. C 5, 323.

57. Co 2, 187; V 2, 121–124; Hales, *Revolution and Papacy*, 159.

58. Pietro Stella, *Crisi religiose nel primo Ottocento piemontese* (Turin: Società Editrice internazionale, 1959), 14–20. The four Gallican propositions, drafted by an assembly of French clergy in 1682, "(1) denied the right of the Church to interfere in civil and political affairs in France; (2) asserted . . . the authority of General Councils over the Pope; (3) insisted that the exercise of the apostolic power in France had to be in conformity with the laws and customs of the Gallican [French] Church; (4) maintained that even in questions of faith the ruling of the Pope was not infallible unless the consent of the Church had been given it." Hales, *Pio Nono: A Study in European Politics and Religion in the Nineteenth Century* (Garden City, N.Y.: Image Books, 1962), 349, n. 15.

59. P, 630.

60. P, 620. Papal infallibility was not yet defined as Catholic doctrine.

61. P, 601.

62. C 3, 334.

63. C 2, 143–145.

64. B, 243–244.

65. B, 244; P, 124. "The other supporter . . . was most likely Don Bucelli." B, 244.

66. John Carey, "The Letters of Fr. Lanteri to Ricasoli: An Example of Oblate Spiritual Direction," typescript, 1995, vi.

Chapter 7: Laborers in the Vineyard

1. B, 252–256; V 2, 163–167.

2. C 2, 147.

3. C 2, 147.

4. C 2, 147.

5. C 2, 147.

6. P, 186–194; V 2, 175–177.

7. P, 187–194.

8. P, 193.

9. P, 193.

10. P, 193.

11. P, 193.

12. P, 189.

13. P, 190-191.

14. P, 192.

15. P, 599.

16. P, 619-620. Giuseppe Loggero likewise affirmed: "He strove to form young priests in fidelity to the Holy See, and for that purpose supplied them with every possible means of books, conferences, etc. He further encouraged them with great energy to prepare the meditations of the Spiritual Exercises according to the method, spirit, and order of St. Ignatius of Loyola, for the conversion of the people and to sustain in them a living faith." P, 630-631.

17. P, 639.

18. B, 253-254; V 2, 177-180.

19. C 2, 150.

20. C 2, 151.

21. P, 104-105; V 2, 180-182.

22. P, 104-105.

23. P, 105; V 2, 182.

24. C 2, 168.

25. B, 248-252.

26. B, 249-250.

27. P, 105.

28. B, 249.

29. C 2, 153; B, 249.

30. B, 251, 255.

31. C 2, 154.

32. P, 105; cf. P, 93-96.

33. C 2, 155.

34. C 2, 157.

35. C 2, 158.

36. P, 40; V 2, 225-227; B, 294, n. 128.

37. P, 40; "Cenni sulla vita del P. Giuseppe Loggero Oblato di M. V.," in Giuseppe Loggero, O.M.V., *Nel regno della bontà: Tesori di confidenza in Dio* (Turin: Libreria del Sacro Cuore, 1931), XV.

38. P, 40; B, 294, n. 128; V 2, 226. Loggero would continue his theological studies after 1809 under Bruno's guidance.

39. B, 294, n. 128; V 2, 226.

40. P, 41.

41. P, 607.

42. P, 104.

43. S 1, 645; cf. Gallagher, *Gli esercizi*, 217, n. 23.

44. S 1, 645.

45. S 1, 645.

46. S 1, 645.

47. S 1, 646.

48. S 1, 646.

49. S 1, 646.

50. S 1, 646.

51. S 1, 646.

52. C 2, 160.

53. C 2, 161.

54. C 2, 160–161.

55. C 2, 161.

56. C 2, 161.

57. C 2, 162.

58. C 2, 163.

59. C 2, 164.

60. C 2, 164.

61. C 2, 165.

62. C 2, 165.

63. C 2, 166.

64. C 2, 166.

65. C 2, 166.

66. C 2, 166.

67. C 2, 166–167.

68. C 2, 167.

69. C 2, 168.

70. C 2, 170.

71. C 2, 170.

72. C 2, 170.

73. C 2, 172; cf. Co, 2, 237–241; V 2, 240–243.

74. E. E. Y. Hales, *Napoleon and the Pope: The Story of Napoleon and Pius VII* (London: Eyre & Spottiswoode, 1962), 93.

75. Hales, *Napoleon and the Pope*, 94.

Chapter 8: "Our Stand Is Irrevocable"

1. Angelo Montonati, *Giulia Colbert di Barolo: Marchesa dei poveri* (Milan: Paoline, 2011), 11, 16.

2. G, 172; Montonati, *Giulia*, 34.

3. Co 2, 314.

4. Co 2, 255–256, 260, 316–318.

5. C 2, 214.

6. C 2, 215–216.

7. C 2, 216.

8. C 2, 217–218.

9. C 2, 222.

10. P, 620–622, 632–633, etc.

11. C 2, 233.

12. C 2, 235.

13. C 2, 197.

14. C 2, 235.

15. C 2, 257.

16. C 2, 257.

17. C 2, 258.

18. C 2, 258.

19. C 2, 259; cf. C 2, 260, 262, 265, 269.

20. S I, 154.

21. P, 55; V 2, 363–364. For the same reason, Bruno asked permission to celebrate the Mass of the Blessed Virgin Mary and the Mass of the Dead on many days of the liturgical calendar. See: P, 55, 363–364.

22. Co 2, 324.

23. Leflon, *La crise*, 241–242; Hales, *Revolution and Papacy*, 173–174.

24. Leflon, *La crise*, 241–242.

25. Leflon, *La crise*, 242; Hales, *Napoleon and the Pope*, 85–86.

26. For centuries, and until Italian unification some decades later, the pope was temporal sovereign of the central part of Italy.

27. Leflon, *La crise*, 242–243.

28. Hales, *Napoleon and the Pope*, 94.

29. Leflon, *La crise*, 245.

30. Hales, *Napoleon and the Pope*, 96.

31. Leflon, *La crise*, 244–247.

32. Leflon, *La crise*, 246.

33. Leflon, *La crise*, 246.

34. Leflon, *La crise*, 248; Co 2, 324–325.

35. P, 651. Giovanni Battista Biancotti (1810-1870) entered the Oblates of the Virgin Mary on June 26, 1830. He would be the fifth Rector Major of the Oblates (1862-1870).

36. C 2, 180-181.

37. C 2, 177-178.

38. S 1, 647; Gallagher, *Gli esercizi*, 217.

39. S 1, 647.

40. S IV, 432, f. 66.

41. S IV, 432, f. 66, 71.

42. S 1, 647.

43. C 2, 216. This was the Shrine of St. Ignatius situated at the summit of Mount Bastia, above Lanzo, forty kilometers northwest of Turin.

44. B, 280-283; Andrea Brustolon, O.M.V., *Guida ai luoghi del ven. Padre Pio Bruno Lanteri e dell'origine degli Oblati di Maria Vergine*, typescript, 2010, 284.

45. P, 560.

46. B, 282.

47. Giovanni Pignata, *Il Santuario di S. Ignazio* (Genoa: Edizioni d'arte Marconi, 2003), 18-19.

48. P, 620-621.

49. C 2, 210, 216 (n. 1), 220-222, 232, etc.

50. C 2, 207-209, 234, n. 3.

51. C 2, 234, n. 3.

52. C 2, 208.

53. C 2, 208.

54. C 2, 208.

55. C 2, 208.

56. C 2, 208-209.

57. C 2, 234.

58. C 2, 234.

59. C 2, 234.

60. C 2, 235.

61. C 3, 197.

62. C 3, 197.

63. C 3, 197-198.

64. C 3, 198.

65. C 3, 198.

66. C 3, 198.

Chapter 9: The Pope in Captivity

1. Bartolomeo Pacca, *Historical Memoirs of Cardinal Pacca, Prime Minister to Pius VII*, trans. George Head (London: Longman, Brown, Green, and Longmans, 1850), vol. 1, 140; Hales, *Napoleon and the Pope*, 113–114; Hales, *Revolution and Papacy*, 189–190.

2. Pacca, *Historical Memoirs*, 1, 140–141.

3. Leflon, *La crise*, 250.

4. Lestra, *Histoire Secrète*, 169; Leflon, *La crise*, 250–251.

5. Hales, *Napoleon and the Pope*, 118–119; Pacca, *Historical Memoirs*, 1, 149–163.

6. Leflon, *La crise*, 251–252.

7. RSVCE.

8. RSVCE.

9. Pacca, *Historical Memoirs*, 1, 162–163.

10. Leflon, *La crise*, 255.

11. Leflon, *La crise*, 255.

12. Leflon, *La crise*, 255.

13. Leflon, *La crise*, 255.

14. Leflon, *La crise*, 256–265; Co 2, 336–365.

15. By present-day roads, Turin lies approximately 140 kilometers from Savona, north and to the west.

16. Co 2, 343.

17. These were the "canons" of the "cathedral chapter" (hence the term "capitular" for the vicar they elected).

18. B, 288; P, 601, 632–633.

19. P, 632; C 5, 23; cf. B, 288–289; V 2, 531–536.

20. P, 632.

21. G, 203; Co 2, 344; B, 288; V 2, 545–546.

22. B, 288.

23. P, 621.

24. P, 20, 23.

25. P, 632.

26. P, 601.

27. P, 601; cf. G, 200–201; V 2, 519–525.

28. Co 2, 344.

29. P, 633; G, 204; B, 294–295; V 2, 579–580.

30. C 3, 113.

31. B, 299, 301.

32. Esp, 71, 73.

33. Esp, 77.

34. P, 604.

35. P, 620.

36. P, 623.

37. S III, 405ff; G, 209, n. 1; V 2, 671-674.

38. C 2, 333; P, 602.

39. C 2, 322. See above, chapter 1.

40. P, 52.

41. P, 52.

42. P, 621-622.

43. V 2, 656.

44. C 2, 301, 305, 314, 357; cf. G, 201.

45. S 1, 757.

46. S 1, 761.

47. C 2, 323.

48. C 2, 323.

49. C 2, 323-324. On the Latin *nunc coepi* in Bruno's writings, see John Carey, *The Spiritual Doctrine of the Venerable Father Bruno Lanteri in His Letters of Spiritual Direction to Sir Leopoldo Ricasoli,* thesis for the degree of master of arts, St. John's Seminary, Brighton, Massachusetts, 1993, typescript, 82-85.

50. C 3, 113.

51. C 3, 113.

52. C 3, 113. As noted above, these currents of thought fostered rigorism in pastoral practice (Jansenism) and sought to undermine papal authority (Richerism, Febronianism).

53. S I, 209, digital page 68.

54. S I, 209, p. 68.

55. S I, 209, p. 68.

56. S I, 209, p. 74.

57. S I, 209, p. 74.

58. S I, 209, p. 75.

59. S I, 209, p. 75.

60. S I, 209, p. 75.

61. B, 297.

62. B, 297-298; cf. G, 202, 210-211; P, 16.

63. P, 621; B, 298.

64. P, 621.

65. P, 621. See Guerber, *Le ralliement*, 194–195, and note 64, for a discussion of Craveri's testimony, and of the authorship of the *Dissertation*. Guerber concludes that although Craveri is a "witness worthy of faith," this question "remains most obscure." See *Le ralliement*, 195–196, n. 64.

66. Gunther Rothenberg, *The Napoleonic Wars* (New York: Harper-Collins, 2006), 160–173.

Chapter 10: Restoration

1. C 2, 300–301.

2. C 2, 305.

3. C 2, 315.

4. C 2, 322.

5. C 2, 332.

6. C 2, 339.

7. C 2, 357.

8. Massimo d'Azeglio, *My Recollections: Recollections of Massimo d'Azeglio*, trans. Count Maffei (London: Chapman and Hall, 1868), vol. 1, 168.

9. C 1, 14; Brustolon, *L'azione*, 235.

10. *Nel regno della bontà*, XVI. Both popes suffered exile at the hands of the French.

11. Francesco Cognasso, *Storia di Turin* (Florence: Giunti Gruppo Editoriale, 2002), 442.

12. Cognasso, *Storia di Turin*, 442–443; Co 3, 40–41.

13. Giacomo Martina, S.J., "Il contesto storico dell'azione evangelizzatrice del Lanteri," *Lanterianum* 2, no. 1 (1994): 95–99.

14. Martina, "Il contesto storico," *Lanterianum* 2, no. 1 (1994): 99.

15. Martina, "Il contesto storico," *Lanterianum* 2, no. 1 (1994): 99. This was the period known in European history as the Restoration. Brustolon writes: "The term 'Restoration' refers to the political and social system imposed in the various nations after the fall of Napoleon . . . as determined in Paris and Vienna (1814–1815), where it was decided to restore the 'former order of things.'" *L'azione*, 43. In Piedmont, the Restoration lasted until 1848: Martina, "Il contesto storico," 91.

16. B, 319ff.

17. B, 322.

18. B, 370–371.

19. B, 369.

20. P, 250.

21. P, 195; B, 307. Luigi Felici was a "former Jesuit" because of the suppression of the Society of Jesus in 1773.

22. P, 197; Gallagher, *Gli esercizi*, 252.

23. B, 307; P, 197.

24. P, 197.

25. C 3, 114.

26. C 3, 114.

27. *Nel regno della bontà*, XII; *Elenco*, 1817-1843.

28. C 3, 114.

29. V 3/1, 84; Brustolon, *Guida*, 190. The writer was Felice Giordano, a future Oblate of the Virgin Mary.

30. P, 599.

31. P, 58; cf. P, 599, 630-631; V 3/2, 185-186.

32. C 2, 379.

33. P, 604.

34. C 2, 379.

35. B, 305.

36. P, 622; B, 305.

37. P, 602.

38. Antonio Lanteri "may have been a distant relative of the Theologian Lanteri." Paolo Calliari, O.M.V., *Gli Oblati di Maria. Vol III: Primi quattro anni di vita* (n.p.: Editrice Lanteriana, 1980), 187.

39. Andrea Brustolon, O.M.V., *Alle origini della Congregazione degli Oblati di Maria Vergine: Punti chiari e punti oscuri* (Turin: Edizioni Lanteri, 1995), 98-99; Brustolon, *L'azione*, 234-236; C 2, 354, n. 3.

40. Antonio Lanteri was the assistant priest in Craveri's parish in Andezzeno, near Turin.

41. C 3, 18.

42. C 3, 18.

43. C 3, 18.

44. C 3, 35.

45. C 3, 35.

46. C 3, 35-36.

47. OM, 12-16; Brustolon, *Guida*, 338-339.

48. OM, 16-17.

49. OM, 24; S I, 245.

50. S I, 245, 257b; OM, 28-30.

51. S I, 245; Gallagher, *Gli esercizi*, 253.

52. S. Carignano, vol. 1, fasc. 1. Published in Claretta, "Origini degli Oblati," *L'Oblato di Maria Vergine* 6 (1962): 80. For the archival reference, see Andrea Brustolon, O.M.V., *Storiografia lanteriana ed Archivio storico della Congregazione degli Oblati di Maria Vergine: Approcci mentali ed indice dei documenti* (Turin: Edizioni Lanteri, 1995), 75.

53. S. Carignano., vol. 1, fasc. 1; Brustolon, *Storiografia*, 75; Claretta, "Origini degli Oblati," *L'Oblato di Maria Vergine* 6 (1962): 82.

54. S I, 257c.

55. P, 259.

56. S I, 257a; P, 259–260; OM, 44–48.

57. S I, 257a.

58. S I, 257a.

59. S I, 257a; OM, 51–56.

60. Montonati, *Giulia*, 26.

61. G, 172.

62. G, 172.

63. G, 172.

64. G, 172.

65. G, 172; Montonati, *Giulia*, 34–35; Brustolon, *Guida*, 237; V 3/1, 86–89; Brustolon, *L'azione*, 235.

66. Montonati, *Giulia*, 46.

67. Montonati, *Giulia*, 46.

68. Montonati, *Giulia*, 46.

69. Montonati, *Giulia*, 47–48.

70. Montonati, *Giulia*, 49ff.

71. Montonati, *Giulia*, 62–68.

72. Montonati, *Giulia*, 6, 73.

73. V 3/1, 89.

74. Co 4, 50.

75. Co 4, 50; Montonati, *Giulia*, 210–212; Brustolon, *Guida*, 255–257.

76. Montonati, *Giulia*, 199.

77. Montonati, *Giulia*, 7, 213.

78. Rothenberg, *The Napoleonic Wars*, 194.

79. Azeglio, *My Recollections*, 177–178.

Chapter 11: Carignano

1. S I, 257c; OM, 53–54.

2. S I, 257c.

3. S I, 257c; OM, 55–56; cf. S I, 257b.

4. OM, 56.

5. S I, 257a; OM, 57–59.

6. S I, 257c; OM, 59.

7. S I, 257c; OM, 59.

8. S I, 257a; S I 257c.

9. P, 260; OM, 62–63, 401–402.

10. S I, 257c; P, 260.

11. OM, 64.

12. S I, 1359.

13. S I, 257c; P, 273.

14. S I, 257c; P, 273.

15. S I, 1359; cf. S I, 257a.

16. S I, 1359.

17. C 4, 179.

18. S I, 275c; P, 273–274.

19. S I, 257c; V 3/1, 48–51.

20. S I, 257a.

21. C 3, 133.

22. C 3, 134.

23. C 3, 136–137.

24. P, 263–265; Esp, 97–99.

25. Esp, 97.

26. Esp, 97–98.

27. P, 270–272. Archbishop Giacinto della Torre died in 1814, and no successor was named until 1818. In the intervening years, Vicar Capitular Emmanuele Gonetti administrated the archdiocese.

28. Candido Bona, I.M.C., *La rinascita missionaria in Italia: Dalle "Amicizie" all'Opera per la Propagazione della Fede* (Turin: Edizioni Missioni Consolata, 1964), 51.

29. Bona, *La rinascita*, 44.

30. Bona, *La rinascita*, 44.

31. Bona, *La rinascita*, 44. Pope Paul VI canonized Elizabeth Seton in 1975.

32. Bona, *La rinascita*, 44; V 3/1, 112.

33. Bona, *La rinascita*, 45.

34. C 3, 127–128.

35. C 3, 127–128.

36. Bona, *La rinascita*, 56; B, 314, n. 63.

37. B, 314, n. 63.

38. C 3, 128.

39. The return of the Jesuits to the kingdom of Piedmont was imminent at the time: Bona, *La rinascita*, 52. In 1816, Loggero entered the Jesuit novitiate in Genoa, then part of the kingdom of Piedmont. He remained only a short time before returning to Turin. See C 3, 111–114, with notes.

40. Bona, *La rinascita*, 52–53; 141–142.

41. Bona, *La rinascita*, 142.

42. Bona, *La rinascita*, 53.

43. C 3, 128–129.

44. C 3, 129.

45. C 3, 28.

46. C 2, 361–362.

47. S II, 116b; C 3, 51–95; S 1, 677–719.

48. C 3, 20.

49. C 3, 20. Bruno's answer has not been conserved. Chateaubriand's *Atala* was published in the 1802 edition of the *La Génie du Christianisme*.

50. C 2, 393.

51. C 2, 393–394. Hugues-Félicité-Robert de Lamennais (1782–1854) was a French priest and celebrated writer. He would later meet Bruno: see below, chapter 20.

52. C 3, 24.

53. C 3, 108, n. 8; 115–124.

54. S IV, 432.

55. S IV, 432.

56. Esp, 151.

57. C 3, 150.

58. C 3, 161.

59. C 3, 167–168.

60. C 3, 195–197.

61. C 3, 168, 197. Bruno's answers to this and the preceding letter from his cousin have not been conserved.

62. C 3, 164–165.

63. C 3, 165.

64. C 3, 165.

65. C 3, 142.

66. C 3, 142.

67. P, 276–277.

68. S I, 257c.

Chapter 12: The Oblates of Mary

1. Acts 15:26, RNAB.
2. P, 275–281.
3. P, 280.
4. P, 280.
5. Esp, 152.
6. Esp, 153. As Bruno notes, the reference is to Ephesians 4:15.
7. Esp, 154.
8. Esp, 137.
9. P, 350.
10. P, 350.
11. C 3, 150; S I, 257c.
12. S I, 257c; G, 233–237.
13. S 4, 2804–2806.
14. S I, 257c.
15. S 4, 2812.
16. S 4, 2815.
17. S I, 255.
18. S I, 271.
19. S I, 257c.
20. S I, 257c.
21. Santoro, *Il cammino*, 279; cf. P, 262.
22. S I, 260b.
23. S I, 260a.
24. C 3, 248–249.
25. C 3, 249.
26. C 3, 249.
27. C 3, 249.
28. C 3, 191; P, 372–373.
29. C 3, 191; P, 372.
30. C 3, 192.

31. Bruno's draft of the letter just cited contains various revisions of the text. Responding to the invitation to join the Oblates in Carignano, Bruno first wrote and later cancelled the following: "But for very grave reasons that I cannot share, with the greatest regret, I must tell you that this is not possible for me." S II, 233a; see the transcription in C 3, 191, n. 1. In no other surviving document does Bruno explain more explicitly the reason for his decision to remain in Turin and, from there, direct

the Oblates. My best sense of Bruno's motive is that, once the priests in Carignano embraced his chosen ministries—Ignatian retreats and parish missions, diffusion of good books, combatting current errors, confessions and catechesis for the poor, ill, and imprisoned—Bruno enthusiastically adopted them and, with great energy, guided and supported them. Nor did he fail to consider a move to Carignano. In 1816, he told Reynaudi that "he might with time resolve to join them" in Carignano (see above, chapter 11), and, as we have just seen, in 1819 wrote to Reynaudi that "had I been able to do so before now, I myself willingly would have taken the initiative" to join the community in Carignano. Bruno was not prepared, however, to abandon his multiple apostolic relations and works in Turin, which also accomplished great good. Thus, in his relationship with the Oblates of Carignano, Bruno essentially continued what he had long done: from his residence in Turin, he guided a group of priests in the classic works of the *Amicizie*. The secrecy with which he did so was characteristic of Diessbach's *Amicizie*, conformed to Bruno's own inclination, and valuable in disarming potential resistance to the congregation. On this last, see Calliari in C 3, 191, n. 1. Bruno did not judge opportune, at this time, the further step of leaving Turin, canonically joining the new congregation, and publicly assuming its leadership.

32. B, 310; C 3, 162.

33. *Écrits Oblats* (Rome: Postulation générale O.M.I., 1982), VI, 206. De Mazenod met Bruno and Guala in 1825: see below, chapter 16.

34. C 2, 185.

35. P, 200.

36. B, 313.

37. P, 201.

38. P, 201.

39. In the Archdiocese of Turin, priestly ordination did not of itself permit the newly ordained to hear confessions. Archdiocesan practice required that these priests study the pastoral applications of moral theology for three further years before such permission was granted.

40. P, 205; B, 312.

41. P, 202–203.

42. P, 203.

43. The University of Turin, the archdiocesan seminary, and, as of 1814, San Francesco d'Assisi, all offered approved programs ("conferences") of moral theology.

44. P, 204–205.

45. P, 205.

46. "Oblati di Maria Santissima Addolorata," literally, "Oblates of Mary Most Holy of Sorrows." P, 207; C 3, 145. I have rendered the title in the more common English-language equivalent.

47. B, 311; P, 212.

48. B, 311.

49. B, 311; P, 212-215.

50. *Il Convitto Ecclesiastico di Torino* (Turin: La Palatina, 1940), 11-12.

51. *Il Convitto*, 13-14.

52. *Il Convitto*, 14.

53. Quoted in Giuseppe Orlandi, "La recezione della dottrina morale di S. Alfonso Maria de Liguori in Italia durante la Restaurazione," *Spicilegium Historicum CssR* 45 (1997): 371.

54. *Il Convitto*, 15-16. Gallicanism tended to limit the authority of the Holy Father with respect to diocesan bishops and civil government.

55. Penco, *Storia*, 266-267.

56. Santoro, *Il cammino*, 275, n. 9.

57. Santoro, *Il cammino*, 275.

58. G, 241-242; V 3/2, 178.

59. P, 65; cf. V 3/2, 201, n. 24.

60. G, 242.

61. S Generali, vol. Elenchi, fasc. 6, 28; Brustolon, *L'azione*, 246-247.

62. *Il Padre Filippo Simonino*, transcription Calliari, 20.

63. *Il Padre Filippo Simonino*, 21-22.

64. *Il Padre Filippo Simonino*, 22; V 3/2, 174; *Lanterianum* 6, no. 1 (1998): 48.

65. C 3, 193.

66. *Elenco/Nota*, 16.

67. S Generali, vol. Elenchi, fasc. 6, doc. 28.

68. *Elenco/Nota*, 15.

69. P, 351.

70. V 3/2, 258-259; C 3, 158-159.

71. V 3/2, 259-260; C 3, 159.

72. S 1, 747. In this and in the following quotations, the emphasis is in the original.

73. S 1, 752.

74. S 1, 752.

75. S 1, 752.

76. S 1, 754.

77. C 3, 264.

78. C 3, 264; V 3/2, 260; G, 467.

79. C 3, 264–265.

80. From the Latin of the Our Father: *Dimitte nobis debita nostra* ("Forgive us our trespasses").

81. C 3, 265.

82. C 3, 158.

83. C 3, 159.

84. C 5, 198.

Chapter 13: Growth and Crisis

1. *Elenco/Nota*, 15.

2. *Elenco/Nota*, 15–18.

3. S I, 257c.

4. C 3, 178; V 3/2, 209–210.

5. V 3/2, 210.

6. ASCR, *Atto capitolare*.

7. ASCR, *Atto capitolare*.

8. Gallagher, *Gli esercizi*, 153, n. 125.

9. From the author's visit to the cathedral, and local consultation.

10. ASCR, *Atto capitolare*; P, 334.

11. ASCR, *Atto capitolare*.

12. G, 250; V 3/2, 213.

13. ASCR, *Atto capitolare*.

14. ASCR, *Atto capitolare*.

15. ASCR, *Atto capitolare*.

16. C 3, 190; cf. C 3, 187.

17. *Il Padre Filippo Simonino*, 30.

18. *Elenco/Nota*, 15.

19. S I, 322.

20. C 3, 187–188.

21. C 3, 188.

22. S I, 322.

23. S I, 322.

24. C 3, 189.

25. *Elenco/Nota*, 15.

26. S I, 257c.

27. S I, 257c.

28. *Elenco/Nota,* 15.
29. C 3, 174.
30. C 3, 225.
31. Co 3, 49.
32. Aldo Giraudo, *Clero, Seminario e società: Aspetti della Restaura-*
zione religiosa a Torino (Rome: LAS, 1993), 51.
33. Giraudo, *Clero, Seminario e società,* 52.
34. Giraudo, *Clero, Seminario e società,* 54.
35. P, 336–342; V 3/1, 124–129.
36. P, 341–342.
37. P, 341.
38. P, 341.
39. P, 337.
40. C 3, 55.
41. P, 344, 388.
42. *Elenco/Nota,* 16.
43. P, 388–389.
44. P, 351.
45. P, 352.
46. P, 352.
47. P, 352.
48. OM, 492.
49. P, 280; Esp, 152–153.
50. P, 354; cf. P, 354–361.
51. P, 391.
52. S I, 257c.
53. P, 391.
54. S I, 257c.
55. P, 391–392.
56. *Il Padre Filippo Simonino,* 32.
57. *Il Padre Filippo Simonino,* 32–37. See also, G, 256–260. Gastaldi
writes: "Filippo, who had given so many singular examples of virtue
when healthy, gave them equally when ill. He radiated gentleness, peace
of spirit, and acceptance of God's will, and, in his pain, thought only of
paradise." G, 258.
58. C 3, 245.
59. C 3, 245.
60. P, 351, 362–364, 389–390.
61. P, 362–364.
62. P, 362.

63. P, 362.
64. P, 363.
65. P, 363.
66. P, 363.
67. P, 363.
68. P, 363.
69. P, 391.

Chapter 14: Dispersal

1. C 3, 261.
2. C 3, 261.
3. *Elenco/Nota*, 18.
4. P, 351; C 3, 267.
5. ASCR, *Atto consolare*; G, 264–266, n. 1; C 3, 268–269, n. 1.
6. ASCR, *Atto consolare*.
7. ASCR, *Atto consolare*.
8. P, 394; C 3, 268.
9. C 3, 270–271.
10. C 3, 270.
11. C 3, 270.
12. C 3, 270–271.
13. C 3, 271.
14. P, 393.
15. S II, 236c. See Gallagher, *Gli esercizi*, 284, n. 172.
16. P, 378; cf. P, 351, 377, 379–380.
17. P, 378.
18. C 3, 272; V 3/2, 376–377.
19. *Elenco/Nota*, 19.
20. *Elenco/Nota*, 19–21.
21. V 4/2, 1–14; C 3, 296, n. 1.
22. See C 3, 293–294. Little is said in AOMV about their brief sojourn with the Jesuits, and efforts to find further details in Jesuit archives bore no result.
23. C 3, 294; cf. S I, 212, Nov. 13, 1821.
24. V 4/2, 13; Esp, 180.
25. C 3, 295.
26. Esp, 180; S 3, 1953; V 4/2, 13.
27. V 4/2, 13; *Elenco/Nota*, 21ff.
28. P, 398.

29. C 3, 296.

30. C 3, 296.

31. C 3, 297.

32. C 3, 297.

33. C 3, 132-133. Biancotti served in the Jesuit colleges of Ferentino, Tivoli, and Spoleto, where he died in 1837.

34. Unanswered letters to Guala from both Biancotti and Antonio Lanteri had left the latter uncertain of whether to write to Bruno. In Tivoli, Antonio Lanteri met Giuseppe Andrea Sineo della Torre, S.J., a former disciple of Diessbach. Fr. Sineo gave Antonio Lanteri word about Bruno, and encouraged him to write. See C 3, 364.

35. C 3, 364.

36. C 3, 365.

37. C 3, 210.

38. Co 3, 57ff.; V 4/1, 9ff.; Cognasso, *Storia*, 451ff.; Chapman, *The Risorgimento*, Humanities-Ebooks, loc. 342ff.

39. Cognasso, *Storia*, 466.

40. Cognasso, *Storia*, 466.

41. Cognasso, *Storia*, 467; Co 3, 63.

42. Co 3, 72-73.

43. Co 3, 73.

44. Co 3, 74-75.

45. C 3, 318-319; V 4/1, 47ff.

46. C 3, 293. "Also," because Pertusati was burdened by the death of a friend as well.

47. P, 588; cf. P, 584-585; C 3, 257-260; V 4/1, 29-33.

48. P, 588.

49. C 3, 334.

50. C 3, 334.

51. C 3, 334.

52. C 3, 341.

53. Co 3, 4.

54. C 3, 342.

55. C 3, 342.

56. C 3, 299.

57. C 3, 299.

58. C 3, 299.

59. Hales, *Napoleon and the Pope*, 207.

60. V 4/1, 202, n. 29.

61. C 3, 369, n.1.

62. V 4/1, 188–190; 201, n. 25.

63. V 4/1, 201, n. 25.

64. C 3, 370.

65. V 4/1, 188, 190.

Chapter 15: "His Ardent Desires"

1. *Réflexions sur la sainteté et la doctrine du Bienheureux Liguori* (Lyons: Perisse Frères, 1823), 1; cf. C 3, 367, and S 2, 1393–1394.

2. *Réflexions*, 1–2.

3. *Réflexions*, 2.

4. S 2, 1392–1494.

5. C 1, 189; Guerber, *Le ralliement*, 104.

6. Guerber, *Le ralliement*, 104, n. 16; C 1, 189.

7. C 1, 189; Brustolon, *L'azione*, 263–266.

8. Guerber, *Le ralliement*, 116–125; C 1, 192.

9. Guerber, *Le ralliement*, 117, 122–125.

10. Guerber, *Le ralliement*, 110–116.

11. C 4, 123.

12. Martina, "Il contesto storico," *Lanterianum* 2, no. 1 (1994): 96.

13. Martina, "Il contesto storico," 96.

14. S 2, 1531–1532.

15. C 3, 235; S 2, 1402–1403.

16. S 2, 1451; Gallagher, "In Defence of St. Alphonsus: The 'Réflexions' of Pio Bruno Lanteri," *Lanterianum* 2, no. 3 (1994): 22. Emphasis in the original.

17. Orlandi, "La recezione," 492; Brustolon, *L'azione*, 264.

18. Guerber, "Le rôle de Pio Brunone Lanteri dans l'introduction de la morale liguorienne en France," *Spicilegium historicum CssR* 4 (1956): 375.

19. Guerber, "Le rôle," 375.

20. Guerber, "Le rôle," 375.

21. Guerber, *Le ralliement*, 116–125.

22. Guerber, *Le ralliement*, 362.

23. Guerber, *Le ralliement*, 4.

24. Guerber, *Le ralliement*, 362. For Bruno's influence on and collaboration with Jesuit Pierre-Charles-Marie Leblanc (1774–1851) in his labors

to translate Alphonsus Ligouri's writings and promote his teaching, see Guerber, *Le ralliement,* 148–170.

25. B, 319ff. On Bruno's assistance to the *Amicizia Cattolica* as theologian and more broadly, see B, 322.

26. Gallagher, *Gli esercizi,* 288.

27. Gallagher, *Gli esercizi,* 288–296; V 4/2, 15–22.

28. Gallagher, *Gli esercizi,* 289; C 3, 114.

29. Gallagher, *Gli esercizi,* 289; C 4, 267.

30. C 3, 308–309; P, 59; Gallagher, *Gli esercizi,* 197, n. 22.

31. P, 58; V 4/2, 20.

32. P, 58.

33. P, 58.

34. P, 58.

35. P, 58.

36. P, 58–59.

37. P, 59.

38. P, 59, n. 1.

39. P, 59, n. 1.

40. P, 59, n. 1; C 3, 406–410.

41. P, 59.

42. P, 59.

43. P, 59.

44. P, 59–60.

45. P, 60.

46. P, 60.

47. P, 60. Italics in Pietro Pirri, S.J., and Ludwig de Jonge, *Epistolae Ioannis Phil. Roothaan Societatis Iesu Praepositi Generalis XXI* (Rome: Apud postulatorem generalem S. I.,1935), vol. 1, 259.

48. P, 60, n.1.

49. P, 60, n.1.

50. P, 60.

51. P, 61.

52. P, 61.

53. P, 61.

54. P, 61.

55. P, 61.

56. P, 61.

57. P, 61.

58. P, 61.

59. V 4/2, 125.

60. V 4/2, 125; C 4, 25.

61. C 5, 261–264; V 4/1, 196–199.

62. Giordano, *Necrologio del p. Pio B. Lanteri*, AOMV, reparto Necrologi (reference as given in V 4/1, 203, n. 35: no more specific reference can be given since this document is uncatalogued in AOMV); V 4/1, 197.

63. V 4/1, 197.

64. C 5, 263–264.

Chapter 16: Beginning Again

1. Pirri, De Jonge, *Epistolae*, 1, 279; P, 62. Emphasis in the original.

2. P, 602.

3. P, 398; G, 267; V 4/2, 36–37.

4. P, 666; Gallagher, *Gli esercizi*, 295–296; Santoro, *Il cammino*, 286, 44; C 4, 236.

5. C 4, 67.

6. V 4/2, 161.

7. Gallagher, *Gli esercizi*, 297; C 4, 20; G, 269–270; S I, 818. Rey describes the Oblate priests as "missionaires," that is, missionaries. He uses the word in the sense of priests who travel continually through an area to preach parish missions and retreats.

8. Pirri, De Jonge, *Epistolae*, 1, 279.

9. C 4, 25.

10. *Elenco/Nota*, 25.

11. C 4, 26.

12. C 4, 26.

13. C 4, 31.

14. P, 406.

15. C 4, 32.

16. C 4, 32.

17. "An institute of consecrated life is said to be of *pontifical right* if it has been erected by the Apostolic See or approved by a formal decree of the Apostolic See; on the other hand an institute is said to be of *diocesan right* if, after having been erected by a diocesan bishop, it has not obtained a decree of approval from the Apostolic See." Canon Law Society of America, trans., *Code of Canon Law: Latin-English Edition* (Washington: Canon Law Society of America, 1983), canon 589, pp. 223–225. Emphasis added.

18. Gallagher, *Gli esercizi*, 28–29.

19. ASCR, *Costituzioni*, September 17, 1825. Bruno spoke habitually of "private" and "public" Spiritual Exercises. "Private" Spiritual Exercises were those given in closed settings—retreat houses, seminaries, monasteries, convents, and the like; "public" Spiritual Exercises were those given in open settings—above all, parishes. I have translated these terms according to their closest English equivalents: private Spiritual Exercises as "retreats," and public Spiritual Exercises as "parish missions." See Andrea Brustolon, O.M.V., *Elenco degli esercizi e tridui dettati dagli Oblati di Maria Vergine e loro aggregati (1817–1843)*, thesis for the degree of licentiate, Pontifical Gregorian University, Rome, 1989, typescript, 54–79.

20. ASCR, *Costituzioni*, September 17, 1825.

21. ASCR, *Costituzioni*, September 17, 1825; cf. Gallagher, *Gli esercizi*, 30–67.

22. ASCR, *Costituzioni*, September 17, 1825.

23. ASCR, *Costituzioni*, September 17, 1825; cf. Gallagher, *Gli esercizi*, 68–75. In the rule of September 1825, Bruno summarizes this aid briefly: "supplying them the opportune means for these tasks, such as books, etc."

24. ASCR, *Costituzioni*, September 17, 1825.

25. ASCR, *Costituzioni*, September 17, 1825; cf. Gallagher, *Gli esercizi*, 75–88.

26. ASCR, *Costituzioni*, September 17, 1825.

27. ASCR, *Costituzioni*, September 17, 1825; cf. Gallagher, *Gli esercizi*, 88–102.

28. ASCR, *Costituzioni*, September 17, 1825.

29. C 4, 141, 179, 333, n. 1, 334; S 3, 1946, 1948.

30. C 4, 67.

31. ASCR, March 14, 1826; Gallagher, *Gli esercizi*, 30, n. 11; C 4, 104.

32. C 4, 42–46. Lambruschini would later serve as nuncio to Paris and as secretary of state under Pope Gregory XVI.

33. C 4, 43: letter of November 15, 1825.

34. Luigi Manzini, *Il Cardinale Luigi Lambruschini* (Città del Vaticano: Biblioteca apostolica vaticana, 1960), 426.

35. Manzini, *Il Cardinale Luigi Lambruschini*, 426.

36. S VII, 1, 1; P, 409; Esp, 167; cf. V 4/2, 54–58.

37. S VII, 1, 1.

38. S VII, 1, 1.

39. S I, 1331b; cf. V 4/2, 63, n. 55.

40. S I, 1331b.

41. P, 402–404.

42. P, 404.

43. P, 399.

44. De Mazenod was canonized in 1995.

45. Joseph Thiel, O.M.I., "Relations du Fondateur avec le P. Lanteri," *Études Oblats* 5 (1946): 130–131. Article reprinted in *Lanterianum* 5, no. 1 (1997): 33–44.

46. Thiel, "Relations," 133–134.

47. Thiel, "Relations,"134. De Mazenod's final words here may mean that Guala, as Bruno's disciple, deferred to Bruno regarding how much he (Guala) might share with de Mazenod. As the "superior," Bruno was subject to no such limitations. Both Bruno and Guala felt great trust in de Mazenod, a trust he reciprocated.

48. Thiel, "Relations,"134.

49. Thiel, "Relations," 135–136; V 4/2, 70–81.

50. In no conserved document does Bruno or any contemporary Oblate of the Virgin Mary mention a proposed union of the two congregations. Such union, entailing the dissolution of the Oblates of the Virgin Mary and their integration into the Oblates of Mary Immaculate, would have been awkward with respect to Bishop Rey who, only two months earlier, had enthusiastically approved the Oblates of the Virgin Mary as a Congregation for his diocese, and now awaited their further approval in Rome. In addition, Bruno's conviction of the unparalleled efficacy of the Ignatian spiritual exercises, and his desire that the Oblates dedicate themselves to this form of retreats and parish missions alone, inevitably would arise as a difference between the two institutes. In fact, six months later, on May 24, 1826, de Mazenod again wrote to Tempier: "Their [the Oblates of the Virgin Mary] system [of giving retreats and parish missions], to which they adhere with great determination, is not compatible with ours. They give only retreats of eight days, and they do in those eight days all that we barely can do in thirty. For the rest, all priests of merit in their area [Piedmont] hold the same opinion . . . that, in practice, eight days for a parish mission are sufficient to meet the need. Only occasionally will they prolong the mission even for fifteen days, and this is the method of all, Jesuits, Passionists, Vincentians, and the religious of all the orders." *Missions de la Congrégation des Missionaires de Marie Immaculée* 10 (1872): 320.

51. C 4, 44.

Chapter 17: Sojourn in Rome

1. C 4, 65–66; V 4/2, 31–32.
2. C 4, 66.
3. C 4, 67.
4. C 4, 85–86.
5. C 4, 90.
6. C 4, 106–107.
7. C 4, 254.
8. P, 410–413; C 4, 97–99.
9. P, 414.

10. P, 413–417; 97–106; Esp, 169–190. In a page of "Observations" sent to the Sacred Congregation of Bishops and Regulars in Rome, Bruno wrote: "Of the four principal works that the Oblates of Mary Most Holy have chosen as their own, that is, giving the Exercises, forming good priests, combatting current errors, and spreading good books, only giving the Exercises is common with the Congregation of the Most Holy Redeemer, and even in this the two congregations follow different methods." Esp, 173. Elsewhere, Bruno noted the focus of the Redemptorists on preaching to the poor in the countryside, and wrote: "The Oblates of Mary do not dedicate themselves only to instructing the simple in rural areas, but go wherever they are requested, with the approval of the Ordinary [bishop of the place]." Gallagher, *Gli esercizi*, 43.

11. C 4, 96.
12. C 4, 92–96.
13. C 4, 94.
14. C 4, 94.
15. C 4, 94.
16. Thiel, "Relations," 139.
17. Thiel, "Relations," 141.
18. C 4, 26.
19. Manzini, *Il Cardinale Luigi Lambruschini*, 426; C 4, 96.
20. C 5, 417.
21. C 5, 417.
22. C 4, 114; V 4/2, 92.
23. C 4, 108, 114; P, 454; V 4/2, 92.
24. C 4, 236; G, 279; V 4/2, 92.
25. C 4, 108–109.
26. P, 454.
27. P, 451ff; V 4/2, 131–149.

28. P, 421.

29. C 4, 159.

30. C 4, 115.

31. P, 446.

32. C, 138.

33. C, 145;Letter of July 1, 1826.

34. P, 461; cf. V 4/2, 165–169.

35. P, 461.

36. P, 461.

37. P, 461.

38. P, 461.

39. P, 461. Calliari comments: "Lanteri's profession at that time, however, had only a personal and private significance, and not a juridical significance. In fact, he would renew his religious profession publicly two years later on August 15, 1828, in St. Clare's, in Pinerolo, together with the small group of the first Oblates." V 4/2, 168. Loggero specifies that these were "simple" vows: P, 461. See John Beal, James Coriden, and Thomas Green, eds., *New Commentary on the Code of Canon Law/* (New York: Paulist Press, 2000), 1417–1418: "The older religious orders (monastic, canon regulars, mendicants, Jesuits) have perpetual solemn vows, and the more recent apostolic congregations have perpetual simple vows. The chief juridical difference between the two is that religious who profess a solemn vow of poverty renounce ownership of all their temporal goods, whereas religious who profess a simple vow of poverty have a right to retain ownership of their patrimony (an estate, endowment or anything inherited from one's parents or ancestors) but must give up its use and any revenue."

40. P, 446–447.

41. C 4, 139.

42. Mario Bini, "Il 'martello del giansenismo' nei suoi rapporti con Empoli e gli empolesi," *Bolletino storico empolese* 10 (1966): 97.

43. C 4, 281; V 4/2, 208, 221, notes 47, 48.

44. C 4, 176; V 4/2, 221, n. 47. In October 1681, Louis XIV convoked a plenary Assembly of the French clergy, which, on March 19, 1682, proclaimed the four Gallican Propositions.

45. Hales, *Pio Nono*, 349, n. 15. Papal infallibility was not yet defined at this time. It was declared a dogma at the First Vatican Council in 1870.

46. G, 288–289; V 4/2, 206.

47. S 3, 1930.

48. Luigi della Fanteria, "Giovanni Marchetti," in *Continuazione delle memorie di religione, ecc.* (Modena, 1836), vol. 5, 290.

49. Fanteria, "Giovanni Marchetti," 290-291.

50. C 4, 286.

51. V 4/2, 302.

52. C 4, 176-177.

53. C 4, 177.

54. P, 476.

55. P, 476; V 4/2, 246-247.

56. P, 472, 473.

57. P, 473.

58. P, 474.

59. P, 474.

60. P, 477.

61. V 4/2, 251-252; P, 629-630.

62. P, 478.

63. P, 481.

64. V 4/2, 303; Fanteria, "Giovanni Marchetti," 291-294.

65. P, 489.

66. P, 489.

67. ASCR, Sept. 3, 1826; cf. P, 489-490.

68. ASCR, Sept. 3, 1826.

69. ASCR, Sept. 3, 1826.

Chapter 18: "We Hope, and We Fear"

1. Esp, 196; P, 401.

2. P, 480.

3. P, 481. See Claretta, "Origini degli Oblati," *L'Oblato di Maria Vergine* 6 (1962): 83.

4. ASV, *Etsi Dei Filius:* Segreteria dei Brevi, 1826; cf. P, 447-451; Esp, 195-197. English translation in Directory of the Venerable P. Lanteri, Constitutions and Directive Norms Approved "ad experimentum" by the XVII and XVIII General Chapters (Rome: Tipografia Agostini, 1974), 13-18.

5. ASV, *Etsi Dei Filius.*

6. ASV, *Etsi Dei Filius.*

7. ASV, *Etsi Dei Filius.*

8. P, 493. Bruno made several personal requests, and gave the Holy Father "the rescript for the Office and Mass" of the Heart of Mary, and of Blessed Alphonsus Liguori.

9. C 4, 210–211.

10. C 4, 211.

11. C 4, 211; cf. C 4, 181.

12. C 4, 201, n. 1; V 4/2, 278; C 4, 196–198.

13. C 4, 202.

14. V 4/2, 279-280; C 4, 171–172; AOMV, *Atti, e Deliberazioni de' Capitoli e Consulte della Congregazione degli Oblati di Maria Vergine*, 5.

15. AOMV, *Atti, e Deliberazioni*, 5–6; V 5, 99; Paolo Calliari, *Gli Oblati a Pinerolo* (Pinerolo: Editrice Lanteriana, 1987), 14–15.

16. C 5, 325.

17. C 5, 325.

18. C 4, 227; V 4/2, 288–289.

19. P, 624.

20. V 5, 156, n. 2.

21. Co 1, 72; cf. Filippo Appendino, ed., *Chiesa e società nella II metà del XIX secolo in Piemonte* (Casale Monferrato: Marietti, 1982), 62–64; C 4, 233–235.

22. C 4, 233–241.

23. C 4, 238.

24. C 4, 240.

25. C 4, 240.

26. C 4, 240.

27. C 4, 242.

28. P, 670; Manzini, *Il Cardinale Luigi Lambruschini*, 426.

29. S I, 503.

30. S I, 509.

31. C 4, 324.

32. C 4, 335. Letter of March 10, 1827.

33. C 4, 345–346.

34. C 4, 382.

35. AOMV, *Atti, e Deliberazioni*, 7; C 4, 249, 257–258.

36. C 4, 266–268.

37. P, 624.

38. C 4, 315.

39. C 4, 316.

40. C 4, 382.

41. *Vita del buon Servo di Dio Luigi Craveri, canonico teologo e vicario generale della diocesi di Fossano scritta da un fossanese* (Pinerolo: Giuseppe Chiantore, 1859), 48–58; C 5, 132–134, 146–147.

42. P, 624.

43. *Vita del buon Servo di Dio Luigi Craveri*, 49; C 5, 93, n. 1, 136, n. 1; *Pinerolien. Beatificationis et canonizationis Servi Dei Pii Brunonis Lanteri fundatoris Congregationis Oblatorum B.M.V. Summarium pro introductione causae, Pars secunda* (n.p.: Stab. Typ. "Ars Nova," 1951), Summarium ex officio, De scriptis, 6.

44. C 5, 64.

45. C 4, 314. See C 4, 312.

46. C 4, 193; cf. C 4, 183; C 5, 34; V 5, 112-117.

47. C 5, 34.

48. C 4, 400.

49. C 5, 340-341.

50. C 5, 325.

Chapter 19: Pinerolo

1. Manzini, *Il Cardinale Luigi Lambruschini*, 426-427; see C 4, 281-283, n. 2. The papal document, *Etsi Dei Filius*, was a brief, not a bull, as Lambruschini calls it here.

2. Manzini, *Il Cardinale Luigi Lambruschini*, 427.

3. P, 503, 512; C 4, 376-378; V 5, 11ff.

4. P, 514-516; C 4, 397-398, n. 1.

5. Brustolon, *L'azione*, 324-326. A *simple* vow of poverty (by contrast with a *solemn* vow) allowed the individual to retain possession of his property, but not administration or personal use of it. See Beal, Coriden, and Green, *New Commentary on the Code of Canon Law*, 1417-1418. In the Rule approved by Leo XII, the Oblates had chosen the simple vow of poverty: ASV, *Segreteria dei Brevi*, 1826, Leo XII, *September pars utraque, Costituzioni e Regole della Congregazione degli Oblati di Maria Santissima*, part 1, chapter 1; chapter 3, 1. See P, 433, 437-439; S 3, 1928, 1932-1933; C 4, 401-402. For the manuscript in ASV, see Gallagher, *Gli esercizi*, 31, n. 12.

6. C 4, 390. The Marquis Giuseppe Massimino di Ceva and Count Luigi Amedeo Gattinara di Zubiena were both former members of the *Amicizia Cristiana*, and later of the *Amicizia Cattolica*. B, 341-342.

7. C 4, 401.

8. C 4, 402; cf. C 4, 436-437.

9. C 4, 402.

10. C 4, 402.

11. *Registro degli individui ammessi in noviziato*, AOMV, S Generali, vol. Elenchi, fasc. 2, doc. 7, nos. 1-6.

12. AOMV, *Atti, e Deliberazioni*, 6.

13. P, 671.

14. AOMV, *Atti, e Deliberazioni*, 7.

15. P, 58.

16. S II, 315, 11; Cf. Esp, 242.

17. C 4, 424; G, 321-323.

18. *Elenco esercizi*, no. 221; AOMV, *Atti, e Deliberazioni*, 10; V 5, 96. The *Elenco* gives only the starting date of the retreat. In Oblate practice, such retreats generally lasted from eight to ten days. See Brustolon, *Elenco degli esercizi e tridui dettati dagli Oblati di Maria Vergine e loro aggregati (1817-1843)*, 44; Timothy Gallagher, O.M.V., *The Great Art of Our Sanctification: A Study of the* Direttorio degli Esercizi di S. Ignazio *of Pio Brunone Lanteri*, thesis for the degree of licentiate, Pontifical Gregorian University, Rome, 1980, second typewritten version with English translation of quotes, 33-34.

19. *Elenco esercizi*, no. 221.

20. *Elenco esercizi*, no. 233.

21. V 5, 105, n. 47; Gallagher, *Gli Esercizi*, 301, n. 41, 304, n. 50, 307-308, 309, n. 64. Oblate friend and benefactor Francesco Andrea Gonella, writing most probably in 1830, affirmed that "the Congregation greatly desires to continue to receive retreatants into its house annually, and more often during the year, because of the great good that derives from this for the glory of God." AOMV, S I, 333; transcribed in Gallagher, *Gli Esercizi*, 309, n. 64.

22. *Elenco esercizi*, nos. 220-225. The last retreats had been given in late April-early May 1827: *Elenco esercizi*, nos. 218-219.

23. *Elenco esercizi*, nos. 220-271.

24. C 5, 85. Emphasis in the original.

25. C 5, 239-240.

26. C 5, 242.

27. C 5, 242.

28. C 5, 242; cf. Esp, 237-246.

29. C 5, 242; V 5, 358-361.

30. C 4, 312.

31. C 4, 314.

32. C 4, 316; cf. V 5, 360; Brustolon, *L'azione*, 599; C 5, 351.

33. P, 672.

34. P, 673.

35. C 5, 326; Gallagher, *Gli esercizi*, 306–309.

36. S IV, 432; Santoro, *Il cammino*, 329–335; V 5, 89–91.

37. S IV, 432.

38. Santoro, *Il cammino*, 329–330. These authors are Vincent Huby, S.J. (1608–1693); Luigi Bellecio, S.J. (1704–1757); Giovanni Pietro Pinamonti, S.J. (1632–1703); Alonso Rodriguez, S.J. (1526–1616); Julien Hayneuve, S.J. (1588–1663).

39. S IV, 432.

40. S IV, 432, f. 28.

41. S IV, 432.

42. S IV, 432; Santoro, *Il cammino*, 332–333.

43. S IV, 432.

44. C 5, 29.

45. C 5, 38.

46. C 5, 29–30, 38–39; *Pinerolien. Beatificationis et canonizationis Servi Dei Pii Brunonis Lanteri fundatoris Congregationis Oblatorum B.M.V.: Responsio ad animadversiones Rev.mi P. D. Promotoris Generalis fidei* (n.p.: Stab. Typ. "Ars Nova," 1951), 69–72; G, 358.

47. C 4, 416–417. Teresa Quey died on August 4, 1827.

48. C 4, 433–434.

49. C 5, 38.

50. C 5, 29.

51. C 5, 29.

52. C 5, 29.

53. C 5, 29–30.

54. C 5, 30.

55. C 5, 30.

56. C 5, 30.

57. C 5, 30.

58. C 5, 30.

59. C 5, 38.

60. C 5, 38–39.

61. C 5, 108; cf. C 5, 177, 194.

62. C 5, 375; cf. C 5, 376–377.

63. C 5, 375.

Chapter 20: "His Shadow Is Enough"

1. *Registro degli individui,* no. 10.

2. *Registro degli individui,* no. 12.

3. *Registro degli individui,* no. 24.

4. *Registro degli individui,* no. 27.

5. AOMV, *Atti, e Deliberazioni,* 9; V 5, 179.

6. AOMV, *Atti, e Deliberazioni,* 9; V 5, 191–193.

7. Registro degli individui, nos. 8, 10–13, 17–18, 20.

8. C 5, 326.

9. Thiel, "Relations," 141; *Lanterianum* 2, no. 2 (1994): 96–102; Brustolon, *Alle origini,* 167–169.

10. C 5, 168. Emphasis in the original.

11. C 5, 287.

12. C 5, 288.

13. C 5, 296; Santoro, Il cammino, 336.

14. C 5, 326.

15. C 5, passim; V 5, 339ff.

16. C 5, 214; B, 404–406.

17. Lamennais, at that time a staunch defender of the Church, would end outside the Church and without Christian faith.

18. C 5, 174.

19. C 5, 174–175, n. 4.

20. C 5, 188; cf. C 5, 191–192.

21. C 5, 278.

22. C 5, 279.

23. *Esercizj Spirituali di S. Ignazio di Lojola col Direttorio pel buono uso de' suddetti Esercizj,* 17–42. Much in this volume directly quotes or summarizes the *Ritiramento spirituale* of Camillo Ettore, S.J. (1631–1700). Guerber writes: "Lanteri printed, once again anonymously, a directory for the Exercises of St. Ignatius: Esercizi spirituali di S. Ignazio . . . Turin, 1829. It is a summary of Ettori, with some additions." *Le Ralliement,* 114, n. 36. Vittorio Moscarelli, O.M.V., likewise affirms: "That the book is by the Venerable Lanteri in the sense that he organized the printing is acceptable; but it is not his in the sense of the complete composition, or of his personal and direct reworking of the Exercises of St. Ignatius as they appear in the book by the saintly author." Manuscript cited in Gallagher, *The Great Art of Our Sanctification,* 19. See Gallagher, *The Great Art of Our Sanctification,* 18–22 for a discussion of Bruno's role in the publication of this volume. See also V 5, 355–356; C 1, 193–194. For the text of this

Directory in Italian, see Esp, 235–251, and S 4, 3663–3681; for an English translation, see Gallagher, *The Great Art of Our Sanctification*, 85–110.

24. Bruno used this brief text as a tool to assist the priests he trained to give the spiritual exercises. Earlier forms of the finalized Directory appear in Bruno's writings for the priests of the *Amicizia Sacerdotale*. For the genesis of the Directory of 1829, see Gallagher, *The Great Art of Our Sanctification*, first part.

25. "Direttorio degli Esercizj," 37. Emphasis in the original.

26. C 5, 303; V 5, 340–342.

27. C 5, 345.

28. *Registro degli individui*, no. 10; V 3/1, 135–138; V 5, 135–138.

29. P, 626.

30. P, 626.

31. P, 626.

32. P, 677. See P, 493.

33. P, 606.

34. P, 606.

35. P, 598.

36. P, 606.

37. *Una vita per il nome di Cristo: L'identità dell'Oblato di Maria Vergine nella Chiesa d'oggi* (Cuneo: AGA, 1993), 26–27; English translation: *To Live the Lord Jesus: The Identity of the Oblates of the Virgin Mary in Today's Church* (Cuneo: AGA, n.d.), 27–28; Timothy Gallagher, O.M.V., *Mother, Lady, Teacher and Foundress: Mary and the Oblate Today*, typescript, 2000.

38. P, 598.

39. P, 626–627.

40. P, 627.

41. P, 627.

42. P, 627.

43. P, 627.

44. Esp, 125; S 3, 1855, 1886, n. 10.

45. Esp, 125; S 3, 1855.

46. P, 681. Alphonsus had died in 1787.

47. P, 681; C 5, 336, 364, 373.

48. P, 679; Gardetti mistakenly wrote "1830." Cf. P, 679, n. 2; V 5, 385.

49. S I, 963; V 5, 412, n. 27; *Elenco esercizi*, no. 265.

50. S I, 963.

Chapter 21: "The Lamp Is Going Out"

1. C 5, 304–305.

2. *Elenco esercizi,* no. 253; *Lanterianum* 1, no. 2 (1994): 72–73; V 5, 361.

3. *Elenco esercizi,* no. 253.

4. P, 65.

5. P, 65.

6. P, 65.

7. P, 65.

8. P, 66.

9. Spiritual Exercises, 23. Themes of the meditations most likely would have included: The Goal of Man's Existence, The Means to that Goal, and The Importance of Salvation. See Bruno's "Direttorio degli Esercizj di S. Ignazio," in *Esercizj Spirituali di S. Ignazio di Lojola col Direttorio pel buono uso de' suddetti Esercizj,* 20–21.

10. P, 66.

11. P, 66.

12. P, 66.

13. P, 67.

14. P, 67.

15. P, 67.

16. C 5, 315–316.

17. C 5, 377.

18. By long tradition, each priest may celebrate the three Christmas Masses: Midnight, Dawn, and During the Day.

19. C 5, 377.

20. C 5, 379–380.

21. C 5,385.

22. C 5, 387.

23. C 5, 387.

24. *Lanterianum* 2, no. 2 (1994): 101. See Brustolon, *Alle origini,* 169, n. 10.

25. *Lanterianum* 2, no. 2 (1994): 100.

26. C 5, 375, n.2.

27. P, 680. Cf. G, 351; V 5, 388.

28. *Lanterianum* 2, no. 2 (1994): 101; *Elenco esercizi,* 276.

29. *Lanterianum* 2, no. 2 (1994):101.

30. *Lanterianum* 2, no. 2 (1994):102.

31. P, 680.

32. P, 679–680.

33. *Registro degli individui,* no. 24; P, 675; V 5, 395–399; AOMV, S Pinerolo Santa Chiara, Loggero 2, fasc. 11, Daverio to Loggero, May 30, 1829. Cf. Brustolon, *Storiografia,* 244.

34. The grammatical errors in his writing bear witness to this: see P, 675.

35. P, 675–681.

36. P, 675–676.

37. P, 676.

38. P, 676, for this and other experiences.

39. P, 676.

40. These questions were treated at length in Bruno's cause of canonization. See *Pinerolien. Beatificationis et canonizationis Servi Dei Pii Brunonis Lanteri fundatoris Congregationis Oblatorum B.M.V.: Animadversiones Promotoris Generalis fidei* (no place or publisher given), February 16, 1955, 30–31; *Responsio ad animadversiones Rev.mi Promotoris Generalis fidei* (Rome: Ex Officina Typogr. "Ars Nova," 1955), 45–47.

41. From the discussion of this issue in Bruno's cause of canonization: *Responsio ad animadversiones,* 1955, 45.

42. *Remembering Iñigo: Glimpses of the Life of Saint Ignatius of Loyola. The Memoriale of Luís Gonçalves da Câmara* (St. Louis: Institute of Jesuit Sources, 2004), 63.

43. *Remembering Iñigo,* 62–63.

44. Testimony of Oblate brother Francesco Avvaro (1860–1941): "I spoke much about the Founder with Brother Pietro Gardetti, who also lived an exemplary life, and who had a special veneration for Fr. Lanteri." P, 744. See also *Responsio ad animadversiones,* 1955, 45–47.

45. P, 677; cf. C 5, 215.

46. P, 624.

47. Esp, 66. In the process of canonization, the following considerations were proposed: Gardetti was a novice and spent most of his time with Bruno, who thus felt responsible for his formation; paternal severity is commonly recognized as important for the novice's formation; the fruits of this formation were revealed in Gardetti's long and faithful religious life; that, were Gardetti alive, he would be amazed that anyone might doubt Bruno's virtue on the basis of his testimony. *Responsio ad animadversiones,* 1955, 45–47.

48. P, 624–625; cf. G, 352; V 5, 390, 393.

49. S I, 748; V 5, 389.

50. S I, 750; V 5, 390.

51. S I, 751; V 5, 390.

52. S I, 752.

53. C 5, 400.

54. P, 678; V 5, 390.

55. C 5, 401–402.

56. C 5, 402.

57. C 5, 402.

58. S I, 1380; P, 676; V 5, 393.

Chapter 22: Last Days

1. P, 676.

2. P, 744. Gardetti used this phrase in conversation with Oblate brother Francesco Avvaro.

3. P, 681.

4. P, 676–677.

5. C 3, 289–290.

6. C 3, 290.

7. C 2, 322.

8. C 4, 181, 211.

9. P, 605–606.

10. P, 677.

11. P, 677.

12. P, 678.

13. P, 678; V 5, 389, 413, n. 42; G, 353.

14. P, 597.

15. P, 678. See V 5, 444–446; C 1, reproductions following p. 240.

16. P, 680. During Bruno's cause of canonization, Oblate brother Francesco Avvaro recounted his conversations with Gardetti in the latter's final years: "Brother Gardetti often spoke to me of the attitude almost of contemplation of the Servant of God [Bruno] during his illness, and above all of the vision of Our Lady, to which he [Bruno] referred in these words: 'Did you not see that it was a Lady with a Child?'" P, 744.

17. P, 606; cf. G, 351. I have preferred to quote the accounts of witnesses Gardetti and Ferrero rather than Gastaldi's later version. See G, 354; V 5, 400.

18. G, 351, 354; P, 89*, 119*–120*, 764; V 5, 416, n. 82; Brustolon, *L'azione*, 304.

19. S II, 374; cf. David Beauregard, O.M.V., ed., *The Spiritual Writings of Venerable Pio Bruno Lanteri: A Selection* (Rome: n.p., 2001), 149; C 1, 5; C 4, 81; S 1, 740.

20. Emphasis added. See *The Spiritual Writings*, 149. See also Tommaso Piatti's archival note in S II, 347: "[This page is] Part of another manuscript that has been lost through the jealous devotion of the first fathers. From his [Bruno's] last years."

21. P, 602-603.

22. V 5, 391.

23. V 5, 391.

24. C 3, 106-108.

25. Papal infallibility was not yet defined as a dogma, and was much debated in theological discussion in Bruno's day. It would be defined as Catholic doctrine in the First Vatican Council, in 1870.

26. V 5, 399. Letter of July 28, 1830.

27. P, 680.

28. Chronicle of Oblate Fr. Luigi Dadesso in S I, 1380; see V 5, 414, n. 58.

29. Leflon, *La crise*, 419.

30. Leflon, *La crise*, 419. All details in this paragraph are taken from this source.

31. Co 3, 117. See Andrea Brustolon, O.M.V., *L'Età della Restaurazione: fratture, inganni, ottusità mentali e religiosità* (Foligno: Edizioni Lanteri, 1996), 355.

32. P, 678.

33. P, 607.

34. P, 607.

35. Rodolfo de Maistre, son of Joseph, brother of Constance: C 4, 192, n. 1; G, 362.

36. V 5, 401.

37. Eugenio Valentini, S.D.B., "La santità in Piemonte nell'ottocento e nel primo novecento," *Rivista di Pedagogia e Scienze Religiose* 4 (1996): 373.

38. V 5, 450; cf. V 5, 348; G, 357.

39. G, 357; V 3/2, 261-265; V 5, 348, 450.

40. Amato Frutaz, in Gallagher, "In Defence of St. Alphonsus: The 'Réflexions' of Pio Bruno Lanteri," *Lanterianum* 2, no. 3 (1994): 24. The title "Theologian Lanteri" given Bruno in his lifetime signified that he had earned a doctorate in theology.

41. AOMV, S I-VIII.

42. Guerber, "Le rôle," 360.

43. Guerber, "Le rôle," 358.

44. P, 623.

45. Esp, 127; cf. *Una vita per il nome di Cristo*, 24–26.

46. Esp, 127.

47. Esp, 127.

48. P, 607.

Chapter 23: Final Passage

1. P, 597; C 3, 273, n. 1.

2. The firsthand accounts of Bruno's death are two: Ferrero's, P, 597–598, and Loggero's, P, 607–608. AOMV, *Atti, e Deliberazioni*, 22–23, adds further details, also of firsthand witnesses. To these may be added Dadesso's chronicle in S I, 1380. I have taken the details of Bruno's death from these sources. See also: G, 354–356; V 5, 399–401.

3. P, 607.

4. P, 607.

5. P, 607.

6. P, 597.

7. P, 597.

8. P, 597.

9. P, 597.

10. P, 597.

11. John 17:11, RSVCE, Second Edition; P, 607; cf. P, 597.

12. P, 607.

13. P, 597.

14. P, 597; AOMV, *Atti, e Deliberazioni*, 22.

15. P, 597.

16. P, 597.

17. P, 607, 597.

18. P, 597. Cf. P, 607–608.

19. P, 597, 607, 678; V 5, 444–446.

20. P, 597–598.

21. AOMV, *Atti, e Deliberazioni*, 22; Paolo Calliari, O.M.V., *Gli Oblati di Maria*, typescript, 1985, vol. 4, 24–25.

22. AOMV, *Atti, e Deliberazioni*, 22–23.

23. AOMV, *Atti, e Deliberazioni*, 24–26.

24. P, 598.

25. C 5, 417.

26. C 5, 402-404; G, 359. Cf. *Pinerolien. Beatificationis et canonizationis Servi Dei Pii Brunonis Lanteri fundatoris Congregationis Oblatorum B.M.V.: Positio super non cultu* (Rome: Ex Officina Typogr. "Ars Nova," 1953), Summarium, 29.

27. P, 594. Cf, G, 361-362; C 4, 192-193, n. 1; V 5, 403.

28. P, 594.

29. P, 595. Cf, G, 361; C 4, 251, n.1; V 5, 403.

30. P, 595-596.

31. S I, 1380. Cf, G, 359; V 5, 404-410.

32. S I, 37. Cf, P, 596-606; V 5, 407-409.

33. Cf. Guerber, "Le rôle," 357, for the figure of "tens of thousands" of books spread regarding St. Alphonsus alone.

34. B, 462.

35. Orlandi, "La recezione," 513.

36. Valentini, "La santità in Piemonte," 303.

37. *Il Convitto*, 15-16.

38. Penco, *Storia*, 226.

39. Penco, *Storia*, 226.

40. Giacomo Martina, S.J., *Storia della Chiesa da Lutero ai nostri giorni: III. L'età del liberalismo* (Brescia: Morcelliana, 2009), 115-118.

41. See Tommaso Piatti, O.M.V., *Un precursore dell'Azione Cattolica: Il Servo di Dio Pio Brunone Lanteri, apostolo di Torino, fondatore degli Oblati di Maria Vergine* (Turin: Marietti, 1954).

42. B, 461-462.

43. Valentini, "La santità in Piemonte," 298; V 5, 427; Appendino, *Chiesa e società*, 233-253, and passim.

44. Valentini, "La santità in Piemonte," 298.

45. Valentini, "La santità in Piemonte," 297-373.

46. Aldo Ponso, *Duemila anni di santità in Piemonte e Valle d'Aosta: I Santi, i Beati, i Venerabili, i Servi di Dio, le Personalità distinte. Guida completa dalle origini ai nostri giorni* (Cantalupa: Effatà Editrice, 2001).

47. Valentini, "La santità in Piemonte," 299.

48. Penco, *Storia*, 260-261; Valentini, "La santità in Piemonte," 373.

49. Valentini, "La santità in Piemonte," 300-370; Ponso, *Duemila anni di santità*, 343-406.

50. Valentini, "La santità in Piemonte," 299.

51. Valentini, "La santità in Piemonte," 302. Cf. P, XVIII.

52. Orlandi, "La recezione," 372. Orlandi qualifies Bruno as a "Servant of God"; I have corrected this to "Venerable."

53. For these historical details, see Brustolon, *L'azione*, 348ff.

54. Felice Prinetti (1842–1916), soldier become priest, and founder of the Daughters of St. Joseph; and Raffaele Melis (1884–1943), who gave his life heroically under bombardment in World War II.

55. For information on the Oblates today, see www.omvusa.org and www.oblati.org.

56. P, 748; *Gli Oblati a Pinerolo*, 56–58.

57. P, 748, n.1: original in, S V, 318b. Pechenino confuses Doctor Fer who was present at the second opening of the tomb in 1926, with Doctor Luigi Moresco who was present at this first opening in 1901. See *Lanterianum* 15, fasc. 1 (2007): 279, n. 2.

58. The tomb is located in the back wall of the church and is accessible from both vestibule and church. It was reopened for the cause of canonization on Sept. 18, 1926, and April 27, 1967: *Gli Oblati a Pinerolo*, 59; V 5, 443, n. 34.

59. P, XXII–XXIV; V 5, 434–440. Frutaz names the following reasons for the delay: the nascent condition of the Congregation in 1830, limited numbers, overwhelming pastoral labor, lack of a biography until 1870, laws suppressing religious that caused a struggle for institutional survival, and World War I. Cf. P, XXII–XXIV.

60. S V, 5a; P, XXIV.

61. *Decretum. Pinerolien. Beatificationis et Canonizationis Servi Dei Pii Brunonis Lanteri, Sacerdotis, Fundatoris Congregationis Oblatorum B. Mariae Virginis*, Rome, November 23, 1965. Italian translation in *L'Oblato* 10 (1966): 8–13. See V 5, 439.

62. P, 614.

63. P, 171.

64. P, 171.

Selected Bibliography

Because inclusion of the complete bibliography would unduly lengthen this book, I give here only a limited selection of sources. Much bibliographical information is provided in the endnotes; for the full bibliography, see www.frtimothygallagher.org

Archives

Archive of the Oblates of the Virgin Mary, Rome [thousands of manuscripts, the principal source for this book].

Archive of the Sacred Congregation for Institutes of Consecrated Life and Societies of Apostolic Life, Vatican.

Secret Archive of the Vatican.

Books and Articles

Bona, Candido, I.M.C. Le "Amicizie": Società segrete e rinascita religiosa (1770-1830). Turin: Deputazione subalpina di storia patria, 1962.

———. La rinascita missionaria in Italia: Dalle "Amicizie" all'Opera per la Propagazione della Fede. Turin: Edizioni Missioni Consolata, 1964.

Brustolon, Andrea, O.M.V. L'azione missionaria degli Oblati di Maria Vergine fuori del Piemonte nel quadro storico della Restaurazione e della vita della Congregazione. Rome: Edizioni Lanteri, 2000.

———. Alle origini della Congregazione degli Oblati di Maria Vergine: Punti chiari e punti oscuri. Turin: Edizioni Lanteri, 1995.

Calliari, Paolo, O.M.V. Gli Oblati di Maria. Vol. III: Primi quattro anni di vita. Editrice Lanteriana, 1980.

———. Il venerabile Pio Bruno Lanteri (1759-1830) fondatore degli Oblati di Maria Vergine nella storia religiosa del suo tempo. 5 vols. Typescript, 1978-1983.

Chiuso, Tomaso. La Chiesa in Piemonte dal 1797 ai giorni nostri. Vols. 1-5. Turin: Giulio Speirani e figli, 1887-1892.

Cristiani, Leon. Un Prêtre redouté de Napoléon: P. Bruno Lanteri (1759-1830). Nice: Procure des Oblats de la Vierge Marie, 1957. English translation: A Cross for Napoleon: The Life of Father Bruno Lanteri (1759-1830). Boston: St. Paul Editions, 1981.

de Mazenod, Eugène, *Lettres aux Oblats de France: 1814-1825.* Collection Écrits Oblats VI. Rome: Postulation générale O.M.I., 1982

Diessbach, Nikolaus von. *Le Chrétien Catholique inviolablement attaché a sa Religion par la consideration de quelques unes des preuves qui en établissent la certitude.* Turin: Jean-Baptiste Fontana, 1771.

Gallagher, Timothy, O.M.V. *Gli esercizi di S. Ignazio nella spiritualità e carisma di fondatore di Pio Bruno Lanteri.* Rome: Typis Pontificiae Universitatis Gregorianae, 1983.

————. *The Great Art of Our Sanctification: A Study of the* Direttorio degli Esercizi di S. Ignazio *of Pio Brunone Lanteri.* Thesis for the degree of licentiate, Pontifical Gregorian University, Rome, 1980. Typescript, second version with English translation of quotes.

Gastaldi, Pietro, O.M.V. *Della vita del Servo di Dio Pio Brunone Lanteri, fondatore della Congregazione degli Oblati di Maria Vergine.* Turin: Marietti, 1870.

Guerber, Jean, S.J. *Le ralliement du clergé français a la morale liguorienne: L'abbé Gousset et ses précurseurs (1785-1832).* Rome: Università Gregoriana Editrice, 1973.

Hales, E. E. Y. *Napoleon and the Pope: The Story of Napoleon and Pius VII.* London: Eyre & Spottiswoode, 1962.

————. *Revolution and Papacy 1796-1846.* Garden City, N.Y.: Doubleday & Company, Inc., 1960.

Lanteri, Bruno. *Carteggio del Venerabile Pio Bruno Lanteri (1759-1830), fondatore della Congregazione degli Oblati di Maria Vergine.* 5 vols. Ed. Paolo Calliari, O.M.V. Turin: Editrice lanteriana, 1976.

————. "Direttorio degli Esercizj di S. Ignazio," in *Esercizj Spirituali di S. Ignazio di Lojola col Direttorio pel buono uso de' suddetti Esercizj.* Turin: Marietti, 1829.

————. *Un'esperienza dello Spirito. Pio Bruno Lanteri: Il suo carisma nelle sue parole.* Ed. Timothy Gallagher, O.M.V. Cuneo: AGA, 1989.

————. *Pinerolien. Beatificationis et canonizationis Servi Dei Pii Brunonis Lanteri fundatoris Congregationis Oblatorum M. V. (1830): Positio super introductione causae et super virtutibus ex officio compilata.* Ed. Amato Frutaz. Rome: Typis Polyglottis Vaticanis, 1945.

————. *Réflexions sur la sainteté et la doctrine du Bienheureux Liguori.* Lyon: Perisse Frères, 1823.

————. *Scritti e documenti d'archivio.* 4 vols. Collaboration of the Oblates of the Virgin Mary with the group "Informatique & Bible," Abbey of Maredsous. Rome: Edizioni Lanteri, 2002.

————. *The Spiritual Writings of Venerable Pio Bruno Lanteri: A Selection.* Ed. David Beauregard, O.M.V. Rome: n.p., 2001.

Leflon, Jean. *La crise révolutionnaire 1789-1846.* Vol. 20 of *Histoire de L'Église.* Ed. Augustin Fliche and Victor Martin. Paris: Bloud & Gay, 1951.

Penco, Gregorio, O.S.B. *Storia della Chiesa in Italia. Vol II: Dal Concilio di Trento ai nostri giorni.* Milan: Jaca Book, 1978.

Piatti, Tommaso, O.M.V. *Un precursore dell'Azione Cattolica: Il Servo di Dio Pio Brunone Lanteri apostolo di Torino fondatore degli Oblati di Maria Vergine.* Turin: Marietti, 1954.

Santoro, Armando, O.M.V. *Il cammino spirituale del P. Pio Bruno Lanteri (1759-1830) Fondatore della Congregazione dei Padri Oblati di Maria Vergine.* Rome: Italian Province of the O.M.V., 2007.

Stella, Pietro. *Crisi religiose nel primo Ottocento piemontese.* Turin: Società Editrice internazionale, 1959.

Thiel, Joseph, O.M.I. "Relations du Fondateur avec le P. Lanteri," *Études Oblats* 5 (1946): 130-131. Article reprinted in *Lanterianum* 5, no. 1 (1997): 33-44.

Valentini, Agostino, O.M.V. "Note di archivio: Relazioni delle ricognizioni eseguite sui resti mortali del Padre Pio Bruno Lanteri." *Lanterianum* 15, fasc. 1 (2007): 269-286.

Index

Numbers in *italics* indicate images.

Which Ignatian title is right for you?

Tens of thousands of readers are turning to Fr. Gallagher's Ignatian titles for reliable, inspirational, and clear explanations of some of the most important aspects of Christian spirituality. Whether you're a spiritual director, priest, or minister, longtime spiritual seeker, or beginner, Fr. Gallagher's books have much to offer you in different moments in life.

+ When you need short, practical exercises for young and old: *An Ignatian Introduction to Prayer*

Group leaders who are looking for practical exercises for groups, including groups that may not have much experience in spiritual development, will want to acquire *An Ignatian Introduction to Prayer: Scriptural Reflections According to the Spiritual Exercises.* This book features forty short (two-page) Ignatian meditations, including Scripture passages, meditative keys for entering into the scriptural story, and guided questions for reflection. These exercises are also useful for individual reflection both for experienced persons and beginners: beginners will recognize and resonate with some of the evocative passages from Scripture; those familiar with Ignatian teaching will appreciate the Ignatian structure of the guided questions.

+ When your life is at the crossroads: *Discerning the Will of God*

If you are facing a turning point in life, you know how difficult it can be to try to hear God's will amid the noise of other people's expectations and your own wishes. Ignatius of Loyola developed a series of exercises and reflections designed to help you in these time so that your decision can be one that conforms to God's will for your life. ***Discerning the Will of God: An Ignatian Guide to Christian Decision Making*** is a trustworthy guide to applying those reflections to your own particular circumstances. This guide, which does not require any prior knowledge of Ignatian spirituality, can be used by people of any faith, though some elements will be more directly applicable to Catholic readers.

- When you want classic spiritual discipline to apply every day: ***The Examen Prayer*** and ***Meditation and Contemplation***

Individuals wanting to deepen their prayer lives using a spiritual discipline will find ***The Examen Prayer*** an important resource. The examen prayer is a powerful and increasingly popular resource for finding God's hand in our everyday lives and learning to be receptive to God's blessings. This easy-to-read book uses stories and examples to explain what the examen is, how you can begin to pray it, how you can adapt it to your individual life, and what its benefits for your life can be. Highly practical!

Because ***The Examen Prayer*** draws from the experiences of everyday life, it can stand on its own as a guide to the prayer of examen. Those looking to begin their practice of meditation and contemplation, which for Ignatius is always based on Scripture, may choose their own Scripture passages or draw from the forty examples in ***An Ignatian Introduction to Prayer,*** mentioned earlier.

A second favorite is ***Meditation and Contemplation: An Ignatian Guide to Praying with Scripture.*** Anyone familiar with Ignatian spirituality has heard about meditation and contemplation. In this volume, Fr. Gallagher explains what is unique to each practice, shows how you can profit from both at different times in your spiritual life, and reveals some of the forgotten elements (such as the preparatory steps and colloquy) and how the structure can be adapted to your particular spiritual needs.

- ♦ When you're ready to move more deeply into Ignatian thought
  The Discernment of Spirits and *Spiritual Consolation*

Spiritual directors, directees, and others who want to understand the deeper structures of Ignatian thought have come to rely on *The Discernment of Spirits: An Ignatian Guide to Everyday Living,* and *Spiritual Consolation: An Ignatian Guide for the Greater Discernment of Spirits. The Discernment of Spirits* leads us through Ignatius's Rules for discernment, showing both their precise insight into the human soul and their ability to illustrate the real-life struggles of spiritual seekers today. As Fr. Gallagher writes, his practical goal is "to offer an experience-based presentation of Ignatius's rules for discernment of spirits in order to facilitate their ongoing application in the spiritual life. This is a book about living the spiritual life." Because it forms the foundation for so many other aspects of Ignatian thought, *The Discernment of Spirits* has become Fr. Gallagher's best-selling book and has been the basis for a TV series.

Spiritual Consolation extends this same approach, interweaving stories and principles for a more profound understanding of Ignatius's Second Rules for discernment.

You might also like

The Discernment of Spirits
A Guide for Readers

by Timothy M. Gallagher, O.M.V.

Paperback, 104 pages, 978-0-8245-4985-5

This handy, easy-to-use workbook is chock-full of probing questions, real-life stories, and practical tips on how to apply the profound spiritual insights Father Gallagher draws from the Ignatian tradition of patient, prayerful self-examination. There's space on every page for notes, reflections, and journaling to help the reader track his or her own progress toward a closer, more loving union with God.

"For years I have given many people instructions in the *Discernment of Spirits* using Father Tim Gallagher's book. The new study guide is a valuable resource for both group and individual study. All those who used the study guide told me that it helped them immensely in the study of his book, *The Discernment of Spirits*, and to more effectively enter into the understanding and practice of discernment. I highly recommend it." **—Dennis Brown, O.M.V.**

"my cherished solitude"